Complementary and Alternative Therapies Research

Complementary and Alternative Therapies Research

Tiffany Field

American Psychological Association

Washington, DC

Published by
American Psychological Association
750 First Street, NE
Washington, DC 20002
www.apa.org

To order
APA Order Department
P.O. Box 92984
Washington, DC 20090-2984
Tel: (800) 374-2721; Direct: (202) 336-5510
Fax: (202) 336-5502; TDD/TTY: (202) 336-6123
Online: www.apa.org/books/
E-mail: order@apa.org

In the U.K., Europe, Africa, and the Middle East, copies may be ordered from
American Psychological Association
3 Henrietta Street
Covent Garden, London
WC2E 8LU England

Typeset in Goudy by Circle Graphics, Columbia, MD

Printer: United Book Press, Inc., Baltimore, MD
Cover Designer: Minker Design, Bethesda, MD
Technical/Production Editor: Harriet Kaplan

The opinions and statements published are the responsibility of the authors, and such opinions and statements do not necessarily represent the policies of the American Psychological Association.

Library of Congress Cataloging-in-Publication Data

Field, Tiffany.
    Complementary and alternative therapies research / Tiffany Field. — 1st ed.
        p. ; cm.
    Includes bibliographical references and index.
    ISBN-13: 978-1-4338-0401-4
    ISBN-10: 1-4338-0401-8
    1. Mental illness—Alternative treatment. 2. Alternative medicine. I. American Psychological Association. II. Title.
    [DNLM: 1. Complementary Therapies—methods. 2. Complementary Therapies—psychology. 3. Disease—psychology. 4. Mental Disorders—therapy. 5. Psychotherapy—methods. WB 890 F463c 2009]

    RC480.5.F45 2009
    616.89—dc22

                        2008021014

British Library Cataloguing-in-Publication Data
A CIP record is available from the British Library.

Printed in the United States of America
First Edition

CONTENTS

ACKNOWLEDGMENTS

I thank all the participants in our complementary and alternative therapy studies and all the researchers for helping with the studies, most especially Maria Hernandez-Reif and Miguel Diego. I also sincerely appreciate the support for our multiple studies from a National Center for Complementary and Alternative Medicine grant (AT00370) and senior research scientist award (AT001585), a National Institutes of Health merit award (MH46586) and research scientist award (MH0033), a March of Dimes grant (12-FY03-48), and a Johnson and Johnson Pediatric Institute grant. Finally, I am extremely grateful to Michelle Hudgins and Angela Ascencio for their help with this book.

Complementary and Alternative Therapies Research

INTRODUCTION

Complementary and alternative medicine (CAM) therapies have been valued enough that in 1998 the National Institutes of Health established the National Center for Complementary and Alternative Medicine (NCCAM) to explore these practices scientifically and to disseminate information to professionals and to the public (NCCAM, 2007).[1] In considering CAM therapies, the practitioner is often unclear about which therapies for which conditions under which circumstances are most likely to benefit his or her clients. Because research on CAM therapies is in its infancy, this response is natural. Adding to the confusion is the proliferation of books in these areas that claim results, many of which are not based on hard data. My research with colleagues in the CAM field and interactions with therapists who are interested in CAM interventions convinced me that enough data exist for therapists to make decisions about CAM therapies for their clients.

---

[1]NCCAM does not provide the names of CAM practitioners or treatment centers.

PURPOSE OF THE BOOK

The purpose of this book is to provide clinicians, graduate students, and medical students information and recent research data on CAM therapies (e.g., acupuncture, massage therapy) that have been used effectively with psychological and medical conditions (e.g., depression, cancer). Although there are many complementary and alternative therapies, the ones included in this volume are those that are both widely available and sufficiently researched for their therapeutic effects. They are also those that are relatively simple to incorporate into one's practice through referrals and regular follow-up. These include bodywork therapies (massage therapy, acupuncture), movement therapies (Tai Chi, yoga, Pilates, and aerobic exercise), sensory therapies (music therapy, aromatherapy), and mind–body therapies (relaxation therapy, imagery, meditation, hypnosis, and biofeedback).

Clinicians (e.g., clinical psychologists, psychiatrists, social workers, counselors), other therapists (alternative therapists, physical therapists, occupational therapists, massage therapists), nurses, physicians, medical students, and graduate students can use this book in several ways. First, it can provide an introduction to common CAM therapies and the range of conditions for which they are being used. Second, readers can use the book as a reference to look up which specific conditions have responded to a specific CAM intervention. An outline of these can be found in Appendix A. Other information includes how to locate and evaluate referral sources and how to collaborate with the CAM practitioner. Finally, researchers and graduate students interested in pursuing studies in CAM will learn about the significant research gaps that need to be filled as well as the methodological limitations of current studies.

Readers can identify complementary therapies for different conditions or symptoms, and information about these therapies can then be used to inform clients and make client referrals. For example, therapists have noted clinical problems related to their clients' history of touch deprivation. Many professional codes of ethics prohibit touching clients, so learning more about massage therapy and then making appropriate referrals to qualified massage therapists may be a helpful adjunct for such clients. Other therapists have noted that some clients with depression suffer from being overweight. A movement therapy such as yoga or Tai Chi may reduce weight, increase serotonin levels, and decrease depression.

In addition to describing the CAM therapies and providing current research data from peer-reviewed journals on their effects, this book suggests potential underlying mechanisms for their effectiveness with particular conditions. For example, the current theory that many alternative therapies increase vagal or parasympathetic activity is described. Increased vagal activity is thought to initiate a cascade of biochemical events such as decreasing stress hormones (e.g., cortisol), thereby reducing the experience of stress and pain and enhancing immune function (e.g., natural killer cells and natural killer cell activity).

Finally, details are provided on training, certification, and referral sources for many of the CAM therapies presented in this book (see especially Appendixes B and C). Although some alternative therapies, such as music therapy and aromatherapy, can be incorporated into practice without a referral, most of the therapies described in this book require that the practitioner make a referral.

In summary, this book can be a resource for readers in a variety of ways. First, it can provide an introduction to common CAM therapies and the range of conditions for which they are being used. Second, it can be used as a reference volume for the specific conditions that have responded to CAM interventions. Third, for those who decide that they would like to integrate a CAM intervention into therapy with a particular client, the book provides information on how to locate and evaluate alternative therapists and make referrals. In general, today's graduate and medical students are highly interested in learning about CAM therapies, and this book addresses many of their questions. (Of the medical and graduate programs in which I teach, alternative therapies is often listed as students' "favorite course.") So for researchers and graduate students, it identifies significant research gaps that need to be filled as well as the methodological limitations of current studies.

ORGANIZATION OF THE BOOK

This book comprises 15 chapters. Chapter 1 gives two extended examples of how alternative therapies have been successfully integrated into traditional therapies. In the first example, meditation is incorporated within the context of cognitive–behavioral therapy. In the second example, massage therapy is combined with group interpersonal psychotherapy. These two examples provide readers with helpful guidelines on integrating CAM modalities into their own therapy.

Chapter 2 is written for those interested in the origins of CAM therapies. Most of these therapies derive from Asia, particularly China and India. For example, yoga and massage originated from Ayurvedic medicine and Tai Chi and acupuncture from Chinese medicine.

Each of the next 12 chapters is devoted to a particular CAM modality: massage therapy and acupressure, acupuncture, Tai Chi, yoga and Pilates, exercise, music therapy, aromatherapy, progressive muscle relaxation, imagery, hypnosis, biofeedback, and meditation. These chapters are organized in a similar way. First, the modality is described in general terms. Then, potential underlying mechanisms are suggested for the effects of the therapy. The remainder of the chapter then briefly summarizes studies that have assessed that therapy with different psychological and physical conditions. In some cases, research is included on stress-reducing and performance-enhancing effects of the therapy. The final section of each chapter suggests ideas for referring clients to practitioners of that therapy. The last chapter of the book is devoted to the use of CAM with pediatric clients. This chapter can help therapists and parents of children with psychological or physical problems.

Chapter length is determined by the amount of research that has been done on the CAM therapy. For example, the chapter on massage therapy is the longest in the book because it is one of the most commonly used complementary therapy and the most frequently researched in terms of potential underlying mechanisms for its effects. These mechanisms (i.e., increased vagal activity, decreased cortisol, and increased natural killer cells) may be common to other therapies such as acupuncture and yoga.

CONCLUSION

Certain CAM therapies seem to hold tremendous promise for clients with psychological and medical conditions, not only helping them resolve symptoms but also restoring their general health and emotional well-being. My hope is that by reading this book, practitioners and students will gain an abiding interest in CAM therapies and will be motivated to follow the research that is just now beginning to reach a critical mass. More research is definitely needed on CAM therapies, and funding is available for this research through NCCAM and other sources. Most of all, my hope is that the research that has been done and reviewed in this volume will motivate clinicians to consider CAM therapies for their clients.

1
COMBINING COMPLEMENTARY THERAPIES WITH PSYCHOTHERAPY

Complementary and alternative therapies have rarely been combined with traditional therapies, at least in research studies. I could find only two examples of recent research on combined therapies. Those are one published study that combined cognitive–behavioral therapy and mindfulness meditation and an unpublished study by the research group I work with on the combination of group interpersonal psychotherapy and massage therapy. In this chapter, I describe some traditional therapies that have been combined with a complementary modality to more effectively treat clients with depression. The first example discusses the combination of cognitive–behavioral therapy and mindfulness meditation. The second examines the combination of group interpersonal psychotherapy with massage therapy. I then discuss how complementary and alternative medicine (CAM) therapies can be incorporated into a traditional psychotherapy practice.

COGNITIVE–BEHAVIORAL THERAPY AND MINDFULNESS MEDITATION

Many therapists have turned to Buddhist teachings to learn about the healing effects of mind–body therapies. In their review, Lau and McMain (2005) discussed how Eastern paradigms have been integrated with cognitive–behavioral treatments. In particular, they described mindfulness-based cognitive therapy (MBCT), which is the integration of cognitive–behavioral therapy and mindfulness meditation.

MBCT incorporates cognitive–behavioral therapy with Kabat-Zinn's (1990, 2003) mindfulness-based stress-reduction program. This combination grew out of the awareness that traditional approaches to preventing repeated episodes of depression were not always effective (Lau & McMain, 2005). Notably, clients with an initial episode of depression have a 50% chance of having a second episode, and when more than two episodes occur, the relapse rate increases to as much as 80% (Lau & McMain, 2005).

Major life stressors are considered a strong predictor of the first episode of depression, but dysphoric mood and dysfunctional thinking styles are more correlated with recurring episodes (Lewinsohn, Allen, Seeley, & Gotlib, 1999). For this reason, MBCT aims to help clients increase their awareness of dysfunctional thinking and thus lead to change in thinking style over time. Because mindfulness-based meditation is focused on acceptance of experience, MBCT also aims to help clients accept their illness rather than to fight to eliminate it.

Teasdale, Segal, and Williams (1995) were the first to integrate cognitive–behavioral therapy with mindfulness meditation to prevent recurrence of depressive episodes. The cognitive therapy exercises that are part of MBCT are directed toward early detection of negative thought patterns. Mindfulness meditation uses exercises such as the *body scan*, which focuses on breathing and bodily sensations to allow the client to become more aware of his or her feelings and thoughts. Those thought patterns that contribute to depression are then modified through work with the therapist. The client is encouraged to view negative emotional states as uncomfortable but temporary; accepting these negative emotional states will make them more likely to become less depressed. Thus, MBCT combines the change-oriented approach of cognitive–behavioral therapy and the acceptance-related approach of mindfulness meditation.

In typical MBCT, clients meet weekly in small groups and are taught meditation techniques that focus on physical sensations, feelings, and thoughts. Group sessions last from 2 to 3 hours. Between these sessions, clients practice the mindfulness meditation and change-oriented techniques they have learned by meditating on their own daily for several hours. The group sessions are typically repeated for 8 weeks and are equally divided into the practice of cognitive–behavioral and mindfulness meditation techniques.

Data from two studies have documented the effectiveness of MBCT for reducing recurrence of depression episodes. In a study by Teasdale et al. (2000), clients with recurrent depression were randomly assigned to an MBCT group or a wait-list control group. The relapse rate was significantly reduced for clients in the MBCT group with three or more previous episodes of depression. A later study showed similar results (i.e., that MBCT could reduce the incidence of relapse; Ma & Teasdale, 2004).

The limitations of these studies are that the components have not been separately investigated with a similar client population, so it is not clear exactly how mindfulness meditation contributes to cognitive–behavioral therapy. The development of measures to assess mindfulness will help this future research effort (Lau et al., 2003). MBCT also needs to be compared with other treatments for its effectiveness in reducing relapse in depression. In addition, other researchers need to replicate the data because the studies to date have been conducted only by the developers of MBCT.

GROUP INTERPERSONAL PSYCHOTHERAPY COMBINED WITH MASSAGE THERAPY

Interpersonal psychotherapy is a time-limited form of psychotherapy that focuses specifically on interpersonal relationships and the clients' improvement or changing expectations about relationships (Stuart & Robertson, 2003). Interpersonal therapy was originally developed in a research context as a therapy for major depression and was outlined in a manual by Klerman, Weissman, Rounsaville, and Chevron (1984) that focused on interpersonal problems. An underlying premise of interpersonal psychotherapy is that depression always has an interpersonal component—that is, the symptoms of depression affect people close to the client, resulting in interpersonal patterns that may maintain or increase symptoms of depression (Klerman et al., 1984). The efficacy of interpersonal psychotherapy was investigated by the National Institute of Mental Health Treatment of Depression Collaborative Research Program for the treatment of mild to moderate depression (Elkin et al., 1989). Later, interpersonal psychotherapy was shown to prevent recurrence of depression in some clients who had experienced multiple episodes of depression (Frank et al., 1990).

The first study on the combined use of interpersonal psychotherapy and massage in pregnant women who have depression showed a reduction in depression (Spinelli & Endicott, 2003). Massage therapy (see chap. 3, this volume) also has been shown to decrease depressive symptoms in prenatally depressed women and to reduce their cortisol levels (Field, Diego, Hernandez-Reif, Schanberg, & Kuhn, 2004).

Some practitioners have become interested in seeing whether *group interpersonal psychotherapy*, which is a combination of interpersonal psychotherapy and group therapy techniques (Klerman et al., 1984), could be enhanced when combined with massage therapy. In a recent study on prenatally depressed women (Field et al., 2008), my colleagues and I compared two groups: a group that received both interpersonal psychotherapy and massage therapy (psychotherapy-plus-massage group) and a group that received only group interpersonal psychotherapy (psychotherapy-only group). The group interpersonal psychotherapy sessions for both conditions were held for 1 hour, once per week, for 6 weeks. They were designed to enable the women with depression to process pregnancy experiences and relationship problems. The women in the psychotherapy-plus-massage group received 20-minute massages once per week over the same 6 weeks during which they participated in group interpersonal psychotherapy sessions.

Results of the study indicated that members of the psychotherapy-plus-massage group attended more psychotherapy sessions on average, and a greater percentage of women in the group completed the 6-week psychotherapy program. Also, a lower percentage of women in the psychotherapy-plus-massage group used lack of interest as a reason for leaving the program. In terms of depression, the psychotherapy-plus-massage group had greater decreases than the psychotherapy-only group on depression scores, anxiety scores, and cortisol levels. Women in the psychotherapy-plus-massage group may have been more likely than those in the psychotherapy-only group to stay with the program because they were experiencing less depression and anxiety. Thus, massage therapy may have contributed to the women's greater compliance in this study. More research needs to be done in combining group interpersonal psychotherapy with massage therapy in other populations.

INTEGRATING COMPLEMENTARY AND ALTERNATIVE MODALITIES INTO A TRADITIONAL PSYCHOTHERAPY PRACTICE

Some therapists would like to expand their repertoire to make their sessions more interesting and therapeutic. Some easily integrated CAM therapies are, for example, music and aromas. Other modalities, such as Tai Chi, Chi Gong, yoga, and Pilates, require some training and if incorporated into one's practice would require separate sessions. Therapists would usually refer their clients to these types of therapies. Still other modalities are already practiced by therapists, such as progressive muscle relaxation, imagery, hypnosis, biofeedback, and meditation.

Some Easily Integrated Modalities

Some CAM modalities can be integrated into a therapist's practice relatively easily—for example, playing light music in the background (music therapy) or placing scented candles in the therapy setting (aromatherapy). Of course, these would need to be carefully selected on the basis of the client's preferences for what feels comfortable or, alternatively, on the basis of the modality's presumed effects. Classical music, for instance, may be more calming for an anxious person but more saddening for a depressed person.

In a study my colleagues and I conducted examining the effects of music on adolescent mothers with depression, we were able to shift electroencephalogram (EEG) patterns from the typical pattern of depressed individuals (greater right frontal EEG activation to greater left frontal EEG activation) using Michael Jackson's music (except in 3 of the adolescents who did not like this particular music; Field, Martinez, et al., 1998). In another study, we played classical music for those who were anxious and rock music for those who were depressed (Field, Martinez, et al., 1998). The effects were in the predicted direction, with the rock music making depressed adolescents less depressed and the classical music calming the anxious adolescents.

Aromas can be similarly used for either calming relaxation or for energizing or activating. In one study, we used lavender for relaxing and rosemary for energizing the participants (Field et al., 2005). We expected that performance (in math computations) would be better in the presence of rosemary. We found, however, that performance was faster with rosemary but more accurate with lavender.

Modalities Requiring Some Training and Separate Sessions

Most of the CAM modalities reviewed in this book can be learned in a series of classes or workshops, including the physical exercise modalities of Tai Chi, Chi Gong, yoga, and Pilates. If a therapist thinks these modalities are indicated because the client is experiencing any pain syndrome or the client is obese because of inactivity, the therapist can make referrals to instructors qualified in these modalities and monitor the client's progress.

Trying the CAM therapies personally is an excellent way for therapists to know how and whether they want to integrate these into their own practice. Trying Tai Chi, for example, was a surprise for me. I had been told it was relaxing, but it takes deep concentration. The relaxation seems to come from having to concentrate so hard that you forget your problems.

Other Modalities That Many Therapists Already Use

In contrast to the more physical movement therapies above, many therapists have already learned mind–body therapies in workshops and courses, including progressive muscle relaxation, imagery, hypnosis, biofeedback, and meditation. Some have combined these, as noted in the earlier examples in which mindfulness meditation was combined with cognitive–behavioral therapy. These are more obvious integrations because they are less physical than, say, yoga and Tai Chi, and more focused on the mind, as many of the more traditional therapies are. These would be thought of more as complementary than supplementary therapies. Techniques such as the body scan and focusing on breathing can facilitate awareness of thoughts and can make therapy sessions more interesting than talking alone.

THE NEED FOR REFERRALS

Although increasing numbers of practitioners are receiving training in CAM therapies to broaden their practice, most would need to make referrals to CAM therapies therapists. They may know, for example, that their clients are touch deprived and could benefit from massage therapy or that their clients are experiencing pain, as in fibromyalgia, lower back pain, and chronic fatigue syndrome, and could benefit from acupuncture, but these treatments can be practiced only by those who are licensed. Some CAM modalities, for example, bodywork modalities including massage therapy and acupuncture, require extensive schooling and licensure. Therapists who are not trained and properly licensed or certified in these CAM modalities can make referrals by calling local training schools or national organizations that have geographical lists of licensed therapists. Many of these appear in Appendix C or can be found on the Internet.

2

ORIGINS OF COMPLEMENTARY AND ALTERNATIVE THERAPIES

Many of the complementary and alternative medicine (CAM) therapies described in this volume are derived from ancient systems of healing, primarily Ayurvedic and Chinese medicine. Although therapists may refer clients to CAM therapies and integrate CAM therapies into their practice without necessarily understanding their early origins, to fully appreciate some of the CAM therapies, one may find it useful to understand a little about these two traditional systems.

Because clients may, on their own, go to osteopaths, naturopaths, chiropractors, and homeopathic practitioners, a brief understanding of these forms of practice or manipulative treatment can be helpful in understanding and communicating with the client. In some areas of the United States, practitioners will find clients who believe in Native American medicine and shamanism. Therapists need to have at least a brief understanding of these to begin to converse about them with clients.

AYURVEDIC MEDICINE

Ayurvedic medicine originated in India over 2,500 years ago and is considered the first organized medicinal system that is not based on spiritual phenomena. In the Ayurvedic system, health is believed to depend on a balance between life forces, or *doshas*, including *vata* (symbolized by air), *pitta* (symbolized by fire), and *kapha* (symbolized by earth). Individuals are believed to be born with a single dosha or a combination of two doshas, resulting in their personality and temperament as well as the ailments and chronic disorders they may experience in their lifetime. Certain foods and activities are believed to be associated with health for a dosha-based individual's type, so when illness arises, specific diets and activities are prescribed, typically depending on the time of the year in which the individual seeks help.

To diagnose the illness or imbalance, the Ayurvedic practitioner will ask in great detail about daily habits and preferences of various kinds, including food, weather, people, and activities. He or she will feel the patient's pulse in both wrists (using the first three fingers), where imbalances among the doshas can be detected. The practitioner then may prescribe dietary and herbal remedies, lifestyle modifications (e.g., sleep times), and meditation and massage. In some instances, practitioners also prescribe a group of procedures that are collectively known as *panchakarma*, which includes massage, herbal steam treatments, laxatives, and enemas.

In India, Ayurvedic medicine is firmly rooted in rural areas; in urban areas it may exist alongside Western medicine. Ayurvedic institutes and practitioners can be found throughout the United States. For example, in Fairfield, Iowa, large numbers of people gather to meditate together for a few hours a day in large assembly halls, to practice yoga, and to receive massage. Although the Ayurvedic system of medicine continues to grow in popularity in many geographic areas of the United States, the therapeutic value of Ayurvedic treatment, per se, has yet to be fully supported by empirical research.

CHINESE MEDICINE

Chinese medicine has also existed for more than 2,000 years and, like Ayurvedic medicine, views health and illness in terms of balances and imbalances of life forces. In Chinese medicine, these forces are referred to as *yin* and *yang*, symbolically referring to female and male and night and day, respectively. Preventive Chinese medicine aims at keeping yin and yang energies in balance. As with Ayurvedic medicine, empirical data are lacking for the effects of Chinese medicine aside from the practice of acupuncture, which has received considerable research support.

In Chinese medicine, medical conditions are diagnosed by using smell, vision, hearing, and touch. The practitioner examines the patient's pallor and, in particular, examines the tongue (its size, motion, color, coating, and texture). Different areas of the tongue are thought to correspond to different parts of the body. For example, the tip of the tongue is thought to correspond to the heart and lungs, the center to the stomach, the back to the kidneys, the left side to the gallbladder, and the right side to the liver. The practitioner also listens to the patient's breathing; smells for particular body odors; and palpates different parts of the body, feeling for insensitivity or inflammation.

As in Ayurvedic medicine, pulse taking in Chinese medicine is also a diagnostic tool. Three places on the wrist are felt, with each pulse thought to represent a different part of the body and with pulse qualities reflecting a different kind of imbalance (e.g., in some Chinese systems, up to 28 pulse qualities are believed to reflect different imbalances).

After diagnosis, the patient is typically treated on the basis of a network of meridians that are believed to transport energy (the *Chi* or *Qi*) throughout the body. A problem involving a particular organ (e.g., the heart, the kidney) is thought to be caused by a disruption of the flow of Chi energy. Treatment focuses on unblocking this energy through interventions such as acupuncture, diet, movement therapies (e.g., Tai Chi and Chi Gong), and herbs.

The most widely researched treatment in Chinese medicine is acupuncture, in which needles are inserted into critical acupoints along the meridians to unblock energy flow. Although some medical texts describe some 365 acupoints, others claim there are as many as 2,000 acupoints (Freeman, 2004).

Very little systematic research has been conducted on herbal treatments in Chinese medicine. Some data suggest that the biological activities of plants and their constituents may be relevant to the treatment of chronic disorders, including enhancement of cholinergic function in the central nervous system and contributions to anti-inflammatory and antioxidant activities in the body (Howes & Houghton, 2003).

Herbal medicine has also been used in some studies on patients with diabetes and dermatological conditions. In a study on diabetes, reduced blood glucose and symptom relief were observed in patients who had not responded to oral antidiabetic drugs (Zhao, Tong, & Chan, 2006). A number of studies have similarly shown responses to herbal treatments for skin conditions (Koo & Desai, 2003), especially in atopic dermatitis (Hon, Ma, Wong, Leung, & Fok, 2005; W. Zhang et al., 2005). Immune dysfunction in cancer has also been responsive to Chinese herbal medicine (Ruan, Lai, & Zhou, 2006). Both laboratory experiments and clinical trials have demonstrated that when combined with chemotherapy, Chinese herbal medicine can raise the efficacy level and lower toxic reactions (Ruan et al., 2006).

Some have suggested that traditional Chinese medicine may serve as a useful model for scientific inquiries into other CAM modalities because there is a standardized system of diagnostics and therapies, and the system is practiced worldwide (I. Cohen, Tagliaferri, & Tripathy, 2002). However, the holistic and individualized nature of traditional Chinese medicine presents challenges to rigorous clinical testing. As a result, most of the published work in this field is in the form of anecdotal reports and uncontrolled trials. Other obstacles include the uncertain origin of the supply of herbs and the inconsistency of their quality (Leung, 2006). A more insurmountable barrier to evaluating traditional Chinese medicine is that amounts of a particular herb or plant are not constant within a diagnostic group. The pattern of the yin–yang imbalance determines the treatment for a particular patient.

However, some studies have been attempted. In one study, for example, herbal treatment was applied to patients with cancer who "lacked both yin and yang," and the treatment focused on supplementing yin or yang by using different herbal treatments (Seki et al., 2005). In this study, one group was administered a yang treatment during the day and no treatment at night, whereas the other group was administered a yin treatment at night and no treatment during the day. When the groups were compared, their results suggested that the patients receiving yang treatment during the day lived longer than the patients receiving yin treatment during the night. Furthermore, the patients in the day yang treatment group also appeared clinically better than the patients treated solely by Western medicine. Because the groups lacked both yin and yang, the perfect treatment might have been yang during the day and yin at night.

In the interim, a research group in the United States has developed and evaluated a method for quantitative evaluation of yin and yang in human participants for the purposes of research (Langevin et al., 2004). This has the potential of comparing patients' differential responses to acupuncture, herbs, and other medicine. Early results suggest that yin and yang can be reliably determined in different participants, but further research is needed to establish the usefulness of this classification for research trials.

SHAMANISM

Shamanism is considered by some to be a more primitive form of healing because it focuses on calming agitated "spirits" rather than on the body itself. Healing ceremonies are conducted during which the *shaman*, or healer, using dance, drumming, hallucinogenic plants, or fasting, will go into a trance. Healing ceremonies involving shamanic trances are believed to be critical in communing with the spirit in a helpful way (e.g., calming the spirit or ridding the body of evil spirits) and are often experienced by patients as helpful and supportive.

Shamanism has a following throughout the world, including in the United States. For example, in a study on a Hmong American community in California, some 36 shamans collected data on 924 patients to describe the patients and their complaints (Helsel, Mochel, & Bauer, 2004). The patients sought shamanic help for an array of physical, emotional, and psychological complaints, which were interpreted by the shamans as being caused by loss of soul or bad spirits. Of all the alternative healing systems, shamanism probably has the weakest empirical support (Money, 2001).

NATIVE AMERICAN MEDICINE

Practiced by members of many Native American tribes in North America, Native American medicine is also based on a belief in spirits. It is thought that all things in nature have a spirit and that some of these spirits can cause harm, including medical and psychological illness. Illness is treated by medicinal products that come from plants, such as dandelions and pussy willows. Lore has it that one particular willow was the precursor of the active ingredient in aspirin.

Some Native American healers carry medicine bundles of healing spirits contained in stones, sticks, and animal skins that are used in healing ceremonies. Healing ceremonies are also conducted in *sweat lodges*, which are similar to saunas but more intense and of longer duration, for healing and purification.

Several reviews have been published over the years on Native American medicine and its use with different diseases and conditions. In a review by Nauman (2007), for example, Native American medicine was viewed as a complement to modern medicine treatments for cardiovascular disease. Although cardiac patients in Nauman's study gave strong testimonials to the benefits of Native American medicine, empirical studies on such benefits have been lacking.

Attempts to empirically test the effects of Native American medicine have been generally confounded by the diversity of patients in the samples and by the heterogeneity of treatments. For example, in a qualitative study of patients with different chronic illnesses, the treatment program consisted of a variety of Native American practices lasting 7 to 10 days (Mehl-Madrona, 1999). Of the patients, 80% reported positive benefits, including improvements in their symptoms. However, this system of medicine has not been studied using randomized controlled trials.

HOMEOPATHY

This 200-year-old system of medicine was started by Samuel Hahnemann, a chemist and physician. The word *homeopathy* comes from the Greek words *homos* and *pathos*, meaning "similar sickness." This system uses highly diluted natural substances that in larger quantities would produce symptoms of the disease being treated. Some 2,000 medicines have been derived from various chemicals, plants, minerals, and animal substances, such as honey bee extract, marigold flowers, graphite, and onions. These medications are only thought to be complementary, and most homeopaths recommend using Western medicine for fighting infectious disease.

Although homeopathy is one of the most widespread of the CAMs, it is one of the most controversial and one with the most mixed findings. In a review by Walach, Jonas, Ives, van Wijk, and Weingärtner (2005), for example, nearly 200 reports of clinical trials were summarized, and few of these studies had been conducted on single conditions. Of these, some documented clinical effects, whereas others did not.

In a review of homeopathy, anxiety, and anxiety disorders, eight controlled studies were identified (Pilkington, Kirkwood, Rampes, Fisher, & Richardson, 2006). The disorders that were studied included test anxiety, general anxiety disorder, and anxiety related to medical or physical conditions such as cancer and surgical procedures. Single case reports were the most frequently encountered studies. Randomized controlled trials reported contradictory results, or they were underpowered or provided insufficient methodological details to evaluate them.

In another review, this time on depression, only two randomized controlled trials were found (Pilkington, Kirkwood, Rampes, Fisher, & Richardson, 2005). These uncontrolled, observational studies reported positive results, including high levels of client satisfaction, but because of the lack of a control group, it was difficult to assess the extent to which responses were due to specific aspects of homeopathy. The authors of the review concluded that the highly individualized nature of homeopathic treatment and the specificity of responses may require innovative methods of analysis of individual treatment responses.

NATUROPATHY

Naturopaths, or doctors of naturopathy, receive training in several types of therapy, including traditional Chinese medicine, Ayurvedic medicine, homeopathy, physical therapy, and manipulative therapies. Much of their focus is on healthy habits, including low-fat diets and exercise. They also prescribe massage and hydrotherapy. This form of medicine has never been accepted by the American Medical Association. Nonetheless, the practice of naturopathy has become increasingly popular as more people subscribe to CAM therapies that emphasize healthy diet and exercise.

A literature search on naturopathy research during the past 5 years yielded only one study, which addressed menopausal symptoms (Cramer, Jones, Keenan, & Thompson, 2003). Women who were treated with naturopathy were approximately 7 times more likely than women treated with conventional medicine to report improvement for insomnia. Furthermore, the naturopathy group reported improvement for anxiety, hot flashes, and menstrual changes. Despite these positive self-reports, because there was no standard protocol (i.e., the treatments were individualized), conclusions must be considered in that context.

OSTEOPATHY

The word *osteopathy* comes from the Greek, with *osteo* meaning bone and *pathy* meaning disease. Osteopathy originated with a conventionally trained American physician, Andrew Still, in the late 1800s. Osteopaths are trained as physicians and practice much like traditional physicians (e.g., they are able to prescribe drugs, have hospital privileges, and perform surgery). However, osteopathic training emphasizes the mind–body connection and places a greater emphasis on prevention.

The osteopath focuses on all parts of the body and how the body moves, including posture and gait. The osteopath looks for any abnormal curvatures of the spine or undesirable postures that may contribute to tight muscles, swelling, and pain. Many individuals go to osteopaths for musculoskeletal injuries expecting to receive manipulation that will reduce inflammation from the injuries.

The only research report that could be found for osteopathy in the literature in the past 5 years involved a cost-effective analysis of osteopathy in primary care (N. H. Williams et al., 2004). The results of the study suggested that osteopathy plus usual general practitioner care was more effective but also resulted in more health care costs than usual general practitioner care alone. One reason for the relative scarcity of research on osteopathy is that because of its similarity to conventional modern medicine, it is rarely uniquely identified as osteopathy.

CHIROPRACTIC

Chiropractors focus on the spinal column and its alignment as the cause of pain and disorders. Diagnoses are made by physical examination that often involve X-rays. Treatment consists of adjusting and realigning the spinal vertebrae over a series of sessions. At times, massage therapy is used as a complementary treatment.

Most patients go to chiropractors for back pain; headaches; or pain in joints such as the shoulder, elbow, foot, or hand. As a practice, chiropractic is one of the most popular alternative therapies. Because of the more extensive medical education contemporary chiropractors receive, the field is increasingly associated more with conventional than with alternative medicine. Recognizing this, many health insurers cover chiropractic treatment.

Although it has gained both legitimacy and access to third-party payments, the effectiveness of chiropractic treatment has received only modest support in the research literature with regard to nonjoint problems. In a review by Ernst (2003), eight studies on the use of chiropractic manipulation for nonspinal conditions suggested that it was not an effective therapy for fibromyalgia, carpal tunnel syndrome, infantile colic, otitis media, dysmenorrhea, or chronic pelvic pain. In addition, a report on chiropractic care with asthma and allergies reviewing three randomized controlled studies showed benefits on subjective measures, but no significant changes were noted on any objective lung function measure (Balon & Mior, 2004). It is fortunate, then, that only approximately 19% of chiropractic patients viewed their chiropractor as their primary care physician (Cambron, Cramer, & Winterstein, 2007). It is puzzling, however, that for each "primary care condition" listed in the survey, the percentage of patients who said their chiropractors could treat the condition was as high as 50%.

Chiropractic treatment for back pain does have some support in the research literature (Homola, 2006). In a review of the 43 randomized trials of spinal manipulation for low back pain, 30 showed more improvement than a comparison treatment, and none of the studies showed it to be less effective (DeVocht, 2006). These data are perhaps not surprising because spinal manipulation has been used for low back pain for at least 2,500 years. The outcomes from a low back pain study at the University of California, Los Angeles, also suggested that chiropractic patients were much more likely to perceive improvement in their lower back symptoms compared with patients receiving standard medical care (Hurwitz, Morgenstern, Kominski, Yu, & Chiang, 2006). Noteworthy, however, is the finding that fewer than 20% of the patients in this study were pain free at follow-up 18 months later. In a similar study for patients with low back pain, the use rates for four procedures (surgery, computed tomography/magnetic resonance imaging, radiography, and in-patient care) were lower in the group with chiropractic care. The data also extended to chiropractic care for neck pain (C. F. Nelson, Metz, & LaBrot, 2005).

To better understand potential underlying mechanisms for chiropractic effects, one group of investigators found significant reductions in patients' mean heart rate and increased heart rate variability (vagal activity). The high-frequency component of heart rate (vagal activity) increased after one chiropractic adjustment, and heart rate decreased after 4 weeks of chiropractic adjustments (J. Zhang, Dean, Nosco, Strathopulos, & Floros, 2006). It is not surprising that a reduction in pain was also noted. The relationship between pain reduction and increased vagal activity has been noted for other manipulative therapies such as massage therapy (Field, Diego, & Hernandez-Reif, 2007).

The cost-effectiveness of chiropractic care has been compared with that of conventional medical care for acute and chronic low back pain, and the results suggest that chiropractic office costs were higher for both acute and chronic patients (Haas, Sharma, & Stano, 2005). However, the patients receiving chiropractic care experienced better outcomes on pain, functional disability, and patient satisfaction compared with patients receiving conventional treatment. It should be noted that clinically important differences in pain and disability improvement for chiropractic treatment were found for chronic patients only.

CONCLUSION

Although the CAM therapies that originated in the ancient healing systems discussed in this chapter have gained popularity, there are relatively few empirical studies to support their effectiveness. Anecdotal reports and personal testimonials abound, but randomized controlled clinical trials have been difficult to conduct, in part because of the highly individualized nature of these therapies. A review by Raschetti, Menniti-Ippolito, Forcella, and Bianchi (2005) highlighted this problem. The review noted that 20,209 articles about CAM therapies were published from 1997 to 2002, representing 0.7% of the total number of Medline-listed articles. Approximately 50% of those articles appeared in journals with a no-impact factor, meaning that those journals were rarely cited. The proportion of randomized clinical trials accounted for only 8% of the total number of articles. Thus, although there seems to be an upward trend in the number of articles, the number of controlled experimental studies was extremely low, and more than half of the articles were published in journals without an impact factor.

However, as will be seen in the chapters that follow, some of the CAM therapies that have derived from these systems (e.g., massage therapy, acupuncture, Tai Chi) have been subjected to empirical scrutiny. They have been found, under specific circumstances, to be highly effective alternative and complementary treatments for therapists to consider.

3

MASSAGE THERAPY, ACUPRESSURE, AND REFLEXOLOGY

Massage therapy involves manipulation of muscles and ligaments, typically using hand and elbow motions, to improve circulation, muscle tone, and range of motion. The most popular type of massage in the Western world is Swedish massage. However, many other types and techniques of massage therapy exist, some of which are described here. *Acupressure* is the application of finger pressure on specific points of the body, similar to those targeted in acupuncture (see chap. 4, this volume). *Reflexology* involves stimulating pressure points, called *acupoints*, on the feet and hands. In addition to describing these three body therapies in this chapter, I review empirical data on the effects of massage therapy, acupressure, and reflexology on a variety of psychological disorders and physical conditions.

POTENTIAL MECHANISMS OF ACTION FOR MASSAGE THERAPY, ACUPRESSURE, AND REFLEXOLOGY

Many studies have noted that massage therapy increases vagal activity. The *vagus* is 1 of the 12 cranial nerves in the brain, and it has many branches throughout the body, including a branch to the heart, where it slows heart

described here because they are popular and are different from the better known Swedish methods.

Thai massage is the traditional massage of Thailand, although its roots date back to India some 2,500 years ago. The techniques of Thai massage are similar to those used in Shiatsu and acupressure, which are based on Chinese, Japanese, and Indian massage. The therapist applies pressure with palms and fingers as well as the forearms, elbows, knees, and feet. Passive stretching movements are also used to stretch the client into different yogalike positions to increase range of motion. Thai massage may be a more desirable form of massage for those who are more comfortable being fully clothed during the therapy, because the clients are generally massaged in loose clothing on a mat on the floor. The sessions are also often longer (60 to 90 minutes) than other types of massage done on a table.

The *Rosen method* was designed by a physical therapist who believed that forgotten memories are stored in the body and cause muscular tension, constriction, and physical dysfunction. Therapists using the Rosen method attempt to detect areas of muscle tension and apply pressure to reduce resistance in these areas. Attention to breathing patterns is also a part of the Rosen method. During the massage, the therapist encourages clients to verbally express what they are feeling as the therapy releases muscle tension. Verbal support by the therapist is aimed at helping the client bring old memories to the fore. A typical session lasts 60 to 90 minutes.

The *Trager* therapist uses rhythmic rocking, shaking, vibrating, and stretching movements. A typical session lasts 60 to 90 minutes, after which the client is assigned homework exercises, called *mentastics* (mental gymnastics). The Trager approach has been used frequently by athletes and their trainers to enhance performance.

The *Rubenfeld method*, like the Rosen method, combines the practices of touching and talking. Rubenfeld believed that many disorders are caused by emotional "holding" (suppressing the expression of emotion) in the body, which can be detected by postural habits and breathing patterns. The therapist using the Rubenfeld method helps the client become conscious of the causes of such holding. Through touch, verbal expression, and movement, the client then releases the emotional holding. A typical session lasts 45 minutes.

The *Feldenkrais method* is designed to correct poor physical habits that are believed to place strain on the joints and muscles. The therapist using this method focuses on helping clients become conscious of automatic and unhealthy habits of movement. Then the therapist manipulates the client's body to model more adaptive patterns of movement. The typical session, which often occurs in the context of a group, lasts about 45 minutes.

The *Alexander technique* is focused on postural problems that are believed to result in muscular tension and pain. Common problems include slouching and hunching over. The therapist using this technique focuses on aligning the client's body properly, particularly when walking. Exercises are also taught for stretching the back and pulling the torso upward by pretending that the body is a marionette and being pulled by a string in a vertical direction. Other exercises involve draping the body in a supine position over a large ball to stretch the back. In addition, clients are taught such pragmatic skills as how to carry luggage without straining the neck and shoulders and how to lift weights by bending from the knees and keeping the back straight. Although the Alexander technique is used to treat such conditions as neck and back pain and chronic headache, many dancers, actors, and professional athletes have found that it improves their performance.

Empirical Support for the Effects of Massage Therapy

Positive effects of massage therapy have been shown in the areas of emotional symptoms and disorders, such as anxiety and depression; physical symptoms and disorders, such as cardiovascular and pulmonary disorders; and exercise and sports performance. Each of these are considered in turn. Different massage techniques were used in the studies, although most of the studies were done in the United States, and U.S. researchers typically use Swedish massage techniques. To date, most of the studies in the literature have been conducted by me and my colleagues at the Touch Research Institutes. Although we typically measured mood states and stress hormone levels in each study, we also included a "gold standard" clinical measure unique to the condition studied, for example, range of motion in a back pain study, glucose levels in a diabetes study, and pulmonary function in a study on asthma.

Psychological Symptoms and Disorders

Anxiety. Many of the recent studies on the use of massage to reduce anxiety were conducted in the workplace. One study, for example, reported that an onsite chair massage therapy program of six massages reduced anxiety levels of employees (Shulman & Jones, 1996). In another study, hospital staff received eight workplace-based, 15-minute Swedish massage treatments (Katz, Wowk, Culp, & Wakeling, 1999). Pain intensity and tension levels were significantly lower after massage, and relaxation levels and overall mood state improved significantly after massage sessions. In a study by Cady and Jones (1997) using the same procedures, participants' systolic and diastolic blood pressure decreased significantly after 15-minute chair massages at work.

In a study on hospital employees conducted by our research group, chair massage was used with one group (i.e., massage group), whereas the control group simply relaxed in a massage chair (Field et al., 1996). Both groups did this for 15 minutes, twice a week, for 5 weeks. As seen in Figure 3.1, the massage group showed decreased frontal alpha power, suggesting enhanced

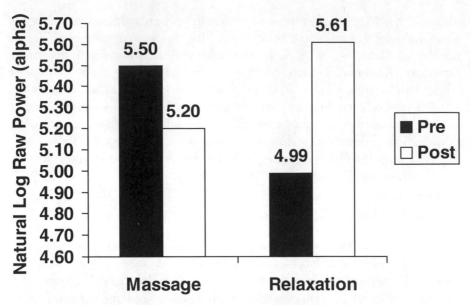

Figure 3.1. Decrease in alpha electroencephalogram power following massage therapy indicating enhanced alertness in the massage therapy group compared with the relaxation group.

alertness, whereas the control group showed increased alpha power, suggesting increased activity. The massage group also showed increased speed and accuracy on math computations after the massage, whereas the control group did not. In addition, anxiety levels of the massage group were lower after each session, but those of the control group were not. Saliva cortisol levels decreased in the massage group but not in the control group. At the end of the 5-week period, depression scores were lower for both groups, but the job stress score was lower only for the massage group.

Depression. In another study by our group, mothers with depression received either ten 30-minute sessions of massage therapy or ten 30-minute sessions of relaxation therapy that involved relaxing each of the muscles or body parts that were being massaged over a 5-week period (Field et al., 1996). Although both therapy groups reported less depression and anxiety following their first and last therapy sessions, only the massage therapy group showed decreased anxious behaviors and other indicators of decreased anxiety, such as decreased pulse rates and salivary cortisol levels. Following the 5 weeks of therapy, only the massage therapy group showed a decrease in urine cortisol levels, suggesting a decrease in the experience of stress, a risk factor for depression.

In another study, mothers with depression were randomly assigned either to a group that attended infant massage classes and support sessions (massage group) or to a support-session-only group (control group; Onozawa, Glover, Adams, Modi, & Kumar, 2001). Each group attended five weekly sessions. Depression scores fell in both groups; however, improved mother–infant interactions were only observed in the massage group.

Giving someone else a massage may have equally beneficial effects as receiving a massage. In one study by our group, older (>65 years) volunteers participated in two conditions that were compared (Field, Hernandez-Reif, Quintino, Schanberg, & Kuhn, 1998). In one condition, the volunteers received massage therapy; in the other condition, the volunteers provided massage therapy to infants at a nursery school. Each volunteer participated in one condition three times a week for 3 weeks and then in the other condition, also for 3 weeks. Immediately after the first and last sessions in which they gave massages to the infants, the volunteers had less anxiety and depression and lower saliva cortisol levels. Over the 3-week period of giving massages, their depression scores and catecholamine (norepinephrine and epinephrine) levels decreased, and their responses to questions on lifestyle and health improved. These effects were also observed for the 3-week period when the volunteers received massage therapy themselves, although they were not as strong as for the conditions when they were massaging the infants.

Prenatal Depression. Depression and elevated cortisol can lead to preterm delivery, and massage therapy has the potential to decrease cortisol and thus lower prematurity rates. In a study we conducted, pregnant women were assigned to a massage therapy or a relaxation therapy group (Field et al., 1999). The therapies consisted of 20-minute sessions twice a week for 5 weeks. Both groups reported feeling less anxiety after the first session and less leg pain after the first and last sessions. Only the massage therapy group, however, reported reduced anxiety, improved mood, better sleep, and less back pain by the last session. In addition, urinary levels of norepinephrine decreased for the massage therapy group, and they had fewer complications during labor and fewer premature births.

In a second attempt to study the effects of massage on premature delivery, we recruited pregnant women who were diagnosed as depressed during the second trimester of pregnancy and randomly assigned them to a massage therapy group, a progressive muscle relaxation group, or a control group that received standard prenatal care alone (Field, Diego, Hernandez-Reif, Schanberg, & Kuhn, 2004). These groups were compared with each other and with a nondepressed group at the end of pregnancy.

Women in the massage therapy group received two 20-minute massage therapy sessions by their significant others each week for 16 weeks of pregnancy, starting during the second trimester. Women in the relaxation group used progressive muscle relaxation on the same time schedule. Immediately after the massage therapy sessions on the first and last days of the 16-week period, the women reported lower levels of anxiety and depressed mood and less leg and back pain. By the end of the study, women in the massage group had higher dopamine and serotonin levels and lower cortisol and norepinephrine levels.

There was also reduced fetal activity and better neonatal outcome for the massage group (i.e., a lesser incidence of prematurity and low birth weight), and infants in the massage group performed better on the Brazelton Neonatal Behavior Assessment Scale (Brazelton, 1973), which measures, for example, the newborn's responses to stimulation, motor activity, ability to self-regulate, and irritability.

Posttraumatic Stress Disorder. In a study on women who had experienced sexual abuse, the women were given a 30-minute massage twice a week for 1 month and were compared with a standard treatment control group (Field, Hernandez-Reif, Hart, et al., 1997). Immediately after the massage, the women reported being less depressed and less anxious, and their salivary cortisol levels had decreased, suggesting decreased stress. Over the 1-month treatment period, the massage therapy group experienced a decrease in depression and in life events stress. Although we had anticipated the women might find touch aversive because of their earlier sex abuse, the women reported liking the massage.

Insomnia. In a study on insomnia, participants were randomly assigned to one of three conditions: a back massage; a teaching session on relaxation; and an audiotape session including muscle relaxation instruction, mental imagery instruction, and relaxing background music. Following 1 month of weekly sessions, sleep improved in the back massage group but not in the other two groups (K. C. Richards, 1998).

Eating Disorders. The effects of massage on eating disorders have also been researched. In one study, women diagnosed with anorexia nervosa received massage therapy twice a week for 5 weeks, and a control group received standard therapy (group therapy; Hart et al., 2001). The women in the massage group reported lower stress and anxiety levels and showed lower cortisol levels immediately following the massage. Over the 5-week treatment period, they also reported decreased body dissatisfaction on the Eating Disorder Inventory and showed increased dopamine and norepinephrine levels.

In another study, women diagnosed with bulimia were randomly assigned to a massage therapy or a standard treatment control group (group psychotherapy; Field, Schanberg, et al., 1998). The massage group received massages twice per week for 4 weeks and showed immediate reductions in anxiety and depression (both self-report and behavioral observation) after the massage sessions. In addition, by the last day of the therapy, they had lower depression scores, lower cortisol levels, and higher dopamine levels, and they showed improvement on depression and eating disorder scales.

Addictions. Surprisingly little massage therapy research has been conducted on the effects of massage on addictions. One exception is a smoking study by Hernandez-Reif, Field, and Hart (1999) in which smokers were randomly assigned to a self-massage treatment group or a control group that received the same assessments. The treatment group was taught to conduct a hand or ear self-massage (the men preferred rubbing their hands, and the women preferred rubbing their ears). The rubbing occurred during three cravings a day for 1 month. Self-reports revealed lower anxiety scores, improved mood, and fewer withdrawal symptoms. In addition, participants in the self-massage group smoked fewer cigarettes per day by the last week of the study, and 28% of the group quit smoking entirely.

Physical Conditions and Diseases: Pain Syndromes

Massage therapy has been studied in patients with common pain syndromes. Some studies reviewed here include low back pain, carpal tunnel syndrome, fibromyalgia, chronic fatigue syndrome, headaches, premenstrual syndrome, labor pain, and trauma pain.

Low Back Pain. Low back pain is one of the most common pain syndromes treated with massage therapy. In one study, patients who had persistent back pain received acupuncture, massage therapy, or self-care educational materials for up to 10 massage or acupuncture visits over 10 weeks (Cherkin et al., 2001). At 10 weeks, massage was superior to self-care on the Symptom Scale and the Disability Scale. Massage was also superior to acupuncture on the Disability Scale. The massage group used the least pain medications and had the lowest costs of subsequent care.

In a study by our group, adults with low back pain were randomly assigned to a massage therapy group or a progressive muscle relaxation group (Hernandez-Reif, Field, Krasnegor, & Theakston, 2001). Sessions were 30 minutes long, twice a week, for 5 weeks. By the end of the study, the massage therapy group reported less pain, decreased depression and anxiety, and improved sleep compared with the relaxation group. When tested for range of motion by having them stand tall and bend over to touch their toes, participants also showed improved standing, increased trunk flexion, and a higher pain threshold.

In a replication study on low back pain, my colleagues and I again examined massage therapy effects on pain, depression, anxiety, sleep disturbances, and trunk range of motion (Field, Hernandez-Reif, Diego, & Fraser, 2007). Once again, by the end of the study, the massage therapy group, compared with the relaxation group, reported experiencing less pain, depression, anxiety, and sleep disturbance, and they showed improved trunk and pain flexion performance. Even massage performed by automobile seat massagers has been assessed for its effects on low back pain (Kolich, Taboun, & Mohamed, 2000). The dependent variable was the change in the *electromyogram signal* (electrical signal from the muscle). One minute of lumbar massage every 5 minutes had a beneficial effect on low back muscle activity compared with no massage.

Burn Pain. Our research group has examined use of massage with burn-related pain (Field, Peck, et al., 1998). In one of our studies, adult patients with burns were randomly assigned before *debridement* (skin brushing) to either a massage therapy group or a standard treatment control group. Compared with the control group, the massage therapy group had greater decreases in anxiety and cortisol levels and greater changes in behavior ratings of mood, activity, vocalizations, and anxiety after the massage therapy sessions on the first and last days of treatment. Longer term effects were also significantly greater for the massage therapy group, including decreases in depression, anger, and pain.

Another study by our group focused on itching pain associated with burn healing. Patients with burn injuries were randomly assigned to a massage therapy or a standard treatment control group during wound healing (Field et al., 2000). The massage therapy group received a 30-minute massage with cocoa butter to a closed, moderate-sized scar tissue area twice a week for 5 weeks. The massage therapy group reported reduced itching, pain, and anxiety and improved mood immediately after the first and last therapy sessions.

Carpal Tunnel Syndrome. Carpal tunnel syndrome is the second most common work-related pain problem after low back pain. In one of our studies, adults with carpal tunnel syndrome were randomized to a 4-week self-massage group or a control group (Field, Diego, Cullen, et al., 2004). Participants in the self-massage group were taught a 10-minute massage routine that was done daily at work or at home. These same participants were also massaged once a week by a trained therapist for 10 minutes. Participants in the self-massage group improved on median peak latency (a measure of nerve conduction) and grip strength. They also reported lower levels of pain, anxiety, and depressed mood compared with the control group.

Fibromyalgia. Patients with fibromyalgia experience generalized pain throughout their bodies, and this condition is of unknown etiology. In a study by our research group, patients diagnosed with fibromyalgia were randomly assigned to a massage therapy, a transcutaneous electrical nerve stimulation (TENS), or a transcutaneous electrical nerve stimulation no-current group (sham TENS) for 30-minute treatment sessions two times per week for 5 weeks (Sunshine et al., 1996). Patients in the massage therapy group reported lower anxiety and depression, and their saliva cortisol levels were lower immediately after the therapy sessions on the first and last days of the study. By the last week of the study, they reported less pain, stiffness, and fatigue as well as fewer nights of difficult sleeping.

In a replication study, we again randomly assigned fibromyalgia patients to a massage therapy group or relaxation therapy group. This time we assessed the hypothesis that sleep deprivation was leading to *Substance P* (a chemical that causes pain and can be measured in saliva) release, in turn leading to pain (Field et al., 2002). Both groups participated in 30-minute sessions twice a week for 5 weeks. Across the course of the study, only the massage therapy group reported an increase in the number of sleep hours, and their activity watches registered fewer sleep movements. In addition, Substance P levels decreased, suggesting that patients in the massage therapy group were experiencing more deep sleep. Physicians of the massage therapy patients assigned lower disease and pain ratings and rated fewer tender points for these patients than did physicians of patients in the relaxation therapy group.

Chronic Fatigue Syndrome. Chronic fatigue syndrome is similar to fibromyalgia in terms of symptoms, although it appears to be accompanied by greater depression. In a study on chronic fatigue syndrome by our research group, we randomly assigned patients to a massage therapy group or a sham TENS control group (Field, Sunshine, et al., 1997). The massage therapy group had lower depression, emotional distress, and somatic symptom scores. They also had more hours of sleep and lower urinary epinephrine and cortisol levels.

Headaches. In a study on chronic headaches, individuals with a self-reported history of chronic headache (i.e., at least one headache per week for at least 6 months) received Trager massage (see earlier description) and were compared with a standard medical treatment group (K. A. Foster et al., 2004). Participants randomized to Trager massage experienced less frequent headaches and less need for medication than those in the standard-treatment group. In a similar study, adults with chronic tension headaches received massage therapy of the neck and shoulder muscles during a 4-week period (Quinn, Chandler, & Moraska, 2002). Massage therapy reduced the number of weekly headaches.

In a study by our research group, adults with migraine headaches were randomly assigned to a massage therapy group, which received twice-weekly 30-minute massages for 5 consecutive weeks or to a wait-list control group (Hernandez-Reif, Field, Dieter, Swerdlow, & Diego, 1998). The massage therapy group reported fewer distress symptoms, less pain, more headache-free days, and fewer sleep disturbances. They also took fewer analgesics and showed increased urinary serotonin levels. Figure 3.2 shows the percentage of reduced migraine days from the first day to the last day for participants in the massage therapy group.

Labor Pain. In a study on labor pain, women were randomly assigned to either a massage therapy group or a control group that practiced breathing exercises (M. Y. Chang, Wang, & Chen, 2002). The women in the massage therapy group reported less labor pain than the women in the control group. Our research group conducted a similar labor pain study, but the women were randomly assigned to receive both massage and coaching in breathing exercises from their partners or just to receive coaching in breathing exercises from their partners (Field, Hernandez-Reif, Taylor, Quintino, & Burman, 1997). The women in the massage group reported a greater decrease in depressed mood and anxiety and more positive affect following the first massage during labor. They also had significantly shorter labor, a shorter hospital stay, and less postpartum depression.

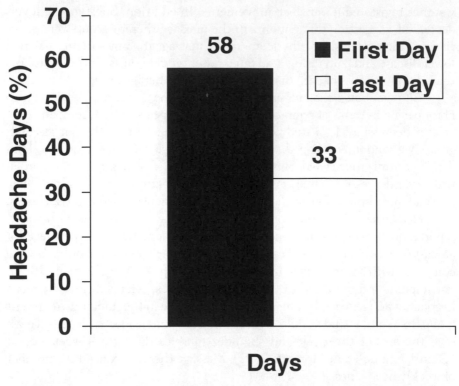

Figure 3.2. Decrease in percentage of headache days from the first day to the last day of massage therapy study for individuals with migraine headaches.

Postoperative Pain. A prospective randomized clinical trial compared pain relief after major operations in patients who received one of three nursing interventions: massage, extra attention from the nursing staff, or routine nursing care (Piotrowski et al., 2003). Interventions were performed twice daily starting 24 hours after the operation through 7 days postoperation. Patients in the massage group reported the greatest pain relief.

In another postoperative study, patients received 20-minute foot and hand massages (5 minutes to each extremity) 1 to 4 hours after a dose of pain medication (H. L. Wang & Keck, 2004). Participants reported decreased pain intensity, and decreased sympathetic responses to pain were observed (i.e., decreased heart rate and respiratory rate).

Trauma Pain. In a study by Kubsch, Neveau, and Vandertie (2000), emergency department patients (who have typically experienced severe injuries or trauma) received massage therapy to relieve pain. Following massage, patients reported significantly reduced pain, and reduced heart rate and blood pressure readings were observed.

Long-Term Joint Pain. Patients suffering from long-term joint pain were randomized to either a massage therapy group or a relaxation group

(Hasson, Arnetz, Jelveus, & Edelstam, 2004). The 30-minute sessions held weekly for 1 month led to decreased muscle pain in the massage therapy group but not the relaxation group.

In a study on shoulder pain, patients referred to physical therapy for shoulder pain were randomly assigned to receive six treatments of massage around the shoulder or to a standard medical treatment control group (van den Dolder & Roberts, 2003). The massage therapy group showed increased range of motion and decreased shoulder pain compared with the control group.

Premenstrual Syndrome Pain. Women with premenstrual syndrome were randomly assigned to a massage therapy group or a relaxation therapy group for 1 month of weekly 20-minute sessions (Hernandez-Reif, Martinez, Field, Quintero, & Hart, 2000). The massage therapy group showed decreased anxiety, depressed mood, and pain immediately after the massage sessions. By the last day of the study, women in the massage therapy group reported reduced menstrual distress symptoms including pain and water retention.

Musculoskeletal and Neurological Conditions

Patients with musculoskeletal and neurological conditions, including multiple sclerosis, Parkinson's disease, and spinal cord injuries, have benefited from massage therapy. In a study conducted by our research group, adults with multiple sclerosis were randomly assigned to a standard treatment control group or to a massage therapy group, which received massage therapy in addition to standard treatment. The massage therapy group received 45-minute massages twice a week for 5 weeks (Hernandez-Reif, Field, & Theakston, 1998). This group had lower anxiety and less depressed mood immediately following the massage sessions, and by the end of the study they had improved self-esteem, better body image, slower disease progression, and enhanced social functioning.

Another study by our group showed that patients with Parkinson's disease also receive benefits from massage therapy (Hernandez-Reif et al., 2002). Patients received either 30-minute massage or 30-minute progressive muscle relaxation sessions twice a week for 5 weeks. Physicians rated the massage therapy participants as more improved in daily living activities by the end of the study, and the participants reported being more effective and having less disturbed sleep.

In a study we conducted on spinal cord injury (Diego et al., 2002), the massage therapy group received two 40-minute sessions per week for 5 weeks, whereas the control group practiced a range of motion exercise routine targeting the arms, neck, shoulders, and back two times per week for 5 weeks. Although both the massage and exercise groups appeared to benefit from treatment, only the massage therapy group had lower anxiety and depression scores and had significantly increased muscle strength and range of motion in their arms.

Dancers also have musculoskeletal problems. In a study on dancers, our research group compared massage therapy with relaxation therapy (Leivadi et al., 1999). The therapies consisted of 30-minute sessions twice a week for 5 weeks. Both groups reported less neck, shoulder, and back pain after the treatment sessions and reduced back pain across the study. However, only the massage therapy group showed increased range of motion across the study, including greater neck extension and shoulder abduction.

Hypertension and Cardiac Conditions

Our research group also studied the effects of massage on hypertension. We randomly assigned individuals with hypertension to either a massage therapy group or a progressive muscle relaxation group (Hernandez-Reif, Field, et al., 2000). Those in the massage therapy group were given twice-weekly, 30-minute massages for 5 weeks, and the progressive muscle relaxation group sessions were conducted on the same schedule. Results showed that although both groups had lower anxiety levels and lower levels of depression, only the massage therapy group showed decreased diastolic and systolic blood pressure and decreased saliva and urinary cortisol levels. In a similar study, a 10-minute back massage three times a week for 10 sessions led to decreased systolic and decreased diastolic blood pressure (Olney, 2005).

A study by M. S. Kim, Cho, Woo, and Kim (2001) showed that even hand massage can be effective in reducing blood pressure. In this study, patients were divided into those given a hand massage 5 minutes before surgery and those not receiving a hand massage. After the hand massage, anxiety levels, systolic and diastolic blood pressures, and pulse rates were significantly lower than before the massage. The hand massage group also showed decreased epinephrine and norepinephrine (stress neurotransmitter) levels.

Immune Conditions

Breast Cancer. One of the most positive effects of massage therapy is the reduction in cortisol levels and a related increase in natural killer (NK) cells, suggesting improved immune function. In a study by our group, women diagnosed with Stage I or II breast cancer were randomly assigned postsurgery to a massage therapy group (receiving 30-minute massages three times per week for 5 weeks) or a standard treatment control group (Hernandez-Reif et al., 2003). Immediately after the massage therapy sessions, anxiety, depressed mood, and anger levels were lower. At the end of the study, women in the massage therapy group had lower depression and hostility levels and increased urinary dopamine, serotonin levels, NK cells, and lymphocytes.

In a replication study, women with breast cancer received one of three treatments to control for the possibility that the effects of massage could simply derive from the attention the women would receive from the therapist during the massages. They either received massage therapy or progressive muscle relaxation for 30-minute sessions three times a week for 5 weeks or served as a standard medical treatment control group (Hernandez-Reif et al., 2005). The massage therapy and relaxation groups reported less depressed mood, anxiety, and pain immediately after their first and last sessions. By the end of the study, however, only the massage therapy group reported being less depressed and less angry and having more vigor. Dopamine levels, NK cells, and lymphocytes also increased from the first to the last day of the study for the massage therapy group.

In a study to evaluate the effectiveness of massaging the arms following lymph node dissection surgery, Forchuk et al. (2004) first taught patients' significant others how to massage the patients' arms, and the partners then performed arm massage on the women as a postoperative support measure. The massage group was then compared with a standard medical treatment control group. The women who had been massaged by their partners had reduced pain in the immediate postoperative period and better shoulder function. Arm massage not only decreased pain and discomfort related to surgery but also promoted a sense of closeness and support between the women and their significant others.

Another study examined the effects of massage on pain, sleep quality, and anxiety in patients hospitalized for various types of cancer versus a control group who received nurse interaction (M. C. Smith, Kemp, Hemphill, & Vojir, 2002). Pain, sleep quality, and anxiety improved from baseline for the patients who received massage.

HIV. In two studies on male HIV patients conducted by our research group, patients who received massage therapy showed an increase in NK cells. In the first study, men with HIV were provided daily 45-minute massages for 1 month (Ironson et al., 1996). At the end of the month, the men receiving massage had decreased cortisol levels and increased NK cells and NK cell activity compared with the standard medical treatment group. Decreased anxiety and increased relaxation were significantly correlated with increased NK cell number.

In a second study on less immune-compromised HIV individuals, we hoped to show massage effects on the disease marker (CD4 cells). HIV-positive adolescents were randomly assigned to receive massage therapy or progressive muscle relaxation two times per week for 12 weeks (Diego, Hernandez-Reif, Field, Friedman, & Shaw, 2001). The adolescents who received massage therapy reported feeling less anxious and depressed compared with those who received relaxation therapy. By the end of the study, not only did those in the massage therapy group have increased NK cells, but their HIV disease progression markers CD4/CD8 ratio and CD4 number also increased, suggesting a slowing of the disease in these less immune compromised adolescents.

Exercise and Sports Performance

Massage is frequently used to improve exercise or sports performance and to reduce soreness after exercise sessions. In an exemplary study on improving performance, massage was used to improve power grip in adults (Brooks, Woodruff, Wright, & Donatelli, 2005). After 3 minutes of isometric exercise, power grip was consistently fatigued to at least 60% of baseline, but massage therapy was shown to have a greater effect than no massage or than placebo on grip performance after fatigue. In another exercise study, participants lay prone on a table and were instructed to extend their trunks until the inferior portion of their rib cage no longer rested on the table (H. Mori et al., 2004). Participants held this position for 90 seconds. They were then assigned to either a massage therapy group that received massage on the lumbar region for 5 minutes or a control group that simply rested for the same time. The increase in blood volume was higher after massage than after rest, and increased blood flow was only observed during the massage condition. An increase in temperature was also greater after massage than after rest, and a Visual Analog Scale score on fatigue was lower during massage.

Delayed-onset muscle soreness has also been reduced by massage therapy. In one study, participants performed 10 sets of six isokinetic exercises with each arm on a dynamometer (Zainuddin, Newton, Sacco, & Nosaka, 2005). One arm received 10 minutes of massage 3 hours after exercise, whereas the contralateral arm received no treatment. Delayed-onset muscle soreness was significantly less for the massaged arm.

In another study, volunteers were randomly assigned to a massage group or a control group (Hilbert, Sforzo, & Swensen, 2003). Two hours after bicycling exercise, participants received either 20 minutes of massage or sham massage (control). Intensity of soreness was significantly lower in the massage group compared with the control group at 48 hours postexercise.

ACUPRESSURE AND REFLEXOLOGY

Acupressure and reflexology are similar in that they both involve application of moderate pressure to pressure points. Reflexology, however, is typically applied to the feet and acupressure to the upper back region.

Acupressure

Acupressure, like acupuncture, has origins in Chinese medicine. Acupressure and Shiatsu (a Japanese form of acupressure) are similar to acupuncture in that they focus on pressure points that are similar to those that are targeted by acupuncture. Applied pressure on the pressure points is thought to rebuild energy at those points so that energy can flow freely through the body's meridians. Acupressure was used before acupuncture was developed, basically treating the same pressure points but using parts of the body such as thumbs and elbows to apply the stimulation rather than needles.

A typical acupressure or Shiatsu session lasts 30 to 90 minutes. The therapy takes place on the floor to enable the therapists to use full-body weight and to provide a deeper level of pressure. The client usually lies on top of a blanket, rug, mat, or other padded surface.

Self-acupressure can also be used by applying pressure with one's hands to various body parts. One of the most common pressure points is the area about 2 inches above the wrist, which is thought to relieve nausea. Pressing the thumb on that area is a common technique for relieving the nausea that is associated, for example, with seasickness. Another pressure point is the one in the web between the thumb and the forefinger, which when pressed is thought to relieve headaches. A third point about a hand width up from the inner ankle is believed to relieve menstrual cramps when pressed. Pressure to the back of the ankle on the Achilles' tendon during pregnancy is thought to stimulate premature contractions and so should be avoided.

Reflexology

Reflexology is a technique of applying pressure to specific points on the hands; feet; and, less commonly, the ears. It is most often used on the feet because reflexologists view the foot as a microcosm of the body, with reflex areas on the foot corresponding to major organs. For example, the ball of the foot is thought to correspond to the chest and lungs, the heel to the sciatic nerve and the pelvic area, and the toes to the head and neck. The left foot is thought to represent the left side of the body and the right foot to represent the right side of the body. Reflexologists believe that applying pressure to specific areas of the foot will channel energy to the corresponding part of the body.

Reflexology is thought to be older than acupuncture. Some have suggested that reflexology stimulates sensory receptors that then travel to the spinal cord (Freeman, 2004). Others have suggested that it promotes relaxation and thereby improves circulation. Still others have suggested that the beneficial effects of reflexology are due to the pressure applied that dissolves crystal deposits in the body that are settled in the feet. Some have contended that pressure on areas of the feet releases a group of pain-blocking chemicals called *endorphins* into the bloodstream and thus eases pain.

Empirical Support for the Effects of Acupressure and Reflexology

Compared with massage therapy, acupressure and reflexology have not been studied as broadly or as frequently. However, a number of studies have looked at the effects of acupressure on nausea, and a few studies have been conducted with regard to other conditions.

Nausea

One study on patients receiving endoscopic sinus surgery under general anesthesia evaluated the use of acupressure points to prevent postoperative nausea and vomiting (Ming, Kuo, Lin, & Lin, 2002). Patients were randomly assigned to a finger-pressing group (actively applying stimulation), a wrist-band group (passive application of stimulation by the wrist band), or a control group of patients who were engaged in conversation. The acupoints were similar in the finger-pressing group and wrist-band group. In both acupressure groups, the incidence of nausea decreased from 73% to 43% and the incidence of vomiting decreased from 90% to 43%.

Acupressure has also been linked to less nausea in postoperative gastric cancer patients receiving their first cycle of chemotherapy (Y. H. Shin, Kim, Shin, & Juon, 2004). The finger acupressure maneuver was performed for 5 minutes on the point located at three-finger widths up from the first palmar crease of the hand at least three times a day before chemotherapy. Patients in the acupressure group had less severe nausea and vomiting compared with those in the control group.

Acupressure wristbands have been linked to alleviation of nausea and vomiting in early pregnancy. In one study, 71% of women in the group who wore the acupressure bands routinely reported both less intensive morning sickness and reduced duration of symptoms than those who did not (Norheim, Pederson, Fonnebo, & Berge, 2001). Similar effects were noted by another group using the same procedure (Werntoft & Dykes, 2001).

Lower Back Pain

Reflexology was used on patients with lower back pain in a study by Degan et al. (2000). Sixty-three percent of the reflexology group versus the standard treatment control group reported a reduction in pain following only three 30-minute reflexology sessions over 1 week.

Acupressure has been compared with physical therapy in reducing low back pain (Hsieh, Kuo, Yen, & Chen, 2004). The mean posttreatment pain score after a 4-week period of once-weekly, 1-hour treatments was lower in the acupressure group than in the physical therapy group. At the 6-month follow-up assessment, the mean pain score in the acupressure group was still lower than that of the physical therapy group.

Chronic Obstructive Pulmonary Disease

In one study, acupressure was linked with improved pulmonary function in chronic obstructive pulmonary disease (H. S. Wu, Wu, Lin, & Lin, 2004). Patients were randomly assigned either to a true acupoint acupressure group or a sham acupressure (pressure applied to an area not considered a pressure point) group. Both groups received five sessions per week, lasting 16 minutes per session for 4 weeks, for a total of 20 sessions. Pulmonary function, 6-minute walking distance measurements, and state anxiety scale scores improved significantly for the true acupoint acupressure group compared with those of the sham acupressure group.

Multiple Sclerosis

A study of patients with multiple sclerosis showed that reflexology can alleviate some symptoms of the disease (Siev-Ner, Gamus, Lerner-Geva, & Achiron, 2003). The reflexology treatment included manual pressure on specific points on the feet and massage of the calf area over a 30-minute weekly session over an 11-week period. Significant improvement in symptoms of multiple sclerosis, including paresthesias, urinary symptoms, and spasticity, occurred in the reflexology group. The reduced intensity of paresthesias persisted at a 3-month follow-up.

Cancer

Foot reflexology has also been shown to alleviate anxiety and pain in patients with breast and lung cancers (Stephenson, Weinrich, & Tavakoli, 2000). Following one session of foot reflexology, patients with breast and lung cancer experienced decreased anxiety, and patients with breast cancer experienced decreased pain.

Renal Disease and Sleep Disturbance

A study by Tsay, Rong, and Lin (2003) assessed the effects of acupressure on patients with end-stage renal disease who were experiencing sleep disturbances. The patients were randomly assigned to an acupressure group, a sham acupressure group, and a control group. Acupressure group patients received acupressure on specific acupoints and sham acupressure group patients received sham acupressure three times a week for 30-minute sessions for 4 weeks during hemodialysis treatment. Sleep log data revealed that the acupressure group had improved quality of sleep compared with the sham acupressure or control group.

REFERRING CLIENTS TO MASSAGE THERAPY, ACUPRESSURE, AND REFLEXOLOGY PRACTITIONERS

Most states require licensure for massage therapists that is based on approximately 1,000 hours of coursework. Thus, most therapists are more interested in referring their clients to massage therapists rather than receiving training and being licensed themselves. Referrals are most often based on local recommendations. If those are not available, most cities have massage therapy schools that can be contacted for referral sources, and the American Massage Therapy Association (http://www.amtamassage.org/) provides contact information for local massage therapists.

4

ACUPUNCTURE

Acupuncture involves stimulating very specific points (i.e., selected among several hundred potential acupoints) on the skin, usually with a specially designed needle, for therapeutic purposes. As a component of Chinese medicine, lore has it that acupuncture evolved from bloodletting. In China, as early as 8000 BC, bloodletting and abscess draining were done by primitive stones shaped into knives.

Later, Chinese physicians noticed that acupuncture or pressure on certain parts of the body led to feelings of tickling, numbness, or anesthesia. Acupuncture was first introduced in the United States by the grandson of Benjamin Franklin in 1825. However, it did not become popular until 1971, when an actor named James Reston described how acupuncture alleviated his postoperative pain following an emergency appendectomy. (For historical information about acupuncture, see Freeman, 2004.)

As practiced in the Western world, acupuncture usually involves anywhere from 3 to 10 needles that are inserted fairly quickly into specific acupoints to treat the condition in question. The angle and the depth of the insertion at each point are critical. Small heated cones of earth may also be applied at acupoints, a procedure that is called *moxibustion*. Although puncturing the skin with the needle is the usual method of acupuncture, acupuncturists can also apply heat, pressure, friction, or suction. Electrical stimulation is another way of stimulating the acupoints.

Insertion of the needle may or may not cause mild discomfort but not usually pain. The penetration varies according to the point being needled. The therapist can locate the optimal point by feeling the surface of the skin. Once the needle is inserted, the patient typically describes feelings of tingling, numbness, warmth, or aching. The needles are typically left in place for about 10 to 20 minutes (Ceniceros & Brown, 1998).

Different durations of needle insertion have been evaluated using functional magnetic resonance imaging (fMRI; K. Li et al., 2006). The stimulation of manual acupuncture with different durations has been shown to induce different effects on the central nervous system. Longer duration manual acupuncture has the most effect on activity in different areas of the brain. Trigger points or points that are painful to touch have been considered possible acupoints. Some have suggested that acupoints are a form of electrical energy because they show decreased skin resistance (Salzberg, Miller, & Johnson, 1995).

POTENTIAL MECHANISMS OF ACTION FOR ACUPUNCTURE

Several writers have suggested that acupuncture works by correcting the balance of energy, or Chi (Qi), in the body, which flows through 12 channels or meridians to organs and organ systems. Six of the meridians are considered yin channels and six are considered yang channels (see chap. 2, this volume, pp. 14–15). Each meridian is named for an organ or function (e.g., lungs, heart, large intestine).

Chi flows freely if the person is balanced and healthy, but if Chi is blocked, the person may become mentally or physically ill. Inappropriate expressions of anger, grief, or fear are thought to signal an imbalance of Chi. To restore health, the acupuncturist stimulates the points that produce balance. Although many points are linked by nerves, blood vessels, or lymphatics, it is surprising that no channel (meridian) "connects" organs, suggesting that there may not be specific meridians for specific organs (Wharton & Lewis, 1986).

Others have suggested that acupuncture effects can be explained by the "gate theory" (J. Foster & Sweeney, 1987). Metaphorically, the gate theory holds that pain messages travel more slowly than pressure messages, which reach the brain faster and close the "gate" to the pain message. A more specific biological explanation is that cells in the dorsal horn of the spinal cord act like a switch between the nerve impulses from the different neuronal fibers. Pain is carried more slowly by the less insulated (*unmyelinated*) C neurons, whereas acupuncture, touch, or vibration signals are carried more rapidly by the A neurons (*myelinated*), which closes the gate to the C impulses and allows the A signals through. In this way, the acupuncture stimulation (A fibers) closes the gate to the pain stimulus (C fibers; Melzack & Wall, 1965).

Another possible mechanism, one that may be shared with the mechanism of massage therapy, is that the stimulation of pressure receptors under the skin by either acupuncture or massage may increase vagal activity that leads to reduced cortisol levels and increased serotonin levels (for a review, see Field, Diego, & Hernandez-Reif, 2007). Indirect support of this was provided by a review showing that acupuncture was less effective in relieving physical pain of patients with depression, who typically have lower serotonin levels than nondepressed individuals (Sims, 1997).

Others have suggested that acupuncture releases endogenous opioid peptides that kill pain (Murray, 1995). The problem with this theory is that acupuncture effects are only partially reversed by *naloxone* (an endorphin antagonist), suggesting that other systems may also be involved (Murray, 1995). The dominant explanation for how acupuncture might work involves neurochemical responses in specific portions of the brain. In this model, acupuncture is not reported to be dependent on specific acupoints or on the means or method of stimulation (Moffet, 2006). In support of this explanation, G. Li, Jack, and Yang (2006) conducted a study of somatosensory acupuncture points in stable stroke patients and in control patients who had not had a stroke and assessed the differences in brain responses to needling and to electrical acupuncture stimulation using fMRI. Needling stimulation in both stroke patients and controls produced significant activation in primary and secondary sensory and motor cortical areas and the cerebellum. There was greater activation in the somatosensory cortex in stroke patients than in controls with both the needling and the electrical acupuncture point stimulation, with needling stimulating more than the electrical acupuncture stimulation in both groups.

One of the problems associated with acupuncture research in general is that the sham procedures often produce as much effect as real acupuncture. Superficial needle insertion is typically thought to be a form of placebo treatment. However, some researchers have suggested that superficial needle insertion may be as effective as real needling (Furlan et al., 2005). Sham acupuncture supposedly produces analgesia in 40% to 50% of patients compared with real acupuncture, which produces analgesia in approximately 60% of patients. For example, in a systematic review of acupuncture for low back pain, although it was concluded that acupuncture was more effective for giving relief than nontreatments or sham treatments, the average reductions of pain were on the order of 32% for the acupuncture group and 23% for the sham intervention. Similarly, in a large trial on neck pain, the real acupuncture treatment was compared with a placebo that involved mock electrical stimulation of acupuncture points (P. White, Lewith, Prescott, & Conway,

2004). In this trial, there was a 60% reduction in pain for the acupuncture group and a 42% reduction for the placebo group.

It may simply be that there are so many acupoints along meridians that virtually any place in the body where acupuncture is applied, as long as it is deep enough to stimulate pressure receptors (as in massage therapy), will lead to therapeutic effects. One major problem in exploring this hypothesis is that those in the typical sham or placebo condition receive superficial needling at points not considered critical acupoints. Thus, it is impossible so far to tease out whether the critical factor for the effects of acupuncture is deep insertion of needles or insertion of needles at specific acupoints or both.

Research has also been hindered because control groups have not been standardized across studies. In addition, many of the acupuncture studies are limited because they are underpowered, nonrandomized, or unblinded. Nonetheless, a National Institutes of Health (1994) consensus conference on acupuncture research established that acupuncture was effective for improving immune function, for postoperative and chemotherapy-induced nausea and vomiting, and for postoperative dental pain. In addition, the conference data indicate that acupuncture may be useful for treating headaches, low back pain, and paralysis resulting from stroke.

EMPIRICAL SUPPORT FOR THE EFFECTS OF ACUPUNCTURE

Earlier research on the effects of acupuncture had largely focused on treatment of pain syndromes and addictions, possibly because these conditions have been most responsive to acupuncture. However, studies in other areas were found in the literature on the use of acupuncture with psychological and neurological disorders such as stroke and nausea.

Psychological Symptoms and Disorders

Anxiety

In a study on anxiety, patients having dental extractions were randomized to *auricular* (ear) acupuncture, placebo acupuncture, and intranasal midazolam (a drug used for muscle relaxation and sedation) and were compared with a no-treatment group (Karst et al., 2007). Patients in the auricular acupuncture group and the midazolam group were significantly less anxious at 30 minutes after the treatment compared with patients in the placebo acupuncture group. In addition, patient compliance assessed by the dentist was significantly improved if auricular acupuncture or application of intranasal midazolam had been performed.

Another study explored the effects of acupuncture on women experiencing anxiety (Arranz, Guayerbas, Siboni, & De la Fuente, 2007). The acupuncture protocol for this study was manual needle stimulation of 19 acupoints, with each weekly session lasting 30 minutes over a period of 1 month. Anxiety was immediately reduced. The most favorable effects of acupuncture on immune function appeared 72 hours after a single session and persisted 1 month after the end of the complete treatment. Although anxiety often dampens immune function, and both were changed by acupuncture, it is unclear whether these effects lasted beyond the treatment period.

Addictions

Acupuncture is notably effective for addictions such as smoking. The results of controlled trials of auricular acupuncture or acupressure for smoking cessation were combined in an exploratory meta-analysis (A. White & Moody, 2006). Comparisons of three higher quality studies in this meta-analysis suggested that "correct" and "incorrect" acupoint acupuncture were no different, and two studies showed that "incorrect" acupoint acupuncture may be more effective than other interventions. Thus, auricular acupuncture appears to be effective for smoking cessation, but the effect may not depend on acupoint location.

Acupuncture has also been used with cocaine-using individuals (Avants, Margolin, Chang, Kosten, & Birch, 1995). Daily acupuncture was provided in four "correct" auricular sites, and daily acupuncture in a second group was provided in three sites but 2 to 3 millimeters from the "correct" site. Cocaine use decreased significantly for both groups, but the only statistically significant difference was noted for the category of cravings, which improved more for the "correct" site group. In a psychiatric unit study, the effects of auricular acupuncture were assessed in substance-abusing patients (Gurevich, Duckworth, Imhof, & Katz, 1996). The treatment group did significantly better than the control group in several ways, including compliance with treatment (75% vs. 20%) and remaining in follow-up treatment for at least 4 months (58% vs. 26%).

Physical Conditions and Diseases: Pain Syndromes

Acupuncture has been predominantly and most effectively used with pain syndromes such as osteoarthritis and headache. Although it is widely used in relieving pain, the mechanisms and effects of acupuncture on pain are not completely understood. In a study by Tsuchiya, Sato, Inoue, and Asada (2007), increased nitric oxide (NO) was found in meridians and acupoints. Because NO is a key regulator of local blood circulation, and because change in circulation can affect the development and persistence of pain, Tsuchiya et al. proposed that acupuncture might regulate NO levels. Patients in the treatment group received acupuncture five or more times compared with patients who refused acupuncture or had four or fewer treatments (the control group). NO concentration in the plasma from an acupunctured versus a nonacupunctured arm was significantly increased. Blood flow in palmar subcutaneous tissue of the acupunctured arm also increased, and this correlated with the NO increase.

Some positive results of acupuncture on pain, however, may be caused by positive expectations of the treatment. For example, in a recent study of acupuncture's effects on a variety of chronic pain syndromes, patients received either 12 sessions of acupuncture or sham acupuncture (nonacupuncture points) over an 8-week period (Linde et al., 2007). Patients were asked at baseline whether they considered acupuncture to be an effective therapy in general and what they personally expected from the treatment. A significant association was shown between decreased pain and higher outcome expectations, and no differences were noted between the sham and real acupuncture groups.

Osteoarthritis

Patients with chronic pain due to osteoarthritis of the knee or hip were randomly assigned to 15 sessions of acupuncture over a 3-month period or to a control group receiving no acupuncture (Witt et al., 2006). Pain severity and health-related quality of life were assessed. At 3 months, pain severity had decreased more in the acupuncture group than in the control group. Similarly, improvements in quality of life were more pronounced in the acupuncture group than in the control group.

In a meta-analysis, studies were included in which adults with chronic knee pain or osteoarthritis of the knee were treated with acupuncture (A. White, Foster, Cummings, & Barlas, 2007). Across five studies that together included 1,334 patients, acupuncture was superior to sham acupuncture for both pain and for functional improvement. In another meta-analysis conducted to evaluate the evidence for the effectiveness of acupuncture for peripheral joint osteoarthritis (Y. Kwon, Pittler, & Ernst, 2006), 10 studies demonstrated greater pain reduction in the acupuncture groups.

Fibromyalgia

Fibromyalgia is pain experienced over the entire body with no known etiology. In a study by Martin, Sletten, Williams, and Berger (2006), fibromyalgia patients receiving true acupuncture were compared with a control group that received simulated acupuncture. Fibromyalgia symptoms were significantly decreased in the acupuncture group compared with the control group during the study period.

Headaches

In an epidemiological study by Melchart et al. (2006), headache patients reported clinically relevant improvements after receiving acupuncture. However, in a randomized trial study, both the acupuncture group and sham group showed improvement, and the groups did not differ on medication use or frequency of headaches (Tavola, Gala, Conte, & Invernizzi, 1992).

In another headache study, migraine patients were randomized either to acupuncture or pain medication (metoprolol) for a 12-week period (Streng et al., 2006). The proportion of responders (reduction of migraine attacks ($\geq$ 50%) was 61% for acupuncture and 49% for metoprolol.

Neck Pain

Neck pain is one of the three most frequently reported complaints involving the musculoskeletal system. In a recent study, acupuncture treatments (10 sessions) for chronic neck pain were more effective than inactive sham acupuncture treatments (Trinh et al., 2007). However, there was limited evidence that acupuncture was more effective than sham acupuncture at short-term follow-up. In a similar procedure study, neck pain and disability decreased (Witt et al., 2006).

Back Pain

Low back pain is notably responsive to acupuncture. In a recent study by Weidenhammer, Linde, Streng, Hoppe, and Melchart (2007), after 6 months of treatment (and a 6-month follow-up), 46% of the patients demonstrated clinically significant improvements in their functional ability scores. The mean number of days patients experienced pain was decreased by half. Patients who were employed reported a 30% decrease from baseline in days of work lost because of pain.

In another study, acupuncture stimulation was applied to the most painful point in patients with low back pain (Inoue et al., 2006). For the acupuncture group, needles were inserted to a depth of 20 millimeters and manually stimulated for 20 seconds. For the sham treatment, a guide tube without a needle was placed at the point and tapped on the skin. Acupuncture at the most painful point gave immediate relief of low back pain.

To evaluate the cost-effectiveness of acupuncture in the management of persistent nonspecific low back pain, Ratcliffe, Thomas, MacPherson, and Brazier (2006) gave 10 acupuncture treatments over 3 months versus usual medical care only. This relatively short course of traditional acupuncture for persistent nonspecific low back pain was cost-effective compared with usual care.

Temporomandibular Joint Pain

Jaw pain (in the temporomandibular joint) can be extremely painful. A recent study compared the effects of real acupuncture and sham acupuncture in the treatment of temporomandibular joint pain over a period of 3 months (P. Smith, Mosscrop, Davies, Sloan, & Al-Ani, 2007). Real acupuncture had a greater influence on reduction of jaw pain than sham acupuncture.

Labor Pain

Labor pain has also been reduced by acupuncture. In one study, women in the active phase of first-stage labor were randomly assigned to either transcutaneous electrical nerve stimulation (TENS) on four acupuncture points or a TENS placebo group (Chao et al., 2006). A visual analogue scale was used to assess pain. The TENS acupuncture group experienced greater pain reduction compared with the TENS placebo group.

Another labor study found that acupuncture reduced pain, the duration of the active phase of labor, and the oxytocin units required for labor progression (Hantoushzadeh, Alhusseini, & Lebaschi, 2007). Acupuncture has also been compared with breathing exercises (control) during labor (Harper et al., 2006). The mean time to delivery occurred 21 hours sooner in the acupuncture group than in the breathing exercise group. Women in the acupuncture group were also more likely to labor spontaneously without being given medication to accelerate labor and less likely to deliver by cesarean section.

Breech presentation has also been treated with acupuncture (Neri et al., 2004). The percentage of cesarean sections indicated for breech presentation in this study was significantly lower in the acupuncture group than in the observation group.

Musculoskeletal and Neurological Disorders

Acupuncture has been used to alleviate symptoms of several musculoskeletal and neurological disorders. Despite the popularity of such use, the evidence to support the use of acupuncture in these conditions is contradictory. For example, in a review designed to summarize and evaluate the available evidence of such acupuncture use, no firm conclusions could be drawn on whether acupuncture treatment was effective for symptoms of epilepsy, Alzheimer's disease, Parkinson's disease, ataxic disorders, multiple sclerosis, amyotrophic lateral sclerosis, or spinal cord injury (H. Lee et al., 2007).

More robust data have been published for acupuncture therapy with patients suffering from peripheral neuropathy (pain and numbness in hands and feet) diagnosed by nerve conduction studies (Schröder, Liepert, Remppis, & Greten, 2007). After 4 months of treatment, 76% of patients in the acupuncture group improved symptomatically and objectively as measured by nerve conduction. However, the study did not include a control group.

Other Medical Conditions

Nausea and Vomiting

Acupuncture has been effective for reducing nausea and vomiting. Results from 26 trials showed acupuncture stimulation to be effective for post-operative nausea and vomiting (Streitberger, Ezzo, & Schneider, 2006). Experimental studies based on fMRI showed positive effects of electrostimulation on gastric myoelectrical activity, vagal modulation, and cerebellar vestibular activity (Streitberger et al., 2006).

In a review of acupuncture and postoperative nausea, chemotherapy-induced nausea and vomiting, and pregnancy-related nausea and vomiting (Ezzo, Streitberger, & Schneider, 2006), the results for postoperative nausea and vomiting were the most consistent, suggesting the superiority of acupuncture stimulation over sham acupuncture. Stimulation seemed to be superior to antiemetic medication for nausea and was equally effective as medication for vomiting. Results for chemotherapy-induced nausea and vomiting showed that electroacupuncture, but not manual acupuncture, was beneficial for first-day vomiting.

Colitis

Joos et al. (2006) investigated the efficacy of acupuncture and moxibustion in the treatment of active ulcerative colitis. All of the patients were treated in 10 sessions over a period of 5 weeks. Scores on the Colitis Activity Index decreased in the acupuncture and moxibustion groups. Acupuncture may be effective in patients with functional gastrointestinal disorders because it has been shown to alter acid secretion, gastrointestinal motility, and visceral pain (Takahashi, 2006).

Sleep Apnea

In one study, patients with sleep apnea received acupuncture or sham acupuncture once a week for 10 weeks (Freire et al., 2007). Scores on the Apnea Index and the number of respiratory events decreased in the acupuncture group but not in the sham group.

Menopausal and Postmenopausal Symptoms

In a study on postmenopausal symptoms, women were assigned to estrogen, acupuncture, or muscle relaxation groups to receive one of these treatments for 12 weeks or were assigned to a placebo control group (Zaborowska et al., 2007). The estrogen, acupuncture, and muscle relaxation groups experienced significantly fewer hot flashes than did the placebo group.

Acupuncture has been assessed with postmenopausal women who had been previously treated for breast cancer and currently had depressed mood and vasomotor symptoms (Nedstrand, Wyon, Hammar, & Wijma, 2006). The women were randomized to receive either 12 sessions of electroacupuncture or muscle relaxation. Over the 12-week study period, hot flashes were reduced by more than 50% and mood improved significantly in the acupuncture group compared with no change in the relaxation group.

REFERRING PATIENTS TO ACUPUNCTURE AND ACUPRESSURE PRACTITIONERS

As noted in Appendix B, acupuncture requires extensive schooling and licensure. Even though many conditions that are accompanied by depression, such as fibromyalgia, chronic fatigue syndrome, and lower back pain, could benefit from acupuncture, therapists do not typically become licensed in acupuncture. Rather, they can make referrals by calling local training schools or national organizations that have lists of licensed acupuncturists by geographical areas. Many of these referral sources appear in Appendix C or can be found on the Internet.

Inasmuch as many people have an aversive reaction to the thought of needling, a referral is difficult to make unless the therapist has confidence that needling will be pain free. Many people who have tried acupuncture have been surprised at the lack of pain associated with needling. Other alternatives may be tried first, such as acupressure on specific acupoints or transcutaneous electrical stimulation that does not involve needles. This may be a way of working up to trying acupuncture.

5

TAI CHI AND CHI GONG

Tai Chi and Chi Gong are both Chinese martial arts. Tai Chi typically involves movement from a standing position and looks like a choreographed dance. Chi Gong typically takes place in a seated position, and movements are confined to the upper body. Chi Gong is focused more on breathing and meditation.

TAI CHI

Tai Chi has been widely practiced in China as a martial art and as a form of gentle exercise. In Chinese, the words *Tai Chi Chuan* mean "supreme ultimate fist," which is thought to refer to its lofty status among the martial arts (Freeman, 2004). It is interesting to note that Tai Chi has become increasingly popular in the Western world as aerobics is becoming more popular in the Eastern world.

Tai Chi consists of a series of postures performed slowly in a sequence, providing a smooth, continuous, and low-intensity activity. The sequences of postures are known as *forms*. The forms vary in complexity, with some involving as few as 18 postures and others more than 100 postures. The forms involve moving from one posture to the next in a flowing motion that resembles dance. Figure 5.1 provides one example of a Tai Chi balancing pose, called *karate pose*.

Although Tai Chi is not considered as physically demanding as other martial arts like karate and judo, a great deal of time is required to master the forms, and each posture requires considerable concentration. Note that unlike other martial arts, Tai Chi is not competitive; there are no colored belts or uniforms to indicate rankings. Postures and forms are learned slowly, but once they are learned, the pace of Tai Chi can increase.

Tai Chi Classes

Tai Chi movements are typically taught and memorized in classes that generally last from 40 to 60 minutes and occur once or twice a week. Classes begin with exercises that prepare the student for the postures, which are then combined into the forms. Once the postures and forms are memorized and mastered, Tai Chi can be practiced at home. Students usually wear loose, comfortable clothing and soft shoes or their bare feet.

Many of the postures and movements have names from nature, such as "grasping the bird's tail," "parting the horse's mane," and "waving hands like clouds." The movements are circular and rhythmic, and each of the postures moves slowly into the next posture following the sequence of the form.

Figure 5.1. An example of a Tai Chi balancing pose, the *karate pose*.

The sequential movements of the postures appear to be opposites. For example, curves are followed by straight movements, movements to the right are preceded by turning slightly to the left, rising up movements are preceded by slight sinking movements, and forward movements are counterbalanced by backward movements. Weight is taken off the lower back and assumed by the thighs. Several of the movements entail bending of the knees and bending of the elbows and wrists.

Preferences regarding the characteristics of Tai Chi classes have been studied. In one study, older adult Chinese participants preferred Tai Chi styles that are slow and feature large motions, and they preferred to practice Tai Chi in groups of 10 to 20 people about twice a week for 30 to 60 minutes in the early morning or late afternoon (K. Chen, Chen, Wang, & Huang, 2005). More research of this kind is needed to design programs to match participant characteristics.

Empirical Support for the Effects of Tai Chi

Students of Tai Chi claim long-term benefits in terms of physical strength and balance. The emphasis in the research literature has been on benefits to muscle tone, flexibility, balance, and coordination, with most research focused on balance, particularly in older adults. However, some studies have focused on mental health benefits, including those pertaining to depression, anxiety, attentional deficits, and sleep problems. Tai Chi effects on physiological functions such as heart rate, respiration, and blood pressure have also been studied, as have its effects on pain syndromes, musculoskeletal disorders, cancer, and HIV.

Psychological Symptoms and Disorders

Stress Levels, Anxiety, and Other Emotions. Decreased anxiety and stress levels following Tai Chi sessions have been noted across several studies (Jin, 1992; Taylor-Piliae, Haskell, Waters, & Froelicher, 2006; Y. Wang, Taylor, Pearl, & Chang, 2004). These effects were measured on Cohen's Perceived Stress Scale, on the Profile of Mood States, and on the State–Trait Anxiety Inventory.

On the basis of similar visual analog mood scales, Tai Chi has also been associated with decreased sadness, confusion, anger, and fear as well as increased energy and happiness (Gemmell & Leathem, 2006). Similar changes in mood state and decreased cortisol have been reported for both beginners and advanced practitioners of Tai Chi (Jin, 1989).

Sleep. Decreased stress, anxiety, and depression may relate to changes in sleep that have been reported following Tai Chi in at least two studies (F. Li et al., 2004; Wall, 2005). In F. Li et al.'s (2004) study, Tai Chi practitioners were compared with low-impact exercise participants. The Tai Chi participants reported significantly greater improvements in the Pittsburgh Sleep Quality Index subscale scores, including sleep quality, sleep-onset latency, sleep duration, sleep efficiency, and sleep disturbances (F. Li et al., 2004). The Tai Chi participants also reported a sleep-onset latency of about 18 minutes less per night and a sleep duration of 48 minutes more per night compared with the low-impact exercise participants.

Attention-Deficit/Hyperactivity Disorder. In a study my colleagues and I conducted on Tai Chi with adolescents with attention-deficit/hyperactivity disorder, 30-minute Tai Chi sessions were held weekly for 10 weeks (Hernandez-Reif, Field, & Thimas, 2001). We found enhanced attentiveness and decreased anxiety levels.

Physical Conditions and Diseases: Pain Syndromes

Fibromyalgia. People with fibromyalgia have responded positively to Tai Chi. Following 6 weeks of 1-hour, twice-weekly Tai Chi classes, fibromyalgia symptoms of Tai Chi participants decreased on the Fibromyalgia Impact Questionnaire (Taggart, Arslanian, Bae, & Singh, 2003).

Osteoarthritis. In a study on women with osteoarthritis, a 12-week Tai Chi program led to less pain and joint stiffness and fewer perceived difficulties in physical functioning (Song, Lee, Lam, & Bae, 2003). In addition, the Tai Chi participants showed greater increases in physical fitness, balance, and abdominal muscle strength. Similarly, in a study on knee osteoarthritis in older adults, 12 weeks of Tai Chi training led to reduced knee pain and stiffness and improved physical function (Brismee et al., 2007).

Osteoporosis

Osteoporosis is a worldwide problem, particularly with menopausal and postmenopausal women, that is increasing significantly as the global population increases in age (Chan et al., 2004). Tai Chi has been used in the treatment and prevention of osteoporosis as well as the general maintenance of women's health during menopause. Bone mineral density is typically measured using dual-energy X-ray absorptiometry (Qin et al., 2002 , 2005; Xu, Lawson, Kras, & Ryan, 2005). In one study, the Tai Chi practitioners had significantly higher bone mineral density than the comparison group, and although bone loss occurred in both groups, decelerated rates of bone loss were noted in the Tai Chi group (Xu et al., 2005). In another study, a significant slowing of bone loss was found in the group that regularly practiced Tai Chi 45 minutes a day, 5 days a week, for 12 months (Chan et al., 2004). Still another study reported an overall higher bone mineral density at all measurement sites, an average of 43% significantly greater strength, and 68% significantly longer single-stance time for the Tai Chi group compared with an age-matched control group (Qin et al., 2005).

Immune Conditions

Breast Cancer. In a study on breast cancer, patients' functional capacity was assessed following 12 weeks of Tai Chi three times per week (Mustian, Katula, & Zhao, 2006). Aerobic capacity, muscular strength, and flexibility improved in the Tai Chi group compared with patients in the control group who received psychosocial therapy.

HIV. One study found that patients with HIV improved on overall functioning measures, including the reach-for-balance test, the sit-and-reach test for flexibility, and the sit-up test for endurance, following 1 month of weekly Tai Chi classes (Galantino et al., 2005). Both the Tai Chi group and the comparison aerobic exercise group showed improved health and enhanced psychological coping. Immune regulation in middle-aged volunteers with HIV was also noted after 12 weeks of Tai Chi (S. Yeh, Chuang, Lin, Hsiao, & Eng, 2006), including a significant increase in CD4 cells (the cells killed by the virus). In a similar study on individuals with *herpes zoster* (shingles), immunity increased 50% from baseline to 1 week following 15 weeks of Tai Chi (Irwin, Pike, Cole, & Oxman, 2003).

Psychological and Biochemical Effects

Blood Pressure. When Tai Chi is practiced, whether two or three times a week or for 6 or 12 weeks, practitioners have invariably shown decreased systolic and diastolic blood pressure. These decreases have ranged from a 10- to a 16-millimeter decrease for systolic blood pressure (Ko, Tsang, & Chan, 2006) and from an 8- to a 10-millimeter decrease for diastolic blood pressure (Lu & Kuo, 2003; Thornton, Sykes, & Tang, 2004; Tsai et al., 2003; Verhagen, Immink, van der Meulen, & Bierma-Zeinstra, 2004; Wolf et al., 2006).

Cholesterol Levels. In at least two of the studies measuring blood pressure changes (Ko et al., 2006; Tsai et al., 2003), cholesterol levels also significantly decreased 6 to 15 mg/dL. In addition, either low-density lipoprotein decreased or high-density lipoprotein increased in these studies.

Heart Rate. In a study demonstrating decreased blood pressure, heart rate also decreased, and body mass index decreased in older adults practicing Tai Chi versus those participating in a wellness education program (Wolf et al., 2006). Such changes have been accompanied by increases in vagal activity in other studies (Lu & Kuo, 2003, 2006; Motivala, Sollers, Thayer, & Irwin, 2006).

Aerobic Characteristics. An increase in peak oxygen uptake was seen in at least one study, suggestive of the aerobic nature of Tai Chi (G. Yeh et al.,

2004). In another study, peak oxygen consumption was 55% of the oxygen consumption peak, and heart rate was 58% of the heart rate range noted during practice (Lan, Chen, Lai, & Wong, 2001). These results demonstrate that Tai Chi is a moderate-intensity exercise and is aerobic in nature. In a meta-analysis on Tai Chi, aerobic capacity was significantly greater for the practitioners in at least seven studies (Taylor-Piliae & Froelicher, 2004). Similar effects have occurred across different age groups and in both genders (Lan, Chen, & Lai, 2004).

When Tai Chi was compared with Chi Gong, both were noted to have aerobic effects, but Tai Chi had greater effects than Chi Gong because of its higher intensity exercise (Lan, Chou, Chen, Lai, & Wong, 2004). This finding was based on measurements of heart rate responses and breath-by-breath measurement during cycling. At the peak exercise, the Tai Chi group displayed higher oxygen uptake.

Brain Waves. In at least one study involving middle-aged women who were either novices or skilled at Tai Chi, brain waves changed in the direction of alertness and relaxation for both groups (Liu, Mimura, Wang, & Ikuda, 2003). In that study, higher beta power was noted along with higher alpha power on electroencephalograms, which is a pattern noted during attentiveness.

Physical Benefits

The most frequently reported benefits for Tai Chi are the physical benefits of increased balance, improved gait, and increased muscle strength. Most of the studies reporting these benefits were conducted with people in their 60s and 70s in nursing homes in villages in Taiwan (Lin, Hwang, Wang, Chang, & Wolf, 2006) and by video conferencing in the participants' homes (G. Wu & Keyes, 2006). The measures used in these studies have included dynamic posturography, electromyograms, the Berg Balance Scale, the Tinetti Balance Scale, the Tinetti Gait Scale, single leg stance time, body sway during quiet stance, the Dynamic Gait Index, functional reach, and speed walking as well as self-reports on the fear of falling and number of injurious falls. Compared with a control group, which typically has been a stretching, a balance and awareness education, or a muscle relaxation group, the Tai Chi training groups have typically shown improved performance on all of these measures, a lesser fear of falling, and fewer falls (F. Li et al., 2005; Lin et al., 2006; Maciaszek, Osinski, Szeklicki, & Stemplewski, 2007). In one study, based on kinematic analysis, the Tai Chi practitioners used a more cautious walking strategy, including slower gait and shorter and slower steps than the control group (Ramachandran, Rosengren, Yang, & Hsiao-Wecksler, 2007).

In reviews on the effects of Tai Chi on balance, gait, and strength, authors have generally concluded that although some studies have limited data (either limited sample size or a limited number of variables), data have suggested that Tai Chi has beneficial effects on balance and gait problems, most particularly those associated with aging (C. Wang, Collet, & Lau, 2004; Wayne et al., 2004). In addition to improved balance and increased musculoskeletal strength and flexibility, the reviews have shown that Tai Chi participants have improved performance on activities of daily living as well as general psychological well-being (Y. Wang et al., 2004; Wayne et al., 2004).

It is interesting that Tai Chi has not been compared systematically with similar forms of movement therapy such as yoga. However, the effects of Tai Chi have been studied in comparison with the effects of golfing. In a study in which older adult Tai Chi practitioners and older adult golfers were compared with healthy older adult participants and young university students, both the Tai Chi practitioners and the golfers had faster reaction times, were able to lean over further without losing stability, and showed better control of leaning trajectory compared with older adult controls (Tsang & Hui-Chan, 2004a, 2004b). The performance of the older Tai Chi practitioners and golfers was comparable with the performance of the young university students.

Methodological Problems

Some methodological problems with these studies include the variability across studies in the Tai Chi form used (varying from 10 to 24 different forms) and the intensity of the Tai Chi protocol (varying from less than 1 hour weekly for 1 month to 1 hour every morning for 1 year). Although virtually all of the studies reported beneficial effects ranging from a reduction of 47% in falls (Verhagen et al., 2004) to clinically significant decreases in blood pressure and cholesterol (Ko et al., 2006), these conclusions were often based on a pre–post analysis rather than a comparison across treatment groups or even across treatment versus wait-list controls.

CHI GONG

Chi Gong (roughly meaning "breath work" or "energy work") is another form of Chinese martial arts that is typically performed in a sitting position on a chair. Although significantly less research has been conducted on Chi Gong than on Tai Chi, the studies that exist suggest robust effects. Evidence indicates, for example, that this low-energy-expenditure movement therapy, derived from traditional Chinese medicine, may benefit patients with cardiac conditions (Pippa et al., 2007). Pippa et al. (2007) carried out a randomized controlled trial to test a 16-week medically assisted Chi Gong training program for the physical rehabilitation of patients with chronic atrial fibrillation. Trained patients walked on average 114 meters more (27% increase) at the end of treatment and 57 meters more (14% increase) 16 weeks later than a standard treatment control group.

Another study examined the effects of Chi Gong therapy on complete blood counts in patients with breast cancer treated with chemotherapy (M. Yeh, Lee, Chen, & Chao, 2006). The experimental group received a 21-day Chi Gong therapy course and was compared with a standard treatment control group. Significant differences in white blood cells, platelets, and hemoglobin over the 3-week period suggested that Chi Gong therapy may decrease leukopenia in breast cancer patients treated with chemotherapy.

REFERRING PATIENTS TO TAI CHI AND CHI GONG PRACTITIONERS

Tai Chi and Chi Gong can both improve posture and reduce pain, effects that contribute to well-being. Reduction of pain in particular can alleviate depression. They are relatively easy to learn, especially the individual exercises, although the forms (combinations of exercises) require more memorization. The exercises could easily be combined with other therapies for their exercise value.

Health clubs and adult education programs often include Tai Chi and Chi Gong classes. Martial arts studios teaching disciplines like karate or judo also feature Tai Chi classes, although they often have waiting lists because of their increasing popularity. As already mentioned, once the postures and forms are mastered and memorized, Tai Chi and Chi Gong can be practiced at home.

6

YOGA AND PILATES

Yoga and Pilates are currently extremely popular forms of movement exercise. Both feature flowing physical movements that are designed to tone different muscles and enhance good posture, rhythmic breathing, and mental concentration. In addition, they improve balance and coordination. They increase flexibility in the muscles and joints and are not injurious to the joints. Their unique features are presented in the following sections of this chapter.

YOGA

Yoga was developed in India at approximately 3000 BC. The word *yoga* comes from the Sanskrit and means "to yoke" or "to join together." Although there are many types of yoga practices, outside of India *yoga* most often refers to Hatha yoga, which combines stretching and exercises in different postures with deep breathing and meditation. The yoga poses are generally done with deep, diaphragmatic breathing that is thought to increase oxygen flow to the brain. Descriptions of the physical yoga postures are found in the *Yoga Sutras*, apparently written by Patajali, a Sanskrit scholar and an Indian physician (Freeman, 2004).

Yoga is designed to stretch and tone all muscles and to keep the spine and joints flexible. Some suggest that the bending, twisting, and stretching movements also massage the internal organs and glands.

Yoga Sessions

Yoga is typically practiced in nonrestrictive clothing and with bare feet on a yoga mat or on the bare floor of a yoga studio. The exercises consist of a series of poses that are called *asanas* in Sanskrit. Most of these poses are performed slowly and with concentration on each movement and on the deep abdominal breathing that accompanies each movement. Figure 6.1 shows one example of a yoga pose (*Natarajasana*, or the Cosmic Dancer pose). The movement between poses is considered as important as maintaining a pose. Traditional writings about yoga suggest that there are as many yoga postures or asanas as there are animals in the world, and many of the poses are named after animals. Experienced yogis suggest that one mimic the animal when in that pose. For example, in performing the cat or the cobra posture, one could feel oneself possessing the qualities of a cat or a cobra while performing that exercise.

Many forms of yoga exist. Hatha yoga (*Hatha* meaning sun/moon) is considered the most relaxing form, and classes described as "Hatha yoga" generally tend to be slower paced stretching classes. Some variations of Hatha yoga include *Iyengar* yoga, which focuses on the physical alignment of the body and involves some strenuous positions such as headstands, and *Bikram* yoga, which is practiced in very high-temperature rooms and consists of a series of 26 yoga postures. The studies described in this chapter involve Hatha yoga unless otherwise indicated.

Potential Mechanisms of Action for Yoga

Although little research has been conducted on potential underlying mechanisms, yoga appears to increase vagal activity and reduce cortisol levels. This may be similar to the underlying mechanism for massage therapy inasmuch as massage and yoga both stimulate pressure receptors under the skin and, in turn, enhance vagal activity and reduce cortisol. It is possible that these physiological and biochemical changes can reduce depression, pain syndromes, and immune problems.

Empirical Support for the Effects of Yoga

Yoga has been shown to reduce anxiety and depression. Studies have also shown that yoga can improve several medical conditions, including back pain, migraine headaches, insomnia, and high blood pressure.

Figure 6.1. Example of a yoga balancing pose (*Natarajasana*, or the Cosmic Dancer pose).

Psychological Symptoms and Disorders

Anxiety. In one study, self-referred women who perceived themselves as emotionally distressed attended two weekly 90-minute yoga classes (Michalsen et al., 2005). Compared with a similar group of women who were on a waiting list, the women who participated in the yoga training demonstrated significant reductions in perceived stress, anxiety, fatigue, and depression as well as increased well-being and vigor. Physical well-being also improved, and women who were suffering from headache or back pain reported marked pain relief.

Depression. Other researchers have studied the effectiveness of yoga for alleviating depression and have found that yoga invariably reduced depression (e.g., Khumar, Kaur, & Kaur, 1993). The depression-alleviating effects may relate to the changes in brain waves and the reduction in cortisol levels that are reported during yoga postures. For example, in one study in which yoga was practiced once weekly, alpha waves increased (sign of increased relaxation) and serum cortisol decreased (Kamei et al., 2000). Figure 6.2 shows the effects of yoga on depression in a group of pregnant women who practiced yoga versus a control group (Field, Diego, Hernandez-Reif, Deeds, & Figuereido, 2008). Center for Epidemiological Studies—Depression (CES–D) scores declined in the yoga group compared with the control group, which showed no change in CES–D scores, and the CES–D scores remained low during posttest for the yoga group.

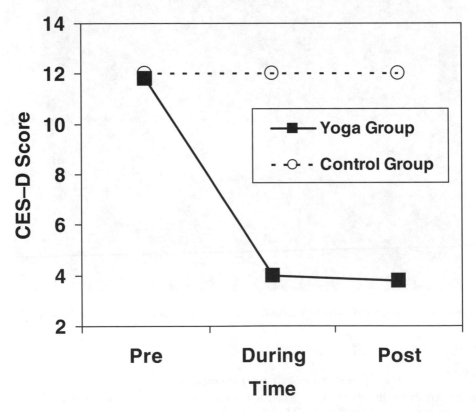

Figure 6.2. Decrease in Center for Epidemiological Studies—Depression (CES–D) scores for the yoga group across the study.

Sleep. The decrease in depression noted following yoga may also be related to enhanced sleep. A simple daily yoga practice was evaluated in a population with chronic insomnia (Khalsa, 2004). Improvements were noted on virtually every sleep measure, including sleep efficiency, total sleep time, sleep onset latency, number of awakenings, and sleep quality measures based on sleep–wake diary entries.

Yoga also improved sleep in a geriatric population studied by Manjunath and Telles (2005). After 6 months of yoga practice, the yoga group versus the standard control group showed, on the basis of rating scales, a significant decrease in the time taken to fall asleep as well as a significant increase in the total number of hours slept and in the feeling of being rested in the morning.

Physical Conditions and Diseases: Pain Syndromes

Osteoarthritis. Patients with osteoarthritis of the hands were randomly assigned to receive either a yoga program or no therapy (Garfinkel, Schumacher, Husain, Levy, & Reshetar, 1994). After once-weekly yoga sessions for 8 weeks, the yoga group improved significantly more than the control group on pain during activity, tenderness of joints, and finger range of motion.

Osteoarthritis of the knee has also been treated by yoga (Kolasinski et al., 2005). Iyengar yoga postures were practiced during 90-minute classes once weekly for 8 weeks. A significant reduction in pain and improved physical function were observed when the participants' status was compared with their precourse status.

Low Back Pain. Chronic low back pain also improved following a course of yoga. In one study, adults with chronic low back pain were randomly assigned to a yoga group (12 weekly sessions of yoga), a therapeutic exercise group, or a self-care group (assigned to read and practice exercises in a book; Sherman, Cherkin, Erro, Miglioretti, & Deyo, 2005). After 12 weeks, back-related function in the yoga group was superior to the book and exercise groups.

In a randomized controlled trial, similar effects were noted for participants with nonspecific chronic low back pain (K. A. Williams et al., 2005). Yoga participants attended weekly yoga sessions for 16 weeks. The control group was given education on low back pain for 16 weeks. Analyses revealed significant reductions in pain intensity (64%), functional disability (77%), and pain medication usage (88%) in the yoga group at the posttest and 3-month follow-up assessments.

Headaches. Patients with migraine headaches without aura were randomly assigned to yoga or self-care (reducing stress) groups (John, Sharma, Sharma, & Kankane, 2007). After 3 months of weekly yoga, the patients' complaints related to headache intensity, frequency, and pain ratings; anxiety and depression scores; and symptomatic medication use were significantly lower in the yoga group compared with the self-care group.

Musculoskeletal and Neurological Conditions: Multiple Sclerosis

In a study by Oken et al. (2004), patients with multiple sclerosis participated in weekly Iyengar yoga classes or regular exercise classes for a month or were assigned to a wait-list control group. The yoga group showed significant improvement on fatigue measures compared with the other two groups.

Hypertension and Cardiac Conditions

Hypertension. Damodaran et al. (2002) used yoga with patients with mild to moderate hypertension. Patients practiced yoga daily for 1 hour for 3 months. Results showed decreased blood pressure, blood glucose, cholesterol, and triglycerides and improved subjective well-being and quality of life.

Coronary Artery Disease. Even patients with advanced coronary artery disease have been shown to benefit from a yoga program (Yogendra et al., 2004). At the end of 1 year of yoga training, total cholesterol was reduced by 23% in the yoga group compared with 4% in the standard treatment control group, and serum low-density lipids cholesterol was reduced by 26% in the yoga group compared with 3% in the control group.

In a similar study, a yoga-plus-dietary-changes group was compared with a control group that included only dietary changes for coronary atherosclerotic disease (Manchanda et al., 2000). After 1 year of weekly sessions, the yoga group had fewer anginal episodes per week, improved exercise capacity, and decreased body weight. Serum total cholesterol, low-density lipoprotein cholesterol, and triglyceride levels also decreased compared with the control group. Revascularization procedures (coronary angioplasty or bypass surgery) were less frequently required in the yoga group. Coronary angiography repeated at 1 year showed that significantly more lesions regressed (20% vs. 2%) and fewer lesions progressed (5% vs. 37%) in the yoga group compared with the control group.

Autoimmune Conditions

Asthma. In a study on asthma, a yoga group was compared with a control group that received education about asthma. Both groups attended a 2-hour session once a week for 4 months (Manocha, Marks, Kenchington, Peters, & Salome, 2002). Scores on the Asthma Quality of Life Questionnaire (AQLQ); Profile of Mood States (POMS); Airway Hyperresponsiveness to Methacholine (AHR); and a diary card based on the combined asthma score reflecting symptoms, bronchodilator usage, and peak expiratory flow rates were measured at the end of the treatment period and again 2 months later. The AHR and the AQLQ mood subscale scores improved more in the yoga group, as did the summary POMS score.

Diabetes. In a study on diabetes, patients were trained to perform yoga asanas 30 to 40 minutes per day for 40 days (S. Singh, Malhotra, Singh, Madhu, & Tandon, 2004). Blood glucose levels as well as glycosylated hemoglobin levels decreased. Pulse rate, systolic blood pressure, and diastolic blood pressure also decreased.

In another study on individuals with diabetes, training in yoga asanas occurred 30 to 40 minutes per day for 40 days (Malhotra, Singh, Tandon, & Sharma, 2005). Fasting blood glucose levels and postprandial blood glucose levels decreased at the end of the training.

Immune Conditions

In one study, patients with lymphoma were assigned to a yoga group or to a wait-list control group (L. Cohen, Warneke, Fouladi, Rodriguez, & Chaoul-Reich, 2004). After participating in 7 weekly yoga sessions, patients in the yoga group reported significantly lower sleep disturbance scores.

Women with breast cancer have also benefited from 1 year of weekly yoga sessions, at least on lowering their levels of pain and fatigue and increasing their levels of invigoration and relaxation (J. Carson et al., 2007). In another study on women with breast cancer, weekly yoga sessions also led to improved quality of life and emotional function ratings (Culos-Reed, Carlson, Daroux, & Hately-Aldous, 2006).

Pregnancy-Related Conditions

Yoga practices, including physical postures, breathing, and meditation, were performed by pregnant women in a yoga group 1 hour daily from early in the second trimester until delivery (Narendran, Nagarathna, Narendran, Gunasheela, & Nagendra, 2005). The control group walked 30 minutes twice a day during the study period. Complications such as pregnancy-induced hypertension with associated intrauterine growth retardation were significantly lower in the yoga group, and the incidence of preterm labor was also significantly lower in the yoga group. These effects are difficult to interpret because the effects of the different yoga practices (physical postures, breathing, and meditation) were not differentiated from each other.

Physiological Effects of Yoga

A number of studies have examined the effects of yoga on heart rate, pulmonary function, parasympathetic activity, body mass, and flexibility in normal individuals.

Heart Rate and Blood Pressure. One study assessed the effects of yoga training on heart rate responses to exercise (Madanmohan, Udupa, Bhavanani,

Shatapathy, & Sahai, 2004). Heart rate was monitored following the Harvard Step Test, a cardiac stress test to detect cardiovascular disease. The participants were asked to step up and down the platform at a rate of 30 steps per minute for 5 minutes or until fatigued. Exercise produced a significant increase in heart rate and systolic blood pressure and a significant decrease in diastolic blood pressure. After 2 months of yoga training consisting of physical postures, exercise-induced increases in heart rate and systolic blood pressure were significantly reduced.

Telles and Naveen (2004) observed similar effects. Both the baseline heart rate and the lowest heart rate achieved voluntarily during a 6-minute exercise period were significantly lower following 30 days of physical postures in the yoga group. In contrast, no changes were noted on the lowest heart rate in the control group following walking exercise.

Another study assessed the effects of yoga on heart rate and blood pressure of healthy men (Harinath et al., 2004) who were randomly assigned to a yoga group or a control group. The yoga group practiced yoga postures for 45 minutes daily for 3 months. The control group performed body flexibility exercises daily for 40 minutes and slow running for 20 minutes in the morning. The men in the yoga group showed greater improvement in heart rate, blood pressure, and aerobic performance compared with men in the control group.

Pulmonary Health. Two yoga practices, one combining calming and stimulating measures and the other using a calming technique, have been compared for their effects on pulmonary measures, including oxygen consumption, breath rate, and breath volume before and after yoga sessions (Telles, Reddy, & Nagendra, 2000). The magnitude of change on all three measures was greater after the calming and stimulating session versus the calming session.

Physical Effects

Flexibility. In a study on older adults, 6 months of weekly Hatha yoga classes were followed by improved physical condition including balance (as measured by one-legged standing) and flexibility (Oken et al., 2006).

Body Mass. Weight reduction has also been associated with yoga. In one study, yoga practice for 4 years was associated with a 3-pound weight loss among normal-weight participants and a 19-pound weight loss among overweight participants (Kristal, Littman, Benitez, & White, 2005).

Exercise and Sports Performance

In a study on runners conducted by Donohue et al. (2006), participants showed significant improvement in running performance after a brief 20-minute yoga session.

PILATES

Pilates was developed by a German named Joseph H. Pilates who suffered from rickets and other illnesses as a child. During World War I, he became an orderly involved in the treatment of patients who were immobile. He developed a series of exercises that the patients could perform in bed, and he attached springs to their beds to increase the efficiency of their exercises. The patients were noted to recover more quickly when they used the springs. After the war, Pilates opened a fitness studio in New York using both the bed exercises and his original system that was based on mat work.

The Pilates system of exercises is concentrated on a focused mind as well as flowing physical movements. The exercises are designed to tone different muscles and condition the body while developing good posture, correct breathing, and mental concentration. Pilates is thought to improve balance and coordination while also increasing flexibility in the muscles and joints.

The Pilates exercises are focused on a centered posture; rhythmic breathing; and flowing, smooth movements. Although this has been referred to as a "yogalike" system, and Pilates did take some inspiration from yoga, the exercises are quite different. The system was originally composed of 34 Pilates movements, but different practitioners have modified these so that many different systems now exist. One of the key ways that Pilates exercises differ from other forms of exercise is that they do not focus on any particular muscle of the 650 muscles in the body but rather focus on many muscles simultaneously.

Pilates believed that strengthening the abdomen was one of the primary ways to increase health. Thus, he taught a method called *thoracic* breathing instead of *abdominal* breathing. The latter involves expanding the abdomen as you breathe, whereas thoracic breathing involves breathing into the back and lower ribs. As the air goes into the lungs and back, the sides of the ribcage expand and contract, and the air is exhaled. Breathing in the thoracic way enables a person to continue tightening the abdominal muscles. Many of the exercises include practicing breathing and tightening the abdomen.

Other exercises are focused on posture and reducing bad postural habits such as *lumbar lordosis*, in which the lower back is pushing too far inward, and *kyphosis*, in which the body is pushed forward, causing compression of the chest and stomach. Other spinal problems include *cervical lordosis*, in which the muscles at the back of the neck contract, those in the front expand, and the chin protrudes; *thoracic spine*, caused by contracting muscles; and *sway back*, in which the back is distorted and muscles are weakened.

In the standing position, the students of Pilates are taught to avoid slumping, jutting the head or chin forward, protruding the stomach, or rounding the upper back. In sitting positions, students are taught to avoid slouching, rounding the shoulders, compressing the chest and lower back outward, and compressing the abdomen. Many of the standing and sitting exercises are designed to improve posture. The movements in Pilates, like those of yoga, do not pause after each repetition but are continuous and flowing.

Empirical Support for Pilates

The clinical research literature on Pilates is extremely limited, perhaps because Pilates has only recently become popular. The few studies that exist suggest that Pilates is an effective complementary movement therapy, perhaps for reasons similar to those of yoga.

In a study on low back pain, patients with at least 3 months of nonspecific low back pain were entered into Pilates therapy or kinesiotherapy (Donzelli, Di Domenica, Cova, Galletti, & Giunta, 2006). In small groups, they followed a daily protocol for 10 days. Evaluations were performed at the start of the study and then at 1, 3, and 6 months after the beginning of treatment. Significant reductions in pain intensity and disability were observed across both groups. However, the Pilates group showed better compliance and a more positive response to treatment.

Another study on the effects of Pilates on low back pain was conducted using a randomized controlled trial with a pretest–posttest design, with 3-, 6-, and 12-month follow-ups (Rydeard, Leger, & Smith, 2006). Physically active participants with chronic low back pain were randomly assigned to a 4-week program on Pilates equipment or to a control group that received consultation with a physician and physical therapists as necessary. Pilates sessions were designed to train muscles thought to stabilize the lumbar–pelvic region. Functional disability outcomes were measured with the Roland Morris Disability Questionnaire and average pain intensity on a rating scale. Following the treatment period, significantly lower levels of functional disability and average pain intensity were noted in the Pilates group than in the control group.

Physiological Effects of Pilates

As with yoga, some research has been done on Pilates in healthy individuals. For example, to assess claims regarding the effects of Pilates on flexibility, body composition, and health status, N. Segal, Hein, and Basford (2004) conducted an observational study on adults who were participating in a Pilates mat class once per week for 2 months. Fingertip-to-floor distance improved from baseline to 6 months, whereas no changes occurred for body composition and health status.

REFERRING PATIENTS TO YOGA AND PILATES PRACTITIONERS

Many referral sources are available at schools, local studios, or health clubs. Some types of yoga need special consideration for safety factors. For example, Bikram yoga's use of high temperatures may not be advisable for individuals with high blood pressure or cardiac conditions, and advanced Iyengar yoga classes include headstands and handstands that may be too difficult for beginners.

7
EXERCISE

As early as 400 BC, Hippocrates, the father of modern medicine, suggested that exercise was an essential activity in maintaining health. He has been quoted as saying, "All parts of the body which have a function, if used in moderation and exercised in labors in which each is accustomed, become thereby healthy, well developed and age more slowly" (Freeman, 2004, p. 483). Physical activity has come to be considered as important as eating a balanced diet, getting a good night's sleep, managing stress, not smoking, and drinking in moderation. Some have estimated that regular, vigorous aerobic exercise allows adults to function physically at levels equal to those of people 10 to 20 years younger than themselves (Arent, Landers, & Etnier, 2000).

POTENTIAL UNDERLYING MECHANISMS
FOR EXERCISE EFFECTS

The two most popular theories for underlying mechanisms for aerobic exercise effects are the opioid theory and the neurotransmitter theory. In the opioid theory, exercise is thought to release endogenous opioid peptides, thus increasing the levels of endorphins (Freeman, 2004). Some have suggested that this causes the emotional high in athletes following intense exercise. A more data-driven theory relates exercise effects to the increase in neurotransmitters, such as serotonin, which is noted to reduce depression and pain levels during exercise sessions of athletes (Strüder et al., 1997).

Not unlike massage therapy effects, exercise effects may be mediated by the stimulation of pressure receptors under the skin, which then increase vagal activity (Field, Diego, & Hernandez-Reif, 2007). With the increase of vagal activity, several biochemical changes occur, including the reduction of cortisol that would lead to enhanced immune function (inasmuch as cortisol kills immune cells) and the increase of serotonin that would reduce depression and pain.

EMPIRICAL SUPPORT FOR THE EFFECTS OF EXERCISE

The recent literature on exercise effects has been predominantly focused on physical effects, including weight loss and increased bone density. Other exercise effects include the reduction of depression, amelioration of cardiovascular and pulmonary conditions, alleviation of pain, and the improvement of some autoimmune and immune conditions.

Psychological Symptoms and Disorders

Depression

Depression has been shown to decrease following aerobic exercise. In a study on the effects of aerobic exercise on depressive symptoms (e.g., insomnia, weight loss, feelings of sadness) and symptoms of seasonal affective disorder (SAD; symptoms include hypersomnia, afternoon or evening slump, weight gain, and carbohydrate cravings), 30-minute daily aerobic exercise sessions for 2 weeks reduced depression symptoms but not SAD symptoms (Leppämäki, Partonen, Hurme, Haukka, & Lönnqvist, 2002).

Similarly, patients with major depression have benefited from aerobic exercise. Participants with a major depressive episode (according to the *Diagnostic and Statistical Manual of Mental Disorders* [4th ed., text revision; American Psychiatric Association, 2000]) who did treadmill exercises for 30 minutes a day for 10 days experienced a significant reduction in depression scores on the Hamilton Rating Scale for Depression (Dimeo, Bauer, Varahram, Proest, & Halter, 2001). In a longer term follow-up study on adults with depression (extending to 10 years), Harris, Cronkite, and Moos (2006) found that more physical activity was associated with less concurrent depression, even after controlling for gender, age, medical problems, and negative life events. Physical activity counteracted the effects of medical conditions and negative life events on depression. In a review of studies on the benefits of exercise for reducing depression (Lawlor & Hopker, 2001), exercise reduced symptoms of depression compared with no treatment.

Other studies have focused on depression in older adults. For example, in a study by Penninx et al. (2002), aerobic exercise significantly reduced depression in older adults with osteoarthritis; in contrast, resistance exercise did not reduce depression. In another study by Kharti et al. (2001) on exercise in older men and women with depression, three supervised 30-minute sessions per week for 16 weeks of continuous cycling, brisk walking, or jogging led to significant reductions in depression and improvements in memory.

Decreased depression following exercise may relate to the effects of exercise on serotonin levels. In at least one study, patients who had been diagnosed with major depressive disorder were noted to have increased prolactin levels following exercise (Kiive, Maaroos, Shlik, Tõru, & Harro, 2004). Exercise may have a strong effect on serotonin release in depressed patients that is reflected in increased plasma prolactin levels.

Quality of Life

In a study conducted on exercise during leisure time, significant training effects occurred after 13 weeks for the participant's emotional well-being and physical strength (Brand, Schlicht, Grossman, & Duhnsen, 2006). Physical strength also significantly improved. However, physical strength and emotional well-being only persisted for those who continued to exercise on their own.

In another study, the participants were assigned to a program of regular aerobic exercise following a 2-month control phase (Oaten & Cheng, 2006). The participants during the exercise phase showed significant improvements on a visual tracking task following a thought-suppression task. They also reported significant decreases in perceived stress, emotional distress, smoking, and alcohol and caffeine consumption and an increase in healthy eating, emotional control, maintenance of household chores, attendance to commitments, monitoring of spending, and improvement in study habits.

Physical Conditions and Diseases

Pulmonary Health and Disease

Exercise has also been notably beneficial to the pulmonary system. Among the effects of exercise are the elimination of toxins and carbon dioxide and more efficient respiration (Freeman, 2004). *Chronic obstructive pulmonary disease* (COPD), which is the persistent obstruction of the airways caused by emphysema or bronchitis, has also responded to increased activity. The exercises have varied, with walking, treadmill, stationary bike, and stair climbing being predominant. Most of the programs have ranged from 4 weeks to 1 year, with the majority of the programs lasting 6 to 8 or 12 to 24 weeks. The outcome measures are typically timed walking tests, incremental treadmill, and stationary bicycle protocols.

Examples of these studies include one in which patients with COPD were randomly assigned to a weight-training group and a control group (C. J. Clark, Cochrane, Mackay, & Paton, 2000). Muscle strength and whole-body endurance that are often compromised in individuals with COPD improved after the weight training. In a similar study, patients with COPD were more likely to improve their exercise capacity, respiratory function, and muscle strength if these were compromised at the onset of the study (Troosters, Gosselink, & Decramer, 2001).

In another study on patients with chronic lung disease, Cheng et al. (2003) measured cardiorespiratory fitness by using a maximal treadmill test and tested respiratory function by spirometry. Actively engaging in aerobic exercise was associated with better cardiorespiratory fitness and respiratory function in both men and women. Men who remained active had higher forced expiratory volume at 1 second and forced vital capacity than the other groups (inactive men, active and inactive women).

Pain Syndromes: Fibromyalgia

In one study on fibromyalgia, Rooks, Silverman, and Kantrowitz (2002) assessed the effects of progressive strength training and aerobic exercise on muscle strength and cardiovascular fitness in women with that condition. Exercise was conducted three times a week for 60 minutes. The first 4 weeks involved water exercises, and the next 16 weeks involved land-based exercises. All sessions consisted of cardiovascular exercise, muscle strengthening, and joint range of motion. Rooks et al. noted that pain decreased and upper and lower body strength and 6-minute walking time improved significantly.

In another study on patients with fibromyalgia, S. C. Richards and Scott (2002) compared an aerobic exercise group with a relaxation and a flexibility training group. After 1 year of three 30-minute sessions per week, fewer of the exercise participants met the criteria for fibromyalgia than the other groups, and the exercise group also had fewer tender points and better fibromyalgia impact scores.

Autoimmune Conditions

Diabetes

The markers of diabetes have also improved following exercise. In one study on aerobic exercise, atherosclerosis-prone men with Type 1 diabetes were assessed for cardiorespiratory fitness and lipid profiles (Laaksonen et al., 2000). These men engaged in a 12- to 16-week exercise program consisting of aerobic and resistance exercises for 30 minutes three times per week. Following endurance training, their lipid profile improved, especially in those patients with low baseline high-density lipoprotein/low-density lipoprotein ratios.

In another study, participants with Type 2 diabetes participated in an 8-week circuit training program of aerobic and resistance exercises (Maiorana et al., 2007). Circuit training consisted of seven resistance exercise stations alternating with eight aerobic exercise stations, each for 45 seconds. Exercise heart rate was significantly lower after the 8-week training, and the ventilatory threshold increased. Muscle strength also increased, and skin-fold thickness, body fat, and waist-to-hip ratio decreased significantly. Peak oxygen uptake and exercise duration increased, and glycosylated hemoglobin and fasting blood glucose decreased.

Immune Conditions

It is striking that no literature could be found within the past 5 years on exercise effects on patients with cancer and patients with HIV. This is particularly surprising because exercise has been noted to decrease cortisol and increase serotonin, ultimately leading to increased numbers of natural killer cells, which in turn are noted to kill viral and cancer cells. Thus, their chronic illness would seem to benefit significantly from aerobic exercise.

Physiological Effects of Exercise

Bone Density

Bone mineral density has been shown to increase following exercise. In one study, for example, premenopausal women were randomly assigned either to an exercise or a control group (Vainionpää, Korpelainen, Leppäluoto, & Jämsä, 2005). The exercise regimen consisted of 30-minute progressive high-impact exercises three times per week for 1 month and an additional home program for 12 months. The exercise group demonstrated a significant increase in femoral neck bone mineral density, in total femoral bone mineral density, and in lumbar vertebrae bone mineral density.

Regular weight-bearing physical activity has been widely recommended for premenopausal women to preserve bone mineral density. However, some researchers have expressed caution regarding this general recommendation. For example, in a meta-analysis by Martyn-St James and Carroll (2006), the effects of progressive high-intensity resistance training on bone mineral density were measured in premenopausal women. High-intensity progressive resistance training was shown to be effective in increasing bone mineral density in the lumbar spine but not the femoral neck in premenopausal women. The authors suggested that the modest treatment effects observed for resistance training on bone mineral density in the studies reviewed may be biased and need to be interpreted with caution. They noted that the randomized control trials may not have been sufficiently long, and also intent-to-treat analyses (to assess the effects of drop-out rate) were not conducted.

Cardiovascular Health

In the large Framingham Heart Study initiated in 1948 and involving 5,209 men and women, physical inactivity was designated one of the highest risk factors for cardiovascular disease and cardiac death (Genest et al., 1991). Other risk factors included male gender, family history of coronary disease, elevated serum cholesterol, hypertension, cigarette smoking, diabetes, obesity, and psychological stress. Of these risk factors, elevated cholesterol, obesity, psychological stress, and physical inactivity were the most modifiable by exercise.

In other more recent studies, diet and different forms of exercise have been compared for their effects on risk factors for coronary heart disease. In a study by Okura, Nakata, and Tanaka (2003), women who were obese (>95th percentile on weight for height) were divided into three groups: diet only, diet plus walking, and diet plus aerobic dance. Reductions were greater in upper body and lower limb fat mass in the diet-plus-aerobic-dance group compared with the diet-plus-walking and diet-only groups. In addition, improvements were seen in leg-extension strength, and reductions were noted in low-density lipoprotein cholesterol and fasting glucose in the diet-plus-aerobic-dance group.

In a similar study, a group of women engaged in progressive, high-impact exercise two to three times per week and an additional home program of the same exercise over the course of 12 months. They were compared with a control group that was not exercising (Vainionpää et al., 2007). The exercise group showed decreased waist and hip circumferences as well as total cholesterol and low-density lipoprotein cholesterol. When a group of athletic women (defined as those playing a sport) was compared with a group of nonathletic women, the athletic group had a higher level of estriol, greater bone mineral density, and higher high-density lipoprotein along with lower low-density lipoprotein, cholesterol, triglyceride, and body mass index (K. T. Chen & Yang, 2004).

REFERRING PATIENTS TO SUPERVISED EXERCISE PROGRAMS

Clinicians often need to encourage their clients to participate in exercise programs. Perhaps the easiest standard to follow is the rule of 20 minutes of fast walking three times per week. Unless individuals are engaged in a particular sport, real discipline is typically necessary for exercise regimes. Belonging to a health club might be the easiest form of self-discipline for clients and the most rewarding for its social features. Like following a diet, keeping an *exercise log* (record of time exercised each day) may also be reinforcing.

8

MUSIC THERAPY

Music therapy is the controlled or prescribed use of music to influence psychological or physical well-being as opposed to simply listening to music. The primary goal of music therapy is to help clients use the expressive experiences of music to improve or enhance their level of physical, psychological, and socioemotional functioning. Most frequently, a music therapist works together with an interdisciplinary team. Typically the music is presented via earphones to the client, and usually classical music is played for its calming effects.

Although studies need to be conducted to explore potential underlying mechanisms for music therapy effects, over the centuries many theories have emerged regarding music. One ancient theory is that music causes vibrations in tissues and influences physiological functions such as heart rate and blood pressure (Dobrzynska, Cesarz, Rymaszewska, & Kiejna, 2006).

Another theory is that one's preferred type of music has calming effects. One of the earliest studies on the effects of music noted blood pressure changes (Vincent & Thomson, 1928). These authors found that although the volume, pitch, melody, rhythm, and type of music all lowered blood pressure, blood pressure decreased the most during the listeners' preferred music.

Different types of music and their comparative effects have also been examined. In a study on subject-selected music, increased cerebral blood flow was noted in the regions of the brain associated with reward and arousal (Blood & Zatorre, 2001). However, a study on pain suggested that the least effective music in reducing pain was the clients' preferred music, and the most effective in reducing pain was *entrainment* music (music designed to synchronize brain waves) that contained both synthesized and acoustic guitar music (Lazaroff & Shimshoni, 2000).

EMPIRICAL SUPPORT FOR THE EFFECTS OF MUSIC THERAPY

Empirical literature on music therapy only emerged after World War II, when the term *music therapy* was first introduced. Michigan State University established a degree program in music therapy in 1944, and the National Association for Music Therapy was established in 1950. Music therapy is now used in many fields of medicine, including mental health, and together with other forms of art therapy, psychotherapy, and physical therapy, music therapy often complements pharmacotherapy.

Although music therapy is a relatively young field, much of the literature about it is based on a scientific approach (Federico & Whitwell, 2001). The conditions that have been most frequently researched for music therapy effects include stress-related psychological symptoms (e.g., anxiety, depression, and sleep problems); dementia; cardiovascular problems; pain; and musculoskeletal, autoimmune, and immune conditions. In a meta-analysis of studies on music therapy, those selected for experimental music therapy groups showed greater improvement on clinical conditions than did control groups (J. Jones, 2006).

Psychological Symptoms and Disorders

Anxiety

In a randomized controlled trial on individuals with high anxiety levels, preoperative anxiety was assessed before and after listening to 30 minutes of patient-preferred music (Cooke, Chaboyer, Schluter, & Hiratos, 2005), and the music was shown to reduce anxiety levels. A study by Haun, Mainous, and Looney (2001) also found that anxiety levels in women awaiting a breast biopsy were lowered by music. After 20 minutes of music, anxiety and respiratory rates were lower compared with a group of women who did not hear music. Music has also been used with patients undergoing radiation therapy. More frequent music sessions produced greater declines in distress (M. Clark et al., 2006). Music played to women prior to cesarean deliveries has also been shown to reduce anxiety (S. Chang & Chen, 2005).

Depression

In a study by Hsu and Lai (2004), patients with major depressive disorder listened to their choice of music for 30 minutes each day for 2 weeks. The participants had significantly lower depression scores at the end of the 2 weeks. Music also appeared to lower depression scores in patients with medical problems, including knee arthroplasty (Giaquinto, Cacciato, Minasi, Sostero, & Amanda, 2006) and multiple sclerosis (Ostermann & Schmid, 2006).

In some studies, physiological and biochemical measures have been used to support the more subjective self-report measures of depression following music. In a study that I conducted with colleagues, for example, rock music was presented for 30 minutes to alter depressed mood state and right frontal electroencephalographic (EEG) activation (typically associated with chronic depression) of depressed adolescents (Field, Martinez, et al., 1998). Cortisol levels decreased and, as can be seen in Figure 8.1, relative right frontal EEG activation was significantly reduced (in a positive direction) during and after the music procedure. In some participants, the EEG shifts did not occur, possibly because the participants said they did not like Michael Jackson's music. In a replication study by our group, the same 20 minutes of rock music reduced right frontal EEG activation and symptoms of depression in depressed adolescent mothers (N. A. Jones & Field, 1999).

In still another study that my colleagues and I conducted, rock music and classical music were compared for their effects on depression and EEG

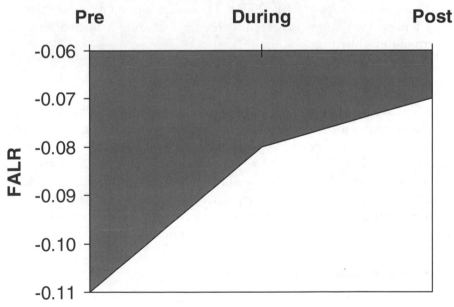

Figure 8.1. Shift of frontal electroencephalographic activation toward symmetry (a positive change) during and following music therapy. FALR = frontal alpha laterality ratio.

patterns in female adolescents with depression (Tornek, Field, Hernandez-Reif, Diego, & Jones, 2003). The EEG patterns were assessed following a 20-minute music session to determine if the music had mood-altering effects. More positive EEG shifts were noted for rock music, perhaps because the subjects were adolescents. Decreased cortisol, anxiety, and depressed mood levels were also noted following the 20-minute rock music sessions.

Music therapy conducted in groups has also been noted to lower depression (Teague, Hahna, & McKinney, 2006). Short-term group psychotherapy for adults with chronic mental illness was enhanced by playing music during the sessions (de L'Etoile, 2002). Anxiety and depression symptoms decreased, and clients reported that the music therapy was helpful and that it improved their attitudes toward help-seeking and openness about their problems.

Posttraumatic Stress Disorder

Abused women who were residing in women's shelters reported lower anxiety levels after listening to a 20-minute recording of participant-selected music, and their sleep quality also improved (Hernandez-Ruiz, 2005).

Schizophrenia

Inpatients diagnosed with schizophrenia who had 12 weeks of individual music therapy plus standard care were compared with those who had standard care alone (Talwar et al., 2006). Those randomized to music therapy experienced fewer symptoms of schizophrenia, including hallucinations and paranoid thoughts.

Sleep

To assess the effects of music on sleep, Lai and Good (2005) asked older adult participants with sleep problems to listen to their choice of music among six 45-minute music tapes daily at bedtime for 3 weeks. Five types of Western music and one type of Chinese music were included. The group that listened to music had significantly better sleep quality than the group that did not. In addition, the music group experienced longer sleep duration, greater sleep efficiency, shorter sleep latency, less sleep disturbance, and less daytime dysfunction. These sleep variables improved weekly, indicating a cumulative dose effect.

Physical Conditions: Pain Syndromes

Back Pain

The pain-alleviating effects of music have been explored in several studies on back pain. In one study, patients listened to 20 minutes of music or had

20 minutes of rest (Sendelbach, Halm, Doran, Miller, & Gaillard, 2006). Anxiety and pain were decreased in the group that received music compared with the resting control group.

In a longer term study by Guetin et al. (2005), patients with low back pain were randomized to receive either physical therapy plus four music therapy sessions on alternate months or physical therapy alone. The combined therapy sessions led to a greater reduction in pain, anxiety, and depression.

Labor Pain

In a study on labor pain, listening to music was an effective part of pre-operative preparation of pregnant women for cesarean section (Sidorenko, 2000a). It also had a powerful antistress effect and reduced the amount of pain medication needed by the women during labor, thus decreasing the negative pharmacological load on the fetus. Furthermore, labor time and hospital stay were decreased.

Another labor pain study examined the effects of music therapy–assisted childbirth on muscle relaxation during labor, perception of pain, and pain medication (Browning, 2001). The music was played for the duration of labor. According to results of the Muscle Relaxation Inventory, women in the music therapy group were significantly more relaxed than those in the control group who did not hear music during the 3 hours prior to delivery.

Operative and Postoperative Pain

In one study, patients undergoing colonoscopy while listening to music had lower saliva cortisol levels than the group not listening to music (Uedo et al., 2004). In another study on music versus no music during colonoscopies, the mean dose of sedative and analgesic drugs used in the music group was lower, as were the levels of anxiety and pain (Ovayolu et al., 2006). Similar data were reported by three other groups on sedation for colonoscopies following music therapy (D. Lee et al., 2002; Sheiman, Gross, Reuter, & Kellner, 2002; Smolen, Topp, & Singer, 2002).

In a meta-analysis of the literature on music therapy and invasive procedures, D. Evans (2002) found 19 studies on hospitalized adults who received music therapy during and following postoperative care for bronchoscopies, sigmoidoscopies, and colonoscopies. Evans concluded that although anxiety, heart rate, and respiratory rate were not reduced during the actual invasive procedures, the need for analgesia during these procedures was reduced in those who received music therapy.

Postoperative music has also been effective in decreasing anxiety level, cortisol level, pain, and the amount of morphine needed (Nilsson, Unosson, & Rawal, 2005). In a similar study, playing music during the first 24-hour postoperative period reduced pain, systolic blood pressure, heart rate, and oral analgesics (Tse, Chan, & Benzie, 2005).

Neurological and Musculoskeletal Conditions

Stroke

In a study by Nayak, Wheeler, Shiflett, and Agostinelli (2000), music therapy was used to improve mood and social interaction after traumatic brain injury or stroke. The brain injury and stroke patients in the music therapy group listened to classical music on a daily basis. After 1 month, they were rated by staff as being more actively involved and cooperative during therapy than those in the control group who did not listen to music. Self-ratings and family ratings of mood also suggested greater improvement in the music group than in the control group.

Dementia

Several studies have investigated music therapy effects on patients with dementia. In one study, patients with dementia received music therapy twice a week for 8 consecutive weeks (Suzuki et al., 2004). The patients' scores for irritability decreased. Other studies on music with dementia patients have found reduction in agitated behavior (Koger & Brotons, 2000; Remington, 2002) as well as depressive symptoms (Ashida, 2000).

Parkinson's Disease

In a study by Haneishi (2001), patients with Parkinson's disease received music therapy, including vocal exercises and rhythmic movements, to improve their speech. Following music therapy, the patients' speech intelligibility, vocal intensity, and vocal range increased, and probably because of these speech improvements, their mood also improved.

Pacchetti et al. (2000) found that music therapy is also effective for improving motor and emotional functions in patients with Parkinson's disease. Following 3 months of weekly music therapy sessions involving choral singing, voice exercise, and rhythmic and free body movements, patients' difficulty controlling limb movements was decreased, and their activities of daily living and quality of life were improved.

Epilepsy

A study by Sidorenko (2000b) found that medical resonance music therapy, which is based on entraining physiological rhythms, is effective in conjunction with the treatment of epilepsy. The frequency and severity of seizures in patients with moderately severe epilepsy changed positively in 80% of the cases.

Cardiovascular Conditions

Studies have shown that blood pressure, heart rate, and respiration are also decreased by music therapy. In one study, participants performed a challenging 3-minute mental arithmetic task and then were randomly assigned to sit in silence or to listen to one of several types of music, including classical, jazz, or pop (Chafin, Roy, Gerin, & Christenfeld, 2004). Those who listened to classical music had significantly lower posttask systolic blood pressure levels compared with those who listened to the other types of music or those who heard no music. In another study, patients who received music therapy notably had lower systolic and diastolic blood pressure but also lower pulse rate and respiration and less pain following 30- to 60-minute sessions (I. S. Kwon, Kim, & Park, 2006).

Autoimmune Conditions

In a study by Kimata (2003), patients with atopic dermatitis listened to Mozart for an hour each day. After 1 month, the patients showed reduced skin wheal responses and positive changes in their immune function, including decreased IgE and a shift in the cytokine pattern toward the positive immune system (the Th1 type) and a decrease in the negative immune system (the Th2 type).

Using a similar protocol, Lazaroff and Shimshoni (2000) found that patients with psoriasis and neurodermatitis also improved following music therapy. In this case, patients' blood pressure, heart rate, and the urge to scratch were reduced following the music therapy.

Cancer

In a study on cancer patients, Burns, Sledge, Fuller, Daggy, and Monahan (2005) assessed the patients' preferences for using two types of music therapy—music making and music listening—and found that the patients were more interested in music listening. Another study on cancer patients showed that the effects of these two types of music experiences did not differ when mood states were measured (Waldon, 2001). After four music-making sessions and four music-responding sessions, mood state scores improved regardless of the type of session.

Chinese music has also been used with cancer patients (in five modes said to be associated with the spleen, lung, liver, heart, and kidney) 30 minutes per day over 15 days (Cai, Qiao, Li, Jiao, & Lu, 2001). Following music therapy, anxiety and depression decreased, and T lymphocytes and natural killer cell activity increased. Increased natural killer cell number and activity were noted following music therapy in at least one other study, which is relevant for cancer patients because natural killer cells are known to kill cancer cells (Hasegawa, Kubota, Inagaki, & Shinagawa, 2001).

REFERRING CLIENTS TO MUSIC THERAPY PRACTITIONERS

Music seems to be a natural therapeutic medium that could accompany any type of therapy session and could be used at home and at work to improve relaxation and mood states. As such, therapists may find it is natural to integrate music into their practice and to encourage its constant use. Some of the studies reviewed here, however, suggest that sophisticated music therapy methods exist—for example, the medical resonance music therapy to entrain rhythms in patients with epileptic seizures. Thus, referrals to music therapists may be appropriate for some patients. Clinicians may even wish to consult with music therapists to learn about relevant conditions for referrals.

9

AROMATHERAPY

Aromatherapy uses essential oils that have been extracted from herbs, plants, and flowers. The oils are used through inhalation or aromatic baths or are mixed with other oils and used in aromatherapy massage. Because essential oils are up to 100 times more concentrated than the plants themselves, they often need to be diluted before being inhaled or applied to the skin. Aromatherapists can tailor-make blends of essential oils to meet a particular individual's emotional and physical needs, such as to be more upbeat and active or more subdued and relaxed. Examples of these oils and their uses are shown in Table 9.1.

Inhalation is the simplest, the fastest, and the oldest method for using essential oils. Clay burners, shaped like miniature tents, are a frequently used way of heating the oil for inhalation. When one inhales these oils, they attach themselves to millions of hairlike receptors that are behind the bridge of the nose just beneath the brain. The receptors are connected to the olfactory bulb. Different odors attach themselves to different receptors, allowing people to discriminate approximately 10,000 odors even though they have only approximately 1,000 odor receptors (Freeman, 2004).

The origins of aromatherapy have been traced back to ancient India, Egypt, Rome, and the Arab empire. Cave paintings in Lascaux, France,

TABLE 9.1
Popular Uses for Essential Oils

Oil	Uses
Basil	For concentration, relief of depression, relief from headaches and migraines
Citronella	Insect repellant, perfume
Eucalyptus	Often used in combination with peppermint to clear the nasal passages in cases of cold or flu
Jasmine	Aphrodisiac
Lavender	To calm and relax, to soothe headaches
Lemon	To enhance mood and relax
Rose	Aphrodisiac
Rosemary	To heighten attentiveness
Sandalwood	Aphrodisiac
Ylang-ylang	Aphrodisiac

suggest that plants have been used for healing since at least 1800 BC. One of the earliest records consists of seeds of aromatic plants that were found near a Neanderthal skeleton dating back 60,000 years. Aromatic medicine was one of the orthodox medicines of the Neanderthal times.

Historically, oils have been used as medicines for urinary and chest infections, and essential oils such as thyme, chamomile, clove, and lemon were used as natural disinfectants and to sterilize surgical instruments, as well as for many other medical conditions until the 1940s, when the pharmaceutical industry was being developed. At around the same time, thymol from the essential oil of thyme was developed by Joseph Lister as the first antiseptic. Listerine (named after Lister), which contains thymol, is still used as a popular mouthwash today.

POTENTIAL MECHANISMS OF ACTION FOR AROMATHERAPY

Reputedly, a person can distinguish one part of the aromatic matter in up to 10,000 billion parts, enabling one to distinguish up to 10,000 different scents (Freeman, 2004). The olfactory nerve that registers these scents is associated with the most primitive part of the brain, the limbic system, which controls people's basic emotional responses.

The limbic system or the "smell brain" is a ring of brain structures below the cerebral cortex that includes the amygdala, septum, hippocampus, inferior thalamus, and hypothalamus. The amygdala and the hippocampus are of particular importance because they involve the emotions, learning, and memory (LeDoux, 1996). Even when smell is affected by a heavy cold or infection, some aromas, such as peppermint and eucalyptus, can still reach the limbic system via the olfactory nerve.

Although essential oils have been used for centuries as a traditional medicine, little research data exist as to potential underlying mechanisms for their effects. However, accumulated evidence on inhaled or dermally applied essential oils (based on molecular, cellular, or animal models) suggests that the effects of essential oils are primarily pharmacological (Perry & Perry, 2006).

EMPIRICAL SUPPORT FOR THE EFFECTS OF AROMATHERAPY

Although aromatherapy is most commonly used for stress, anxiety, depression, insomnia, and chronic pain, the essential oils are also said to have antimicrobial effects against fungal, bacterial, viral, and parasitic infections. Unless otherwise indicated, in the following studies aromatherapy was administered through inhalation.

Psychological Symptoms and Disorders

Some psychological symptoms and disorders have been improved by aromatherapy. These include stress, mood, and cognitive performance.

Stress

Most of the aromatherapy studies in the literature have focused on stress. Typically in these studies, two aromas are compared or an aroma (usually lavender) is compared with an odorless substance such as water. For example, in one study, lavender was assessed for its effects on participants' responses to a stress–arousal adjective checklist (Motomura, Sakurai, & Yotsuya, 2001). Lavender was associated with reduced mental stress and decreased arousal.

In another study, water, lavender, and rosemary scents were compared for their effects on physiology and mood state following an anxiety-provoking task (Burnett, Solterbeck, & Strapp, 2004). Participants in the rosemary condition scored higher on measures of tension–anxiety and confusion–bewilderment compared with those in the lavender and control conditions. The lavender and control groups showed higher mean vigor–activity ratings compared with the rosemary group, whereas both rosemary and lavender scents were associated with lower mean ratings on the fatigue–inertia subscale.

Cognitive Performance and Mood

In one study, Moss, Cook, Wesnes, and Duckett (2003) examined the effects of lavender and rosemary on cognitive performance and mood in healthy adults. In the aromatherapy group, lavender was associated with lower performance involving working memory and impaired reaction times for both memory and attention tasks compared with a control group that did not receive the aromas. In contrast, rosemary enhanced performance on memory and secondary memory factors, although it was associated with less speed of memory compared with controls.

In a study by our research group, electroencephalographic (EEG) activity, alertness, mood, and cortisol levels were assessed in adults who inhaled either lavender or rosemary for 3 minutes (Diego et al., 1998). Participants were given simple math computations before and after the therapy. The lavender group showed increased beta power, suggesting increased relaxation. They also felt less depressed and performed the math computations faster and more accurately after as opposed to before the aromatherapy. The rosemary group, in contrast, showed decreased frontal alpha and beta power, suggesting increased alertness. They also had lower state anxiety scores, reported feeling more relaxed and alert, and were faster (but not more accurate) at completing the math computations after the aromatherapy session.

Sanders et al. (2002) examined frontal EEG asymmetry shifting from baseline in the Diego et al. (1998) sample mentioned earlier. Results revealed significant EEG shifting in the lavender group, with greater shifts from right-to left-frontal EEG activation (associated with greater approach behavior and less depressed affect). Collapsing across aroma groups, those with greater baseline right-frontal EEG activation shifted left (a positive shift) during the aroma sessions.

Similarly, my colleagues and I assessed alertness, mood, and math computations in adults before and after they sniffed a cleansing gel with a lavender floral blend aroma (Field et al., 2005). The lavender fragrance blend had a significant transient effect on improving mood, making people feel more relaxed and performing the math computations faster. The self-report and EEG and heart rate data were consistent with relaxation. Figure 9.1 shows the decrease in participants' mean heart rate during exposure to lavender aroma. (For more information, see Lis-Balchin, 2006.)

Aroma massage (the combination of aromas and massage) has also been used with mothers postpartum (Imura, Ushijima, & Misao, 2005). The mothers' scores decreased significantly on the Maternity Blues Scale, the State–Trait Anxiety Inventory, and each subscale of the Profile of Mood States Scale following the lavender aroma massage.

Lavender has also been combined with other aromas, including chamomile, rosemary, and lemon, for aromatherapy massage. In a study by Rho, Han, Kim, and Lee (2006), each massage with this combination of oils lasted 20 minutes and was performed three times per week for two 3-week periods. The intervention resulted in significantly lower anxiety and higher self-esteem. Park and Lee (2004) tested the effects of aroma inhalation of a

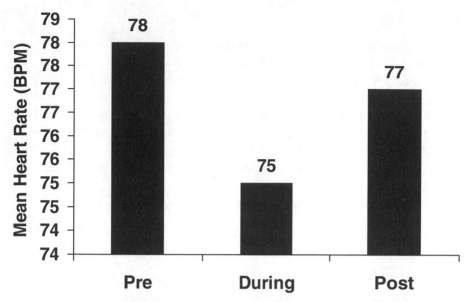

Figure 9.1. Participants' mean heart rate measured in beats per minute (BPM) before, during, and after exposure to lavender aroma.

mixture of lavender, peppermint, rosemary, and clary sage on nursing students. They found that the students' physical symptoms, anxiety scores, and perceived stress scores decreased.

Lavender has also been compared with other oils, such as jojoba and hiba oils. In a study by H. K. Lee (2005), lavender aromatherapy was given to one group and jojoba oil to the other group for 2 weeks, and no treatment was administered to the control group. The lavender group showed a significant decrease in anxious behavior compared with the jojoba and control groups.

Itai et al. (2000) investigated the effects of aromatherapy in three conditions (odorless, lavender, and hiba oil) on mood and anxiety in patients who were being treated with chronic hemodialysis. The effects of aromatherapy were measured using the Hamilton Rating Scale for Depression and the Hamilton Rating Scale for Anxiety. Hiba oil aroma was associated with significant decreases in the mean scores on the depression and anxiety scales, and lavender aroma significantly decreased the mean anxiety scores. Lavender effects were also noted for insomnia. In Lewith, Godfrey, and Prescott's (2005) study, lavender resulted in improved sleep as measured by Pittsburgh Sleep Quality Index scores.

A study on dental patients assessed the effects of orange and lavender on anxiety, mood, alertness, and calmness (Lehrner, Marwinski, Lehr, Johren, & Deecke, 2005). Orange and lavender odors reduced anxiety and improved mood in patients waiting for dental treatment.

Addictions

Aromatherapy massage with lavender has also helped reduce eating and smoking addictions. In a study on overweight individuals, aromatherapy massage using lavender and a placebo oil massage were given for 2 weeks (S. H. Han, Yang, & Kim, 2003). The aromatherapy massage reduced weight, abdominal circumference, and appetite. The urge to smoke has also been reduced through aromatherapy. In one study, sniffing either a pleasant lavender or unpleasant odor (fish odor) reduced the reported urge to smoke compared with a control odorless condition (Sayette & Parrott, 1999).

Physical Conditions and Disorders: Pain Syndromes

Aromatherapy has been used with physical conditions and disorders as well as pain syndromes. These include osteoarthritis, postoperative pain, and dysmenorrhea.

Osteoarthritis

Aromatherapy has reduced pain and depression and enhanced feelings of satisfaction in patients with arthritis (M. J. Kim, Nam, & Paik, 2005). Lavender aroma, in particular, decreased both pain and depression scores.

Postoperative Pain

A study by J. Kim et al. (2006) showed that patients who underwent breast biopsy surgery also benefited from lavender oil aromatherapy. Patients in the lavender group reported higher satisfaction with pain control compared with patients in the control group, who did not receive the aroma.

Dysmenorrhea

In a study on dysmenorrhea, aromatherapy was provided for the experimental group in the form of an abdominal massage using two drops of lavender, one drop of clary sage, and one drop of rose in 5 cubic centimeters of almond oil (S. Han, Hur, Buckle, Choi, & Lee, 2006). The placebo group received the same massage but with almond oil only. Menstrual cramps were significantly less frequent and less intense in the aromatherapy group.

Cardiovascular Conditions

Patients with cardiovascular conditions have also benefited from aromatherapy. In one study by Hwang (2006), lavender, ylang-ylang, and bergamot were blended and presented by the inhalation method once daily for 4 weeks to patients with hypertension. Psychological stress responses, serum cortisol levels, and blood pressure in patients with essential hypertension were reduced. Relaxing odors (such as lavender) have also yielded decreases in heart rate and skin conductance, whereas stimulating odors (such as rosemary) have yielded the reverse effects under equivalent conditions (Campenni, Crawler, & Meier 2004).

In a similar study on cardiovascular responses, the patients inhaled lavender, rosemary, and citronella (Saeki & Mayumi, 2001). The measures included electrocardiograms, *galvanic skin conductance* (blood flow in the tips of the fingers measured by an electrode), and blood pressure readings. The results showed that lavender decreased systolic blood pressure within 10 minutes, decreased galvanic skin response within 2 minutes, and increased blood flow within 6 minutes. Rosemary increased systolic blood pressure and decreased blood flow immediately. In addition, changes in electrocardiogram readings were noted after lavender exposure, and the two frequency components of heart rate variability (the high-frequency component and the high-frequency/low-frequency component ratio) increased immediately, suggesting a calming parasympathetic influence. Citronella did not change blood flow or blood pressure, but galvanic skin response decreased immediately, and heart rate decreased after 10 minutes.

Immune Conditions

In a study on infections, eucalyptus and tea tree oils were shown to be effective against staphylococcus aureus infection when that infection was resistant to penicillin (C. Carson, Cookson, Farrelly, & Riley, 1995). In 22 of 25 cases, the infection was resolved. Carson et al. (1995) also tested these two essential oils in vitro against multiple-resistant tuberculosis, and more than 90% of all five strains of the tuberculosis test were killed within 1 minute.

Aromatherapy for patients with cancer has been researched in terms of its effects on depression and anxiety. In one study, patients with cancer referred for clinical anxiety and/or depression were randomly assigned either to a course of aromatherapy massage in addition to their support group sessions or to the support group session alone (Wilkinson et al., 2007). The patients who received aromatherapy massage had lower anxiety and depression. In another study, Wilkinson, Aldridge, Salmon, Cain, and Wilson (1999) used aromatherapy massage with cancer patients in a palliative care setting. A significant reduction in anxiety occurred after each aromatherapy massage session as measured by the State–Trait Anxiety Inventory.

Skin Aging

Elastase is an enzyme that degenerates dermal elastin, and elastase activity is believed to contribute to cutaneous wrinkling and aging. To examine whether certain aromatherapy oils can inhibit elastase activity and thus prevent wrinkling, M. Mori, Ikeda, Kato, Minamino, and Watabe (2002) experimented with various essential oils. They found that elastase activity was inhibited by oils derived from lemon, juniper, and grapefruit.

REFERRING CLIENTS TO AN AROMATHERAPY PRACTITIONER

Aromas, like music, can be used as background for therapy sessions. Studies need to be done on combining aromatherapy with other therapies, not unlike the studies combining aromatherapy and massage therapy. Of course, some knowledge of the differential effects of different aromas would be important, for example, knowing that lavender is typically relaxing and rosemary is activating or alerting. Workshops on aromatherapy are offered in many massage therapy schools, and books and Internet sites are informative. Although the studies on aromatherapy are based on average (mean) responses of groups to specific aromas, there are probably large individual differences in aroma preferences just as there are for tastes. Most massage therapists who use aroma in their oils will inquire first about client preferences, and most clients who receive aromatherapy probably do so in the context of massage therapy.

10
PROGRESSIVE MUSCLE RELAXATION

Progressive muscle relaxation (PMR) is a technique in which a person is trained to voluntarily relax individual muscles. It induces both physiological and psychological relaxation by reducing the response to stress, reducing skeletal muscle contractions, and decreasing the sensation of pain (McCaffery & Pasero, 1990). PMR was first developed by American physician Edmund Jacobson in 1934. His protocol involved the tensing and relaxation of 16 muscle groups (Freeman, 2004). Because the PMR therapy developed by Jacobson was a long procedure, Joseph Wolpe in 1948 developed a method called *abbreviated progressive relaxation training* (APRT), which focuses on relaxing several muscle groups simultaneously. Wolpe taught students to tense muscles and then relax them as opposed to focusing on tensions and relaxing them (Wolpe, 1990). Several therapists since that time have developed further adaptations, so the art of relaxation therapy is now highly variable.

A brief relaxation strategy has become a standard feature of clinical training (Turner, Calhoun, & Adams, 1992), and its outcomes have compared favorably with those of some psychotherapy studies (C. Carlson & Hoyle, 1993). Heart rate has been reliably and consistently used as a dependent physiological measure in PMR studies for the past 60 years (Hale &

Whitehouse, 1998). Similarly, motor activity has been an important measure of the effects of PMR (Herman & Blanchard, 1998).

POTENTIAL UNDERLYING MECHANISMS
FOR PROGRESSIVE MUSCLE RELAXATION EFFECTS

Little research has been conducted on potential underlying mechanisms for relaxation therapy effects. Through the tensing and relaxing of muscles, PMR may be stimulating pressure receptors and thereby increasing vagal activity, which in turn would lower heart rate and blood pressure and lead to reduced cortisol levels. Although this potential mechanism has not been directly assessed, several studies have reported increased vagal activity and/or decreased heart rate and blood pressure, and some have reported decreased cortisol following relaxation therapy as detailed in the following two studies.

Lucini et al. (1997) compared healthy participants in a relaxation training group with a sham relaxation group. Increased heart rate and blood pressure were induced by having participants stand and perform mental arithmetic exercises. Sympathetic activity in response to the physical stressor (standing) and the mental stressor (arithmetic) was significantly reduced in the group that received relaxation training, and vagal activity was increased. These data support the suggestion that vagal activity might be an underlying mechanism for the relaxation therapy effects.

Another potential mechanism is the increase in endorphins. A study by McCubbin et al. (1996) conducted with men with elevated blood pressure assessed the effects of relaxation therapy on endogenous opioids. The men practiced a brief 25-minute relaxation therapy procedure before being exposed to a laboratory stressor (arithmetic). The men who practiced relaxation therapy showed reduced diastolic blood pressure. When they were given an opioid antagonist to block the opioid receptors, the blood pressure decrease was reversed. These data suggest that relaxation is accompanied by a release of endogenous opioids that may underlie their effects on blood pressure.

One of the most difficult problems in research on PMR is compliance. When home relaxation sessions have been electronically monitored, the compliance rates are extremely low (30%), suggesting that overreporting and noncompliance are common problems. In addition, in many of the studies that were excluded from this review, several types of relaxation therapy were combined with PMR, including meditation, hypnosis, imagery, and biofeedback, making it difficult to know which type or types of relaxation therapy were contributing to the effects.

EMPIRICAL SUPPORT FOR THE EFFECTS
OF PROGRESSIVE MUSCLE RELAXATION

Empirical evidence supports the use of PMR for reducing stress, improving sleep, and managing pain. These conditions include arthritis, irritable bowel syndrome, and cancer (McCallie, Blum, & Hood, 2006).

Psychological Symptoms and Disorders

PMR has been practiced by those who have psychological symptoms and disorders. These include, for example, stress and anxiety.

Stress

PMR is often used to reduce stress. In a study by Pawlow and Jones (2002) that examined whether relaxation training was associated with reduced subjective and physiological stress, participants were led through APRT exercises during two laboratory sessions spaced 1 week apart. Participants in the control group sat quietly for an equal amount of time in two laboratory sessions. The results indicated that the APRT led to lower levels of postintervention heart rate, state anxiety, perceived stress, and salivary cortisol as well as increased feelings of relaxation.

In another study on stress, Ghonchech and Smith (2004) compared the psychological effects of PMR with yoga stretching. Both groups practiced once a week for 5 weeks at home. Practitioners of PMR displayed higher levels of physical relaxation and disengagement at Week 4 and higher levels of mental quiet and joy as a posttraining aftereffect at Week 5.

Anxiety

Undergraduate students in a large-group setting were exposed to 20 minutes of meditation, PMR, or a control condition, followed by 1 minute of stress induction and another 10 minutes of each intervention (Rausch, Gramling, & Auerbach, 2006). The participants in both the meditation and PMR groups decreased more on cognitive, somatic, and general state anxiety compared with the control group. However, the PMR group had the greatest decline of all three groups in somatic anxiety.

In another study, Weber (2004) used PMR, meditative breathing, guided imagery, and soft music to promote relaxation in patients in a psychiatric unit across a month of weekly sessions. Anxiety levels were measured before and after relaxation sessions. Although the effects of each type of therapy were confounded, a significant reduction in anxiety level was noted on the posttest.

Physical Conditions and Diseases: Pain Syndromes

PMR has been used in research on physical conditions and diseases and pain syndromes. These include osteoarthritis and postsurgical pain.

Osteoarthritis

Adults with osteoarthritis must deal with pain that leads to limited mobility and may lead to disability and difficulty maintaining independence. Baird and Sands (2004) conducted a study to determine whether PMR would reduce pain and mobility difficulties of women with osteoarthritis. The treatment consisted of listening twice a day to a 10- to 15-minute audiotaped script that guided the women through PMR. The treatment group reported a significantly greater reduction in pain and mobility difficulties at Week 12 compared with the control group that did not receive relaxation training.

Postsurgical Pain

PMR has benefited patients following different types of surgery. Effects of PMR on postsurgical pain were assessed in patients who had undergone abdominal surgery (Delloiagono de Paula, Campos de Carvalho, & Benita dos Santos, 2002). The results showed a statistically significant reduction in pain after PMR.

In a study by Miller and Perry (1990), patients undergoing coronary artery bypass surgery also experienced less pain following relaxation therapy. In this case, the experimental group received relaxation training before the surgery and practiced the techniques after surgery, and the control group received standard treatment. Self-reported pain levels were lower in the relaxation training group, and they also showed decreased systolic and diastolic blood pressure and respiratory rates.

Cardiovascular Conditions

In a study on cardiac rehabilitation patients, blood pressure and heart rate data and scores on the State–Trait Anxiety Inventory were collected from a group of patients enrolled in cardiac rehabilitation who received relaxation training versus a group who did not receive relaxation training (Wilk & Turkoski, 2001). Analysis of the data revealed positive effects of PMR on heart rate and anxiety. In addition, written evaluations of PMR by patients in the treatment group indicated a high degree of subjective satisfaction with PMR as a means for reducing stress.

In an 8-week randomized, prospective, controlled trial on PMR versus a placebo intervention, Nickel et al. (2006) noted a significant reduction in systolic blood pressure and a significant increase in both forced expiratory volume in the first, second, and peak expiratory flow after PMR of pregnant women with bronchial asthma. A significant increase was also noted in vagal activity, and there was a significant decrease in anger scores on the State–Trait Anger Expression Inventory.

Immune Conditions

Pawlow and Jones (2005) showed that immune function improved following relaxation therapy with a variety of cancer patients. APRT led to the patients having significantly lower levels of postintervention salivary cortisol and significantly higher levels of postintervention sIgA (immune cells) compared with a control group. Similar increases in IgA have accompanied decreased heart rate and cortisol following relaxation therapy (Lowe, Bland, Greenman, Kirkpatrick, & Lowe, 2001).

PMR training has also been used to reduce anticipatory nausea and vomiting and postchemotherapy nausea and vomiting in patients with cancer (Yoo, Ahn, Kim, Kim, & Han, 2005). In this study, patients with breast cancer received relaxation before and after chemotherapy, and the control group received the standard treatment. The relaxation group was significantly less anxious and depressed than the control group, and they experienced less nausea and vomiting. Other studies have shown decreased nausea and vomiting when relaxation therapy preceded and followed chemotherapy (Arakawa, 1995; Mollasiotis, 2002).

Systematic Desensitization

Systematic desensitization is a technique that uses PMR to treat phobias and other extreme fears. With the therapist's support, the client responds to the fearful image or act by producing the state of relaxation. Relaxation then replaces anxiety when the fear is experienced. Because panic reactions can occur, this technique should only be used by a well-qualified, trained professional. Although the underlying mechanisms are unknown and the use of this technique has declined, it is still widely used among therapists (McGlynn, Smitherman, & Gothard, 2004; Tryon, 2005).

REFERRING CLIENTS TO RELAXATION PRACTITIONERS

Learning relaxation techniques is relatively easy, and if workshops cannot be found, clients can be encouraged to try instructional videos, which are widely available. Therapists can also refer clients to yoga classes, which also frequently include PMR segments. Like yoga and Tai Chi, these relaxation sessions can become a home-based or health-club-based daily routine.

11
IMAGERY

Imagery is an imagination process that focuses on the senses, including sound, vision, smell, taste, touch, and the sense of movement. Images are thought to elicit physiological, biochemical, and immunological changes that can prevent or treat symptoms or disease. Imagery has been used in other forms of therapy that are reviewed in this book, including relaxation therapy, meditation, hypnosis, and biofeedback.

Imagery was first used in the 4th century BC in the Asclepian temples of Greece, and the method was used by Aristotle, Hippocrates, and Galen (Freeman, 2004). Imagery in early Greek times was considered a natural state of consciousness that occurred just before sleep, and therefore healers paid close attention to the dreams of their patients or the hypnagogic sleep state that was precursor to what today is known as hypnotic imagery.

TYPES OF IMAGERY

The imagery procedures that are used today can be classified as diagnostic imagery, mental-rehearsal imagery, and end-state imagery. *Diagnostic imagery* is when patients are requested to elaborate how they are feeling in emotional and sensory terms. The therapist typically induces relaxation and often does that by creating a relaxing environment that sometimes features music, candles, and aromas. The therapist then tries to have the patient imagine the components of the disease and the treatment. Typically the session lasts about 30 minutes and desirably leads to images (and drawings) of relaxation, including images that are incompatible with painful procedures such as debridement (brushing the skin following burns).

Mental-rehearsal imagery is a technique that is typically used to prepare the patient for medical procedures such as surgery and childbirth. In this mental-rehearsal imagery, the patient is typically taught a relaxation technique (see chap. 10, this volume), and then the medical procedure is elaborated in a guided imagery that uses sensory terms. The purpose is to relieve anxiety associated with the impending procedure and to reduce pain associated with the procedure and any side effects following the procedure.

End-state imagery is used to induce a physiological or biochemical change in the body, such as a decrease in cortisol or enhanced immune cells. This is also used to alleviate the side effects of chemotherapy, to reduce nausea in early pregnancy, and to control surgical pain.

POTENTIAL MECHANISMS UNDERLYING THE EFFECTS OF IMAGERY

One of the problems in determining mechanisms of action for imagery is that in many of the studies conducted (including those described in this chapter), the effects of imagery are confounded by the effects of progressive muscle relaxation (PMR; see chap. 10, this volume), which is often used in tandem with imagery because it appears that relaxation is necessary to produce effective images. Whether that relaxation is achieved by PMR or simply by a request for relaxation, the simple relaxation of muscles confounds the effects of the imagery itself.

Results of studies that used functional magnetic resonance imaging (fMRI) during motor imagery or motor practice seem to suggest that changes are occurring both in the central nervous system and in the immune system. fMRI has been used to locate activity in different brain regions during imagery that might explain its effects on motor function. For example, Meister et al. (2004) used fMRI to investigate the cortical network that mediates music performance compared with music imagery in music academy students. In both conditions, fMRI activation was noted in the brain's bilateral frontal parietal network comprising the premotor areas and the medial part of Brodmann Area 40. During music performance, but not during imagery, the contralateral primary motor cortex and posterior parietal cortex were bilaterally active. Meister et al. suggested that this reflected the role of the primary motor cortex for motor execution but not for imagery.

Some of the contradictory reports about activation of the motor cortex as measured by fMRI may be explained by another study. Dechent, Merboldt, and Frahm (2004) addressed the participation of the primary motor cortex in motor imagery by using fMRI. Motor execution activated the primary motor cortex as well as other parts of the motor system, such as the supplementary motor area and premotor areas. In contrast, motor imagery did not lead to activation in the primary motor cortex but involved the supplementary motor area and the anterior intraparietal cortex. Thus, the previous contradictory reports in the literature may relate to some investigators measuring the onset of the imagery that does not lead to primary motor cortex activation and other investigators measuring the motor practice during imagery that does lead to primary motor cortex activation.

EMPIRICAL SUPPORT FOR THE EFFECTS OF IMAGERY

Imagery has been effective in the treatment of anxiety and depression and in pain syndromes such as migraine headaches, fibromyalgia, and osteoarthritis. There is also some evidence that imagery can help patients with cancer, diabetes, asthma, and eczema.

Psychological Conditions and Disorders

Research has been conducted on imagery with psychological conditions and disorders, including anxiety, depression, stress, and posttraumatic stress disorder.

Anxiety and Depression

In a study on relaxation and imagery for anxiety and depression, patients with advanced cancer were given 10 months of guided imagery training and were compared with a standard treatment control group (Sloman, 2002). The patients who received the guided imagery training experienced less depression and a greater quality of life.

Stress and Moods

In E. Watanabe, Fukuda, and Shirakawa's (2005) study, participants attended 10 sessions over 7 months on guided imagery and then practiced guided imagery at home for 20 minutes once daily in a quiet place. Those who practiced imagery at home longer had lower negative mood scores and lower stress scores and higher positive mood and general health scores.

The opposite effects can be obtained from negative imagery. In a study by Holmes and Mathews (2005), participants either imagined unpleasant events (*negative imagery*) or listened to neutral descriptions while thinking about their verbal meaning (*benign imagery*). Those in the negative imagery group reported more anxiety and rated neutral descriptions as more emotional than those in the benign imagery condition. When the unpleasant imagery was compared with benign imagery, participants' anxiety increased more after the unpleasant imagery.

Posttraumatic Stress Disorder

Posttraumatic stress disorder (PTSD) has been treated by imagery-rehearsal therapy in a number of studies. For example, in a study by Krakow et al. (2001), women who had been raped or sexually assaulted received three sessions of imagery-rehearsal therapy or were assigned to a wait-list control group. In the imagery group, participants imagined a dream that they would rather have instead of a typical nightmare about the trauma. They were to write down the new dream and rehearse it for 5 to 20 minutes per day for the 3 weeks in therapy. The imagery-rehearsal therapy led to fewer nights per week of nightmares as well as an improvement in other PTSD symptoms. A decrease in symptoms was noted for 65% of the imagery group compared with the control group.

In another study with Vietnam War veterans diagnosed with PTSD who were experiencing nightmares related to their combat (Forbes, Phelps, & McHugh, 2001), four sessions of imagery-rehearsal therapy over 1 month led to a significant reduction in nightmares as well as a reduction in their other PTSD symptoms. In a script-driven imagery study on Vietnam veterans diagnosed with PTSD, positron emission tomography was used to study regional blood flow during the recollection of personal traumatic and neutral events (L. M. Shin et al., 2004). The psychophysiological and emotional self-report data confirmed the effects of script-driven imagery.

Sleep Disorders

Imagery has also been used with sleep disorders. In one study, individuals with insomnia were exposed to a stressor (the threat of giving a speech) prior to going to bed (J. Nelson & Harvey, 2002). One group was instructed to think about the speech and its implications using images. The other group was instructed to think about the speech and its implications using words. The image group reported more immediate distress and arousal compared with the verbal group. However, in the longer term, the image group fell asleep more quickly, and the following morning they were less anxious about giving the speech. The authors suggested that images are more arousing than words because they are more vivid, but it is not clear why the participants were more able to sleep following the imagery.

Addictions

Imagery has also been used with people who have addictions, including eating and smoking addictions. Harvey, Kemps, and Tiggemann (2005) used imagery with people on diets who were attempting to lose weight and were experiencing food cravings. The imagery process involved in food cravings was predominantly visual in nature. Craving intensity increased following instructions to imagine the food, and visual imagery reduced the level of food craving compared with auditory imagery.

Wynd (2005) used imagery for smoking cessation in adult smokers. Smokers were given instructions on guided imagery and were encouraged to practice this imagery at least once per day with a 20-minute audiotaped exercise. Two years after the intervention, smoking abstinence rates were significantly higher for the imagery group (26% abstinence rate) than for the standard treatment control group (12% abstinence rate).

Physical Conditions and Diseases: Pain Syndromes

Pain syndromes are also lessened by imagery. Those that have been recently researched include fibromyalgia and osteoarthritis.

Fibromyalgia

In a study by Fors, Sexton, and Gotestam (2002), patients with fibromyalgia were given either 10 sessions of relaxation training and pleasant imagery to distract them from pain or relaxation training and attention imagery to imagine the internal pain control systems. The pleasant imagery was "beautiful, natural settings on nice summer days," and the attention imagery was visualization of pain-alleviating systems such as endorphins inhibiting neurons to limit pain. Over a 1-month period, patients in the pleasant imagery group but not in the attention imagery group had a significant reduction of pain. Fors et al. suggested that the pleasant imagery may have been more effective than the attention imagery because monitoring of somatic symptoms may actually increase pain.

In another study on patients with fibromyalgia by Fors and Gotestam (2000), a pleasant imagery group listened to an audiotape that encouraged them to practice relaxed breathing while imaging nature, flowers, water, sunny weather, and light, and an attention control group listened to an audiotaped tour of the pain-controlling mechanisms in the body. In the latter condition, patients were asked to imagine pictures of endorphins acting on pain and tender points. These groups were compared with a group of patients who talked freely and emotionally with each other and a therapist about their fibromyalgia problems (control group). After the imagery intervention, both of the imagery groups experienced significant pain reduction both before and after the intervention, but the therapy talk group did not. The pleasant-imagery group experienced a greater reduction in pain than the pain-systems-imagery group, which in turn experienced a greater reduction in pain than the control group.

In still another study on fibromyalgia, patients were randomized to a guided-imagery or a usual-care control group (Menzies, Taylor, & Bourguignon, 2006). The guided-imagery group received audiotaped imagery scripts and was instructed to use at least one tape daily for 6 weeks and to report weekly frequency of use. The Fibromyalgia Impact Questionnaire scores for this imagery group decreased over time, whereas those of the usual-care group did not. Ratings of self-efficacy for managing pain and other symptoms of fibromyalgia also increased significantly over time in the imagery group compared with the usual-care group.

Osteoarthritis

In a study of female patients with osteoarthritis, guided imagery was used with PMR to reduce pain and mobility difficulties (Baird & Sands, 2004). The treatment consisted of listening twice a day to a 10- to 15-minute audiotape script that guided the patients in their imagery and helped them with PMR. Patients in the treatment group reported a significant reduction in pain and mobility difficulties at the 12th week compared with patients in the control group who did not receive imagery.

Neurological and Musculoskeletal Disorders

Patients with neurological and musculoskeletal disorders have also been noted to benefit from guided imagery. Two examples are stroke and Parkinson's disease.

Stroke

Mental practice or visual imagery of a particular motor skill often activates the same muscles as physically practicing the skill (Freeman, 2004). Some research suggests that this intervention should be incorporated into rehabilitation programs for patients who have had one or more strokes.

In Page, Levine, and Leonard's (2007) study, stroke patients with moderate motor deficits either received 30-minute imagery sessions twice per week for 6 weeks or were assigned to a standard treatment control group. The patients in the imagery group showed greater increases in arm function and activities of daily living compared with those in the control group.

Parkinson's Disease

Motor imagery and motor practice have also been effective with Parkinson's disease. Tamir, Dickstein, and Huberman (2007) held 1-hour sessions twice a week for 12 weeks with patients with Parkinson's disease who practiced both imagery and motor exercises, and the control group received only motor exercises. Comparable motor tasks assigned to both groups included calisthenics, functional tasks, and relaxation exercises. The combined treatment group (imagery plus motor exercises) performed movement sequences faster than did the control group.

Autoimmune Conditions

Imagery is frequently used with autoimmune conditions. The examples discussed here are inflammation, asthma, and chronic obstructive pulmonary disease.

Inflammation

Inflammation is at the base of several autoimmune diseases, including asthma, eczema, psoriasis, and arthritic conditions. Acute or chronic stress can activate inflammation. In a study that assessed the effects of mental stress and imagery-based relaxation on the inflammatory process, individuals participated in a mental stress test and then were assigned to a relaxation-imagery video session or a control condition (Sloman, 2002). The relaxation-imagery group had a greater reduction in diastolic blood pressure and less inflammation compared with the control group.

In a similar study, Reid, Mackinnon, and Drummond (2001) used relaxation and imagery with university students who were experiencing examination stress. Following eight sessions over a 4-week treatment period, PMR and guided imagery including imagery of increased immunoglobulin led to decreased symptoms and increased salivary immunoglobulin.

Asthma

Asthma, another inflammatory condition, notably benefits from imagery sessions. In a study by Epstein et al. (2004), adults with asthma were randomly assigned to an imagery group that was given seven imagery exercises that were practiced three times a day for a total of 15 minutes per day over 17 weeks or to a control group that did not receive imagery. The patients in the imagery group had less need for medication or discontinued their medications compared with the control group.

Chronic Obstructive Pulmonary Disease

Patients diagnosed with chronic obstructive pulmonary disease engaged in a guided imagery relaxation task for six practice sessions (Louie, 2004). The imagery group experienced improved pulmonary functions compared with a standard treatment control group.

Immune Conditions

It has been suggested that imagery may increase immune cell count and immune cell migration. Some have suggested that imagery immediately affects immune cell count (e.g., white blood cell count) through cell migration patterns rather than through cell maturation or proliferation (Donaldson, 2000). When neutrophils and lymphocytes are activated, they are thought to migrate from the blood stream to lymphatic and body tissue to combat cancer cells, for example, thereby lowering the number of cells in the peripheral bloodstream.

In Donaldson's (2000) study that examined the way blood cell count increases, patients who were diagnosed with cancer, AIDS, and other viral infections practiced imagery for 30 minutes a day. The imagery included both general imagery ("I relax deeply and easily") and specific imagery ("White blood cells, I call on you"). As predicted, the white blood cell count first decreased as if the cells were migrating to the location of the cancer or viral cells. At 30, 60, and 90 days, the patients in the imagery group demonstrated a significant increase of 17%, 31%, and 38% of the white blood cells, respectively.

Studies have also been performed with patients with breast cancer to determine the effects of guided imagery on immune function and psychological profiles. Bakke, Purtzer, and Newton (2002) measured psychological profiles and natural killer cell number and activity at baseline and after the 8-week imagery training program using both general relaxation imagery and specific imagery focused on increasing immune cells. Patients' depression decreased and natural killer cell number increased.

In another study, patients with terminal cancer practiced a similar guided imagery protocol (Burns, 2001). The patients individually participated in 10 weekly 1-hour imagery sessions. Patients who participated in the imagery sessions scored better on both mood scores and quality-of-life scores at posttest than those participating in the control group who did not receive imagery.

REFERRING CLIENTS TO AN IMAGERY PRACTITIONER

Some practitioners actively use imagery in their therapy sessions. Imagery training, much like relaxation training, is typically offered at workshops that can be found on the Internet, on DVDs, and at national meetings of professional organizations. Also, like relaxation techniques, imagery activities can be practiced in daily sessions at home.

12

HYPNOSIS

Hypnosis is defined as an artificial subjective state in which alterations of perception or memory can be induced by suggestion. It is a process that involves a hypnotist and a person who agrees to be hypnotized (Sharma & Kaur, 2006). The hypnotic state is usually characterized by intense concentration, extreme relaxation, and high suggestibility.

Franz Anton Mesmer (1734–1815) introduced hypnosis in the 18th century on the basis of what he called "animal magnetism" demonstrations (Riskin & Frankel, 1994): He believed that there was a magnetic field around and extending through people and that this animal magnetism could be used for healing. Mesmer would induce a trancelike state with changes in perception, and the patients often lapsed into deep sleep or fainting (Riskin & Frankel, 1994). Students of Mesmer observed that these patients were in a hyperalert state while seemingly being asleep.

In England around 1843, the surgeon James Baird (1795–1860) revisited the phenomenon of mesmerism and renamed it *hypnosis* after the Greek god of sleep, Hypnos. Baird was the first person to attribute the phenomenon to psychological rather than physical variables.

In the 19th century, Scottish physician James Esdaile (1805–1859) used hypno-anesthesia in surgical patients. At around the same time, chemical anesthetics were being introduced. Hypnosis became province of charlatans and stage hypnotists whereas standard clinical drugs were being used for anesthesia. Although Freud used hypnosis in psychotherapy, it was not until 1958 that the American Medical Association endorsed the use of hypnotism by physicians and condemned its use for entertainment (Rosen, 1960). Probably the greatest reawakening of interest in hypnosis came when it was combined with anesthesia. *Hypnoanalgesia* has emerged as a combination of hypnotic techniques and pharmacological analgesia and sedation and is commonly used in medical practice (Lang et al., 2000).

POTENTIAL UNDERLYING MECHANISMS FOR HYPNOSIS EFFECTS

Little is known about the potential underlying mechanisms for hypnosis effects. A psychological explanation that is often given for how hypnosis works is based on a dissociation model (Watkins &Watkins, 1990). This model can be seen in patients with dissociative identity disorder, in which the patient in effect walls off distress in a psychological storage area in the unconscious. When used for pain management, it is possible that dissociation would eliminate the perception of pain by isolating it in a similar psychological storage area away from the primary consciousness of the patient. This model has been referred to as the *hidden observer* model of cognition (Watkins & Watkins, 1990).

A study in the 1970s that compared biofeedback with hypnosis for reducing test anxiety noted that both groups received similar scores, suggesting that there may be a similar underlying mechanism responsible for the effectiveness of both therapies (Spies, 1979). When the results were compared with relaxation training, they were all found to be similar. Because these are all forms of relaxation techniques, relaxation may be the underlying key to the effectiveness of hypnosis. In another study in the early 1990s (Weinstein & Au, 1991), norepinephrine levels were significantly higher during angioplasty of hypnotized patients in comparison with nonhypnotized controls. Because norepinephrine has some effects on sleep states, it is possible that hypnosis increases norepinephrine levels and, in turn, the sleeplike state. The similarity between hypnosis and the REM state of sleep would support a measurable chemical effect of hypnosis.

The major problem for the field of hypnosis is the difficulty finding measurable physiological variables that are associated with the hypnotic state. Hypnotic trances are also difficult to reproduce reliably, and of course, it is impossible to conduct a double-blind clinical study involving hypnosis.

Two studies have documented physiological correlates of hypnosis. Using positron emission tomography, Faymonville et al. (2000) demonstrated specific alterations of metabolic activity and perfusion of the anterior cingulate gyrus that were consistent with changes in pain perception during hypnosis. Schulz-Stubner et al. (2004) showed similar results with functional magnetic resonance imaging (MRI) in volunteers subjected to thermal pain with and without hypnosis.

In another study, Rainville, Duncan, Price, Carrier, and Bushnell (1997) gave two groups of adults—one group that was easily hypnotized and the other group not easily hypnotized—MRIs during hypnosis. The MRI images of the participants' corpus callosum showed significant differences between the groups. Those who were easily hypnotized had a significantly larger rostrum. Thus, the rostrum and the cortices appeared to play a role in attentional control during hypnotism.

SUSCEPTIBILITY TO HYPNOSIS

Although hypnosis has been effective for some clinical conditions, especially the management of pain, not all people are able to enter into a hypnotic state, which limits the clinical utility of this technique. In a study that explored whether hypnotic susceptibility could be increased, Batty, Bonnington, Tang, Hawken, and Gruzelier (2006) used three methods: an EEG neurofeedback protocol that elevated the theta to alpha ratio, a progressive muscle relaxation protocol, and a self-hypnosis protocol. Participants with moderate levels of susceptibility were randomly assigned to each condition and assessed in a pre–post design before and after completing 10 sessions of training. Hypnotic susceptibility increased following training in all three groups, providing further evidence that control over the theta:alpha ratio is possible. All three techniques successfully enhanced hypnotic susceptibility in over half of the participants, and the greater increases occurred in those more susceptible participants. However, enhancement was even noted in some at low levels. This would suggest that the lack of hypnotic susceptibility can be solved.

EMPIRICAL SUPPORT FOR
THE EFFECTS OF HYPNOSIS

Many of the hypnosis studies have small samples, and they lack controls and sometimes physical evaluations. Double-blind studies are impossible, and even single-blinded studies are near impossible, because the participants are required to be active. The interpretation of the results from different studies is also complicated by their lack of standardized procedures and techniques. Nonetheless, there is an increasing body of more robust studies.

Psychological Symptoms

In a study by Saadat et al. (2006) on the effects of hypnosis on preoperative anxiety, adult patients were randomized into three groups: a hypnosis group that received suggestions of well-being, an attention-control group that received attentive listening and support without any specific hypnotic suggestions, and a standard-care control group. On entrance to the operating room, the hypnosis group reported a significant decrease in their anxiety level (56% decrease), whereas the attention-control group reported a 10% increase in anxiety and the control group reported a 47% increase in anxiety.

The effects of hypnosis have also been compared with standard-care effects on pain, anxiety, and analgesia use during conscious sedation for minimally invasive procedures during radiology (Lang et al., 2000). Patients in the hypnosis group experienced less anxiety and decreased pain throughout the procedure, and they required less analgesic medication than the group receiving standard care. Others have reported faster wound healing, earlier postoperative recovery, and less nausea when hypnosis was used as part of preoperative management (Ginandes, Brooks, Sando, Jones, & Aker, 2003; L. E. Moore & Kaplan, 1983).

In several studies, patients who were susceptible to hypnosis reached a deeper hypnotic trance and attained a greater reduction of pain perception in operative stress compared with those who were less receptive to hypnosis (Horton, Crawford, Harrington, & Downs, 2004; Zachariae & Bjerring, 1994). However, even patients who did not reach the state of hypnotic trance benefited from hypnotic suggestion, which could be simply related to the power of suggestion by the anesthesiologist (Egbert, Battit, Welch, & Bartlett, 1964).

A meta-analysis on the effectiveness of hypnosis with surgical patients suggested that hypnosis improved the outcome of their surgeries (Montgomery, David, Winkel, Silverstein, & Bovbjerg, 2002). However, the data need to be interpreted tentatively because of the significant variability of the hypnotic techniques across the studies included in this analysis.

Hypnotic-focused analgesia also is effective in the laboratory. Casiglia et al. (2007) performed cold pressor tests on participants who kept their right hand in icy water until intolerable (pain tolerance). The test was then repeated while the participants were under hypnosis. Hypnosis reduced the participants' perception of pain and the cardiovascular response, suggesting a decrease of sensitivity or a block of transmission of painful stimuli.

Physical Conditions and Diseases: Pain Syndromes

Pain syndromes have been lessened by hypnosis. Some examples are fibromyalgia, irritable bowel syndrome (IBS), and cancer pain.

Fibromyalgia

In a study on fibromyalgia, Castel, Perez, Sala, Padrol, and Rull (2007) compared three conditions: hypnosis with relaxation suggestions, hypnosis with analgesia suggestions, and relaxation. Hypnosis followed by analgesia suggestions had a greater effect on reducing the intensity of pain than hypnosis followed by relaxation suggestions, and hypnosis followed by relaxation suggestions was equivalent to relaxation.

Irritable Bowel Syndrome

IBS is a functional gastrointestinal disorder characterized by abdominal pain, distension, and an altered bowel habit for which no cause can be found. Tan, Hammond, and Joseph (2005) reported that a hypnosis session improved the symptoms of IBS in the majority of patients as well as positively affecting noncolonic symptoms.

On the basis of a review of the literature, hypnosis was found to be (along with cognitive–behavioral therapy) the psychological therapy best researched as an intervention for IBS (Whitehead, 2006). Eleven studies suggested that the median response rate to hypnosis was 87% and that bowel symptoms were generally improved by about half.

Cancer Pain

The National Institutes of Health reviewed outcome studies on hypnosis with cancer pain (Hammond, 2007). They concluded that research evidence for the effects of hypnosis was strong.

REFERRING CLIENTS TO HYPNOSIS PRACTITIONERS

Many therapists receive training in hypnosis and then actively use it in their practice. However, referrals to hypnosis practitioners may be easier and more practical, especially in the case of medical procedures and chronic pain syndromes. For example, many national associations, such as the American Society of Clinical Hypnosis and the Society for Clinical and Experimental Hypnosis, can provide names of local therapists.

13
BIOFEEDBACK

Biofeedback, developed as a therapeutic and research tool, typically uses monitoring instruments to give people feedback on physiological and chemical processes that are occurring in their bodies (Freeman, 2004). Parameters monitored often include heart rate, respiration, electroencephalographic (EEG) patterns, and muscle activity. The therapist attaches the biofeedback instruments (e.g., monitoring leads such as the electrodes for heart rate or EEG) and then uses a visual or auditory monitor to demonstrate the various wave forms as a video feedback to the patient.

From biofeedback, patients learn that they can slow their heart rate, lower their blood pressure, alter their EEG waves, and reduce muscle tension (N. C. Moore, 2000). In this way, patients can learn to have more voluntary control over their physiological processes and can then establish more cognitive control over their behavior or symptoms. Neal Miller, my friend and colleague who was a psychologist at Yale University, was a pioneer (along with his students) of the field of biofeedback in the early 1960s.

THE BIOFEEDBACK PROCESS

After electrodes are attached to a patient, they are connected to a transducer and amplifier to convert the signal to a wave form or digital signal that can then be interpreted by the biofeedback therapist for the patient. The computer interface analyzes these signals and then displays them on a monitor visually or auditorily. Usually, the monitor displays the information in real time so that patients can see the effects of their activity.

The therapist obtains baseline measurements as the patient is adapting to the monitoring devices and equipment. The baseline period ranges from a few to many minutes depending on the intent of the biofeedback (i.e., for therapeutic or research purposes). Although there are several forms of biofeedback, those that are being used most commonly in therapeutic and research situations today are EEG monitoring, heart rate and heart rate variability, electromyography (EMG), and skin conductance. As patients receive feedback on their biorhythms, they can then relax and attempt to alter them, for example, by reducing their heart rate or blood pressure.

Electroencephalographic Monitoring

EEG monitoring measures the electrical activity that occurs between the pre- and postsynaptic spaces in different regions of the brain. The EEG is filtered into different frequency bands, including (a) *delta*, which usually accompanies deep sleep; (b) *theta*, which generally denotes a relaxed state; (c) *alpha*, which typically accompanies a focused state; and (d) *beta*, which usually accompanies an alert–attentive state.

Biofeedback sessions typically are focused on increasing one wave form while decreasing another wave form. For example, for a client with attention-deficit/hyperactivity disorder, the sessions might focus on reducing theta and increasing beta so that the client is more attentive. The feedback screen usually features vertical bars indicating the amplitude of the different bands so that the client can see that beta is increasing while theta is decreasing. In that way, EEG feedback helps clients condition or shape their own brain waves.

Heart Rate and Heart Rate Variability Monitoring

Heart rate variability (vagal activity) is an index of an individual's parasympathetic activity or state of relaxation. *Vagal activity* is the respiratory sinus arrhythmia or the interbeat interval for the time elapsed between heartbeats and has been used as an index of attention because the vagus slows the heart rate during attentiveness and is instrumental in many functions of the body, such as digestion. Low vagal activity is found in people who are depressed, reflected in their low intonation and flat facial expressions, again stimulated by the vagus (both vocal behavior and facial expressions). Thus, training clients to increase their heart rate variability is basically training them to relax, experience a sense of well-being, and have the ability to concentrate.

Electromyography or Muscle Activity Biofeedback

EMG electrodes are usually attached to the forehead area because less muscle tension in the forehead is thought to reflect muscle relaxation in general. The EMG signal derives from the electrochemical changes that take place when muscles are contracting. One sensor is usually placed about an inch above the pupil of each eye, with the ground sensor placed above the bridge of the nose.

Skin Conductance

Skin conductance measures sweat gland activity, which is often indicative of arousal levels. The sweat contains salts that conduct electricity. The skin conductance biofeedback machine applies a small shock to the skin that is so minor that it is not detected by the individual. The sensors are often placed on the palm of the hands or the fingers because those are the areas where sweat glands are concentrated.

POTENTIAL UNDERLYING MECHANISMS FOR BIOFEEDBACK EFFECTS

It is unclear how the effects of biofeedback are mediated. Raymond, Varney, Parkinson, and Gruzelier (2005) suggested that alpha–theta neurofeedback works by raising feelings of well-being. In their study, the participants were given either alpha–theta feedback or mock feedback, and their mood was assessed. Real feedback led to higher overall mood state scores than mock feedback and caused the participants to feel significantly more energetic, whereas mock feedback made them feel more tired.

Although the shifts in heart rate variability noted in the studies that follow suggest that the changes accompanying biofeedback are autonomically mediated, additional research is needed on the physiological and biochemical changes that accompany biofeedback to begin to address underlying mechanisms. Further research is necessary to determine the long-term effects of biofeedback and the mediating effects of mood on the patients' responses to treatment. The patients' perceived success in performing the biofeedback would invariably play an important role in clinical improvement. Other variables that need study are the duration of treatment, the number and type of treatments used, the positioning and number of electrodes, and the effects of medications (N. C. Moore, 2000).

EMPIRICAL SUPPORT FOR THE EFFECTS OF BIOFEEDBACK

Biofeedback is commonly used to reduce stress and improve mood. In addition, biofeedback is used to treat common conditions such as cardiovascular conditions, pain syndromes, and autoimmune problems such as asthma and diabetes. Biofeedback has also been used to improve performance in office work, dance, music, and athletics.

Psychological Symptoms and Disorders

Biofeedback is commonly used for psychological symptoms and disorders, including anxiety disorders and depression.

Anxiety Disorders

In a review by Hammond (2005), EEG biofeedback was a promising methodology for retraining abnormal brain wave patterns in depression and in anxiety disorders, including posttraumatic stress disorder and obsessive–compulsive disorder. The EEG biofeedback (*neurofeedback*) was associated with minimal side effects and was less invasive than other methods of treatment.

Depression

A growing literature suggests that depression is accompanied by reduced heart rate variability and reduced vagal activity. Karavidas et al. (2007) used heart rate variability feedback to treat major depression. Participants attended 10 weekly sessions of heart rate variability biofeedback, and their depression decreased halfway through the treatment.

Physical Conditions and Diseases: Pain Syndromes

Pain syndromes can also decrease following biofeedback. Examples here are fibromyalgia, migraine headaches, temporomandibular joint disorder (TMJ), and chronic pain.

Fibromyalgia

Research by Hassett et al. (2007) suggests that autonomic dysfunction may account for some of the symptomatology in fibromyalgia. In this study,

10 weekly sessions of heart rate variability biofeedback were provided for patients with fibromyalgia. Following the treatment, decreases were noted in depression and pain, whereas increases were observed in heart rate variability and blood pressure variability. In another study on fibromyalgia, patients underwent EMG biofeedback therapy for 12 sessions, twice weekly (Drexler, Mur, & Günther, 2002). Improvement was noted in all the measured parameters (clinical symptoms, sensory and affective pain, and quality of life) after EMG biofeedback.

Migraine Headaches

In a study on migraine headache patients, one group received propranolol on a daily basis and another group received weekly sessions of EMG and temperature biofeedback, assisted diaphragmatic breathing, and systematic relaxation training for 6 months (Kaushik, Kaushik, Mahajan, & Rajesh, 2005). The biofeedback group had fewer migraines compared with the propranolol group over the treatment period.

In another study, migraine headache patients either experienced 12 sessions of biofeedback and relaxation therapy or were assigned to a standard treatment control group (Vasudeva, Claggett, Tietjen, & McGrady, 2003). The biofeedback group showed significant reductions in pain, depression, and anxiety compared with the control group. In a meta-analysis on the effectiveness of biofeedback in treating migraine headaches, Nestoriuc and Martin (2007) reviewed 55 studies and found that the strongest improvement following biofeedback was the reduced frequency of migraine headaches.

Temporomandibular Joint Disorder

In a meta-analysis on biofeedback for TMJ, Crider and Glaros (1999) found that 69% of those treated by biofeedback were noted to improve as opposed to 35% of those in the control groups. A systematic review by Medlicott and Harris (2006) similarly suggested that the programs involving relaxation techniques and biofeedback, specifically EMG biofeedback training, were more effective than placebo treatments or splints for TMJ. In another review, biofeedback-assisted relaxation training and surface EMG training were effective treatments for TMJ (Crider, Glaros, & Gevirtz, 2005).

Chronic Pain

Chronic pain is a common health problem for older adults, with a prevalence twice that in younger adults. In a review of the literature, Middaugh and Pawlick (2002) observed that older pain patients readily acquired the self-regulation skills taught in biofeedback-assisted relaxation training and achieved comparable decreases in pain following biofeedback.

Work-Related Injuries

In a study on repetitive strain injury, biofeedback was used to reduce work injuries and related musculoskeletal disorders (Peper et al., 2003). In another study, Madeleine, Vedsted, Blangsted, Sjøgaard, and Søgaard (2006) provided participants with surface EMG audio and visual biofeedback in a randomized order during computer work, which was performed for 3 minutes with and without time constraints. The duration of muscle activity in the right trapezius muscle that was above a preset threshold was used as a source of biofeedback. The biofeedback led to a significant decrease in the right trapezius EMG and a decrease in the number of errors made by mouse clicks. Audio and visual biofeedback were equally effective. A lowering of the trapezius muscle activity was thought to contribute to a decrease in the risk of developing work-related musculoskeletal disorders.

Hypertension and Cardiac Conditions

Blood Pressure

Nakao, Yano, Nomura, and Kuboki (2003) conducted a meta-analysis on biofeedback training versus clinical visits and self-monitoring by patients with hypertension. Biofeedback resulted in reduced systolic and diastolic blood pressure.

In another hypertension study, adults with Stage 1 or 2 hypertension received 8 weeks of relaxation training coupled with thermal EMG and heart rate variability biofeedback (Yucha, Tsai, Calderon, & Tian, 2005). This combined treatment protocol resulted in significantly lower systolic and diastolic blood pressures.

Cardiovascular Disorders

In a review on cardiovascular disorders, Kranitz and Lehrer (2004) found that biofeedback was notably effective for hypertension, cardiac arrhythmias, angina pectoris, cardiac ischemia, myocardial infarction, and Reynaud's syndrome. In another study, heart rate variability biofeedback was used as a method of improving pulmonary function (Lehrer et al., 2003). The treatment group was given 10 sessions of biofeedback training and was compared with a control group that did not receive the training. Lehrer et al. found increased heart rate variability that correlated with slower breathing during the biofeedback period.

Patients with coronary heart disease typically experience depressed mood and lower vagal activity (Nolan et al., 2005). Myocardial infarction and sudden cardiac death are independently associated with depression and stress as well as reduced vagal activity. Nolan et al. (2005) used heart rate variability biofeedback to enhance vagal activity in coronary heart disease patients. In this study, the patients were randomized to five 1.5-hour sessions of heart rate variability biofeedback or to a control group that was monitored while resting. Both groups showed a reduction in depression symptoms, but the reduction in depression was significantly associated with increased vagal activity only in the heart rate variability biofeedback group.

Autoimmune Conditions

Asthma

A review by Lehrer et al. (2004) suggested promising effects of biofeedback training on asthma. The patients were assigned to a heart rate variability biofeedback plus abdominal breathing group, a heart rate variability biofeedback alone group, or a placebo EEG biofeedback group. The patients recorded daily asthma symptoms and twice-daily peak expiratory flows. Compared with the control group, the patients in both heart rate variability biofeedback groups were prescribed less medication. Measures from forced oscillation pneumography showed improved pulmonary functions in both biofeedback conditions. Thus, these results suggest that heart rate variability biofeedback may be a useful complementary therapy that may help reduce patients' dependence on steroid medications.

Chronic Obstructive Pulmonary Disease

Similarly, in Giardino, Chan, and Borson (2004), patients with chronic obstructive pulmonary disease benefited from combined heart rate variability and pulse oximetry biofeedback. In this study, patients with this disease participated in five weekly sessions of heart rate variability biofeedback and four weekly sessions of walking practice with oximetry feedback. After 10 weeks of training, the patients showed improvements in the distance walked in 6 minutes and heart rate variability amplitude during spontaneous breathing.

Diabetes

In a study on Type 2 diabetes, patients were randomized to either 10 sessions of biofeedback (EMG and thermal) and relaxation or a control group that received education about diabetes (McGinnis, McGrady, Cox, & Grower-Dowling, 2005). Biofeedback and relaxation were associated with decreased blood glucose levels and muscle tension compared with the control group. Both biofeedback and relaxation groups also showed lower scores on depression and anxiety scales.

Skin Conditions

A review by Shenefelt (2003) found that dermatology conditions that responded to biofeedback included acne and atopic dermatitis (eczema), perhaps because the participants received biofeedback that helped reduce itching and scratching.

Enhancing Physical and Other Kinds of Performance

Athletic Performance

In a study by Bisson, Contant, Sveistrup, and Lajoie (2007), balance and reaction time improved in older adults by using biofeedback training. Knee flexion angle was also enhanced along with sports performance as measured by the "intelligent knee sleeve," which is a device that provides immediate audible feedback to the wearer (Munro, Steele, Campbell, & Wallace, 2004).

Dance

Gruzelier, Egner, and Vernon (2006) used alpha–theta protocols to improve dancers' attention, memory, mood, and performance. In one study with ballroom and Latin dancers, alpha–theta EEG feedback was compared with heart rate variability biofeedback (Raymond, Sajid, Parkinson, & Gruzelier, 2005); performance improved in both biofeedback groups.

Music

Egner and Gruzelier (2003) found that musical performance also improved with alpha–theta EEG feedback. Improvements were noted and were highly correlated with learning to progressively raise beta (5 Hz to 8 Hz) over alpha (8 Hz to 11 Hz) band amplitudes. This suggests that the musicians were being shifted to a more focused state. These findings were replicated in an experiment by Zinn and Zinn (2003) in which an alpha–theta training group displayed improved performance enhancement.

REFERRING CLIENTS TO BIOFEEDBACK PRACTITIONERS

Although some clinicians have trained in various forms of biofeedback to increase their repertoire of therapy offerings, biofeedback, like hypnosis, requires considerable training and practice time; biofeedback also requires specialized equipment. It may be more cost-effective to make referrals, especially for clients with chronic conditions. Referral sources can be found on the Internet and from professional organizations such as the Association for Applied Psychophysiology and Biofeedback that have lists by geographical location.

14
MEDITATION

The word *meditation* is generally used to describe the practice of self-regulating the body and mind to induce relaxation and altered states of consciousness. Two of the most common types of meditation are *mindfulness meditation* and *concentrative meditation*. Mindfulness meditation practices involve allowing and observing any thoughts, feelings, and sensations that arise while maintaining a specific emotional stance (i.e., neutral observation). Mindfulness meditation is the most popular example of mindful practices in psychological and medical conditions (Kabat-Zinn, 2003).

Concentrative meditation techniques involve focusing on a specific sensory activity; a repeated sound; an image; or a specific body sensation, such as the breath (Manocha, 2000). These are more often used in yogic meditations and transcendental meditation. Whereas mindfulness meditation tends to encourage open, nonjudgmental awareness of the sensory and cognitive stimulation and includes a mental awareness or observation of ongoing thoughts, concentrative techniques continually direct the attention back to specific objects of concentration.

Meditative practices are derived from traditions in both Eastern and Western cultures dating back many centuries (Manocha, 2000) and are found in the different religions and cultures across the world. The most popular meditation techniques in the West over the past half century have been the Buddhist and Indian yoga forms. Meditation is increasingly being integrated into contemporary clinical and health psychology. Based on Buddhist philosophy and subsequently integrated into Western medical care in the context of psychotherapy and stress management, various forms of meditation such as transcendental meditation and mindfulness meditation are evolving as important therapies. Newer innovations in psychological treatments have, in fact, integrated meditation techniques with traditional cognitive and behavioral therapies using different strategies from each of the modalities to accomplish treatment goals.

One of the recognized forms of treatment using mindfulness meditation today is the mindfulness-based stress reduction (MBSR) program (Kabat-Zinn, 2003). The essence of this program is learning to focus attention on a present-moment experience in a nonjudgmental way. This meditation program teaches three practices: the body scan, Hatha yoga, and the sitting meditation. The *body scan* is a guided exercise (30 to 45 minutes) in which attention is systematically directed throughout the body from one region to another. This is practiced in a quiet state that promotes relaxation. *Hatha yoga* involves stretching movements that are meant to encourage better body awareness. The *sitting meditation* involves directing the attention to various stimuli, including the breath, physical sensations, thoughts, and emotions.

POTENTIAL UNDERLYING MECHANISMS FOR MEDITATION EFFECTS

Several studies have focused on the psychophysiological and biochemical changes accompanying meditation, particularly vagal activity, electroencephalogram (EEG), and magnetic resonance imaging (MRI) changes. One of the neurophysiological models for meditative states has explored the continuum of autonomic arousal from parasympathetic to sympathetic dominance. Parasympathetic activity is generally measured by vagal activity or vagal tone.

Increased Vagal Activity

At least two studies have reported increased vagal activity or parasympathetic tone during or following meditation. In a study by Telles, Mohapatra, and Naveen (2005), the meditation consisted of three 10-minute phases (i.e., breath awareness and awareness of other sensations). Heart rate variability was increased during the breath awareness phase of the 30-minute meditation. Compared with the preperiod, high-frequency power (vagal activity) increased and low-frequency power (sympathetic activity) decreased, suggesting that there was a shift in the cardiac sympathovagal balance during the breath awareness phase of the meditation, with a reduction of sympathetic activity and an increase in vagal activity.

In another study on vagal activity, adults were randomly assigned to a meditation, a progressive muscle relaxation, or a wait-list control group (Ditto, Eclache, & Goldman, 2006). Participants displayed significantly greater increases in vagal activity while meditating or while engaging in progressive muscle relaxation.

Studies on Brain Activity

EEG studies of meditative states have been conducted for decades, although no definitive data have resulted. Some consistent data have been found for EEG frequency effects with increased theta and alpha activity as well as for EEG coherence and symmetry. Functional magnetic resonance imaging studies are also beginning to suggest the specific parts of the brain that are affected by meditation.

Across the studies on EEG, increases have been noted in theta activity and in symmetry of frontal activity during meditation. In a study by Aftanas and Golosheykin (2003), EEG was recorded in novice and experienced meditators at rest and during a happy mood state. Increased theta wave activity (relaxation state) was the happy mood state in experienced meditators.

In another study on experienced and novice meditators by the same research group, the experienced meditators at the lowest level of arousal (eyes closed) showed greater theta-1 (4 Hz to 6 Hz), theta-2 (6 Hz to 8 Hz), and alpha-1 (8 Hz to 10 Hz) activity, suggesting greater relaxation (Aftanas & Golosheykin, 2005). Although increasing arousal (eyes open) led to desynchronized activity in the theta and alpha bands in both groups, the theta-2 and alpha-1 activity in the eyes-open condition remained still higher in the experienced meditators. During the eyes-closed and eyes-open period, the novice group showed greater right than left hemisphere activity, whereas experienced meditators showed hemisphere symmetry. An aversive movie clip viewed by both groups yielded significant alpha desynchronization. In all conditions, experienced meditators showed more modulation of the intensity of emotional arousal.

In another study, meditation-associated increases were observed in fast theta power and slow alpha power on EEG predominantly in the frontal areas (Takahashi et al., 2005). Heart rate variability was also measured, and as in the studies described earlier, increases occurred in the high-frequency power (as a parasympathetic index), and decreases occurred in the low-frequency power and low-frequency:high-frequency ratio (as sympathetic indices).

Other measures derived from EEG are frontal coherence and asymmetry. In a transcendental meditation study, frontal coherence and lateralized asymmetry were higher in meditation participants (Travis & Arenander,

2006). Frontal coherence increased linearly during computer tasks and during eyes-closed rest and as a step function during meditation practice. Coherence was a more sensitive measure of the effects of transcendental meditation practice than lateral asymmetry. EEG changes are also accompanied by neurotransmitter changes. In a positron emission tomography study by Kjaer et al. (2002), increased endogenous dopamine release was noted in the ventral striatum during meditation. A 65% increase was noted in dopamine release, which in turn was correlated with increased EEG theta activity, one of the most notable features of meditation.

This research showing that meditation practices are associated with altered resting EEG patterns suggests long-lasting changes in brain activity. Lazar et al. (2005) explored the meditation-associated changes in brain physical structure, using MRI to assess cortical thickness in participants with extensive meditation experience. The brain region associated with attention and sensory processing, including the prefrontal cortex and right anterior insula, was thicker in meditation participants than in matched controls. Differences in prefrontal cortical thickness were most pronounced in older participants, suggesting that meditation might offset age-related cortical thinning. The thickness of the two affected regions was correlated with meditation experience.

Several methodological problems exist for meditation research, including not having a standardized protocol (specific and not-so-specific techniques being mixed). Among the challenges are the mismatches between questions and designs, the variability in meditation types, problems associated with meditation implementation, individual differences across meditators, and the difficulty of conducting double-blind, placebo-controlled meditation studies (Caspi & Burlesson, 2005). In addition, the inclusion of Hatha yoga in conjunction with meditation sessions could explain the physiological effects.

EMPIRICAL SUPPORT FOR THE EFFECTS OF MEDITATION

Although much of the research on meditation involves mood and anxiety disorders, clinical evidence also exists for positive effects of meditation on epilepsy, symptoms of premenstrual syndrome, and menopausal symptoms. Autoimmune conditions have also benefited (Arias, Steinberg, Banga, & Trestman, 2006).

Psychological Symptoms and Disorders

Stress and Anxiety

Meditation has been shown to decrease stress (E. Carlson, Speca, Patel, & Goodey, 2003), which may relate to the decreased cortisol and catecholamine levels following meditation (E. Carlson, Speca, Patel, & Goodey, 2004; Kamei et al., 2000). In a study on highly stressed adults, K. Williams, Kolar, Reger, and Pearson (2001) compared the MBSR program with educational materials over a 3-month period. Significant decreases were noted in daily hassles, psychological distress, and medical symptoms following meditation.

In another study that involved adults with mixed psychological and physical distress, mindfulness meditation was conducted over an 8-week period, with a 3-month follow-up (Majumdar, Grossman, Dieyz-Waschkowski, Kersig, & Walach, 2002). Significant improvement was noted in physical well-being, emotional well-being, and quality of life.

In a study that assessed anxiety, patients were randomly assigned to an 8-week meditation-based stress reduction management program or an anxiety disorder education program (S. Lee et al., 2007). The meditation group showed significant improvement on all anxiety scales compared with the education group.

In another randomized controlled trial on stress, Jain et al. (2007) assessed the effects of 1 month of mindfulness meditation versus progressive muscle relaxation in students reporting distress. Both the meditation and relaxation groups experienced significant decreases in distress as well as increases in positive mood states over time compared with the control group.

Depression

Mindfulness-based cognitive therapy has been successful in treating depression (Ma & Teasdale, 2004; Mason & Hargreaves, 2001; Rohan, 2003; Z. Segal, Williams, & Teasdale, 2002; Teasdale et al., 2000). In Teasdale et al.'s (2000) study, mindfulness-based cognitive therapy was associated with a decrease in depression relapse in clients who had three or more prior episodes. Thomas and Peterson (2003) noted that the decreased depression was associated with decreased cortisol levels.

In another study, Weiss, Nordlie, and Siegel (2005) compared a group undergoing psychotherapy coupled with training in MBSR with a group undergoing psychotherapy alone. The groups showed a comparable decrease in psychological distress. However, the MBSR group reached their goals and terminated therapy in fewer sessions than did the comparison group.

Physical Conditions and Diseases: Pain Syndromes

Irritable Bowel Syndrome

Participants with irritable bowel syndrome participated in a 1-year follow-up study to determine the effects of mindfulness meditation on irritable bowel symptoms (Keefer & Blanchard, 2002). From pretreatment to a 1-year follow-up, significant reductions were noted in abdominal pain, diarrhea, flatulence, and bloating.

Fibromyalgia

Another example of meditation-associated decreases in pain was noted by Weissbecker et al. (2002) in a sample of women with fibromyalgia. In this study, mindfulness meditation led to reduced pain.

Cardiac Conditions

In two studies, Ditto et al. (2006) examined short-term autonomic and cardiovascular effects of basic body scan meditation, one of the techniques used in mindfulness meditation training. In the first study, adults were assigned randomly to a meditation group, a progressive muscle relaxation group, or a wait-list control group. Each group participated in two laboratory sessions (4 weeks apart) in which they practiced their assigned technique. In a second study, adults practiced meditation or listened to an audiotape of a popular novel during two laboratory sessions. In both studies, participants displayed greater increases in vagal activity while meditating than while engaging in other relaxing activities.

Immune Conditions

In a study using MBSR with adults with cancer, participants spent an average of 30 minutes a day meditating over a 1-month period (Speca, Carlson, Goodey, & Angen, 2000). Reduced stress and mood disturbance were noted in the meditation versus a standard treatment control group.

A review of the literature by Otto, Norris, and Bauer-Wu (2006) on the use of mindfulness meditation with cancer patients identified nine relevant studies published in the past 5 years. Most of these studies were conducted with breast and prostate cancer patients. The results included improved psychological functioning, reduction of stress symptoms, and enhanced coping and well-being.

The effects of meditation on brain activity and immune function were also studied in healthy individuals at their workplace (Davidson et al., 2003). The participants received an 8-week training program in mindfulness meditation. At the end of the 8-week period, participants in both the meditation and wait-list control groups were vaccinated with influenza vaccine. Significant increases in left-frontal EEG activity (a pattern previously associated with positive affect) occurred in the meditators compared with the nonmeditators. Significant increases in antibody titers to influenza vaccine also occurred among participants in the meditation group compared with those in the control group. The magnitude of increased left-frontal EEG activation predicted the magnitude of antibody titer rise to the vaccine.

REFERRING CLIENTS TO MEDITATION PRACTITIONERS

Many clinicians have been trained in meditation techniques and can help their clients learn the techniques. However, the sessions are longer than the typical therapy session and are often done in groups. For these reasons, therapists often refer their clients to meditation programs and workshops.

15

COMPLEMENTARY AND ALTERNATIVE THERAPIES IN PEDIATRIC POPULATIONS

Current estimates of children and adolescents using complementary and alternative medicine (CAM) range widely, from a low of 2% for younger children to a high of 68% for older adolescents (Davis & Darden, 2003). Davis and Darden's (2003) epidemiological study also noted that the children who used CAM therapies were found in each age category, and the mean age was 10 years. In the study, 77% of the users of CAM were White, 54% were female, 32% lived in the West, 66% lived in a metropolitan statistical area, and 36% lived near the poverty level.

In a similar study that also quoted 2% CAM usage by children and adolescents, only 12% disclosed the usual source of care (Yussman, Ryan, Auinger, & Weitzman, 2004). The mean amount spent per person, per year, on CAM visits was US$73 and on remedies, US$13. Factors that were independently associated with CAM visits were female gender, older age, good or very good perceived physical health, and parental CAM use. The respondents (the children's parents) also viewed CAM care as greater in quality than the usual source of care.

In another survey sample, 21% of parents used CAM for their children (Sibinga, Ottolini, Duggan, & Wilson, 2004). Overall, 53% of parents expressed the desire to discuss CAM with their pediatrician, increasing to

75% among those who used CAM themselves and 81% among those who used CAM for their children. Among parents who used CAM for their child, 36% had discussed it with their pediatricians.

In another U.S. study, 33% of parents reported using CAM for their children within the past year, most commonly citing the use of infant massage, massage therapy, and vitamin therapy (Lotman, 2003). White parents who used CAM for themselves and had children school age and older were significantly more likely to provide CAM for their child.

In a sample of U.S. adolescents, 68% of the adolescents reported using one or more of the CAM therapies, most commonly massage therapy (27%), herbal medicines (27%), and megavitamins (22%; Braun, Bearinger, Halcón, & Pettingell, 2005). Alleviation of physical pain in this sample was the most common desired health outcome (66%). Insurance coverage was provided for 10% of the therapies, and out-of-pocket costs averaged $67 per month.

In a much larger sample in South Australia, the 12-month prevalence of CAM use in children under 15 years old was 18% (C. Smith & Eckert, 2006). The children used a wide variety of CAM modalities, including herbal therapies (33%), chiropractic (34%), and massage (20%). Common reasons for CAM use were to prevent illness or to maintain health (39%) and for musculoskeletal conditions (22%), respiratory problems (20%), and skin complaints (18%). There was little difference in the use of CAM treatment modality across child ages. Thus, approximately 1 in 5 children used CAM in South Australia. In New Zealand, a study on a smaller sample suggested an even higher prevalence at 70% (Wilson, Dowson, & Mangin, 2007). Parental use was again predictive of child CAM use in this survey.

EMPIRICAL SUPPORT FOR THE EFFECTS OF COMPLEMENTARY AND ALTERNATIVE THERAPIES WITH INFANTS AND CHILDREN

Physical Conditions and Diseases

In a Canadian study on the use of CAM in children with chronic medical conditions, Samdup, Smith, and Il Song (2006) surveyed children with muscular dystrophy, cystic fibrosis, diabetes, and spina bifida. Popular therapies included massage and dietary or herbal remedies. Within this group, greater severity of symptoms was associated with higher use. The main reason for CAM use was to complement conventional medicine.

Cerebral Palsy

In a study on children with cerebral palsy, 56% of the children used one or more CAM techniques (Hurvitz, Leonard, Ayyangar, & Nelson, 2003). Massage therapy (25%) and aquatherapy (25%) were the most common.

Children with quadriplegic cerebral palsy, those with spasticity, and those who could not walk independently were more frequent users of CAM. Mothers with a college degree had a greater tendency to use CAM for their child than those without. Once again, parents who used CAM for themselves were more likely to try CAM for their child (70% vs. 47%) and were more likely to be pleased with the outcome (71% vs. 42%).

Attention Disorders and Autism

Children with attention disorders including attention-deficit/ hyperactivity disorder (ADHD) and autism have also been frequent users of CAM. In a study on ADHD by Sinha and Efron (2005), of the 23 different therapies reported by 75 families, the most common were modified diet (33 families), vitamins and/or minerals (16), dietary supplements (12), aromatherapy (12), and chiropractic (10). The factors most frequently rated as important in choosing CAM were minimizing symptoms (40 families), adding to the benefit of conventional treatment (30), and avoiding side effects of medications (29).

It has been noted that almost all parents of autistic children in the United States use CAM. This suggests a high incidence given that the prevalence of autism in the country is 1 out of 150 children. In a study by Harrington, Rosen, Garnecho, and Patrick (2006), parents most frequently attributed their child's autism to immunizations (54%), genetic predisposition (53%), and environmental exposure (38%). (Note, however, that none of these causes has actually been proven to cause autism. Immunization and environmental exposure are particularly controversial; see M. J. Smith, Ellenberg, Bell, & Rubin, 2008.) Approximately half of the children were reported as having at least one gastrointestinal, neurological, and/or allergic symptom. More than a third of the children with autism had immunological symptoms. Almost all of the parents (95%) indicated some use of CAM therapies, with most of the self-reported referrals generated from a physician or nurse (44%).

In another U.S. study, 74% of children with autism used CAM (Hanson et al., 2007). Most CAM use was reported by families to be either helpful or without effect but not harmful. The main reasons for choosing CAM were related to concerns with the safety and side effects of prescribed medications.

Asthma and HIV

In a comparison of children with asthma, children with HIV, and well children, Ang et al. (2005) found that the parents of the HIV group were less likely to be employed, less likely to have private insurance, less likely to have a high school or college education, and more likely to be Black. It is interesting that 38% of the well children used CAM compared with 22% in the HIV group and 25% in the asthma group. The children with HIV and asthma in this study possibly had parents with lower SES who could not afford CAM, which is usually not reimbursed by insurance. More than 80% of the three groups paid out of pocket for their children's use of CAM.

In a study on asthma in Turkey, 49% of the children had used some form of CAM previously, and 38% had used CAM within the previous year (Orhan et al., 2003). The most popular forms of CAM were quail eggs (79%), herbal medicine (31%), Turkish wild honey (26%), speleotherapy (5%), and royal jelly (5%).

Thus, the use of CAM by children and adolescents is highly variable except in samples of children with chronic illness and significant attention problems. The therapies that seem to be most commonly used are massage therapy, chiropractic, and herbal therapies. With the exception of massage, the other popular CAM therapies have not been widely researched with pediatric populations.

MASSAGE THERAPY

Most of the massage therapy studies with children have been conducted by my colleagues and me in our lab and have included children with attention problems (autism and ADHD); children and adolescents who are depressed or anxious; adolescents with aggressivity and conduct disorder problems; children with pain syndromes (burns and rheumatoid arthritis); children with auto-immune conditions (asthma, cystic fibrosis, diabetes, and atopic dermatitis); adolescents with eating disorders (anorexia and bulimia); and children and adolescents with immune problems, including children with leukemia and adolescents with HIV (for a review, see Field, Diego, & Hernandez-Reif, 2007). For example, our massage therapy studies have found reductions in glucose level to within the normal range in a group of children with diabetes (see Figure 15.1). These children were massaged at bedtime for a month by their parents, which led to significant decrease in glucose levels. In another study on children with asthma (see Figure 15.2), increases in peak airflow indicated improved respiration. These children had also been massaged at bedtime for a month by their parents, which led to their having better breathing.

The lion's share of massage therapy research in different parts of the United States and the world has been focused on helping premature infants grow (for a collection of these studies, see Field, 2004). In the most recent studies, growth, weight gain, and bone growth have been consistently reported. In one study by Aly et al. (2004) on bone mineralization, premature infants received a daily protocol of combined massage and physical activity. The levels of a peptide that is an index of bone formation increased significantly. In one of our studies, we found that moderate-pressure massage versus light-pressure massage was critical for weight gain in preterm infants (Field, Diego, Hernandez-Reif, Deeds, &

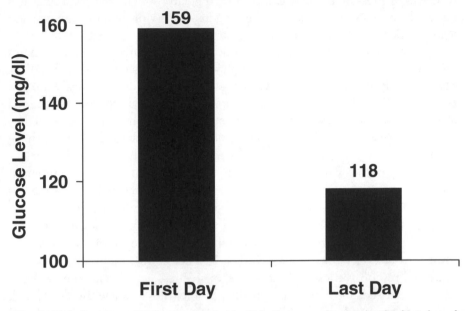

Figure 15.1. Decrease in glucose levels to within the normal range by the last day of the massage therapy study.

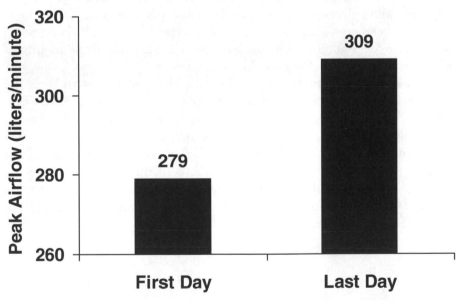

Figure 15.2. Increase in peak airflow indicating improved respiration in children with asthma by last day of massage therapy study.

Figuereido, 2006). In this study, the moderate-pressure massage group as opposed to the light-pressure massage group showed greater weight gain as well as less active sleep; less stress behavior, including fussing, crying, and hiccupping; and a greater decrease in heart rate and a greater increase in vagal activity.

In a study on underlying mechanisms, we compared preterm neonates receiving moderate-pressure versus light-pressure massage (Diego, Field, & Hernandez-Reif, 2005). Greater weight gain as well as increased vagal tone and gastric motility (which would result in more efficient food absorption) were noted after the moderate-pressure massage treatment. The weight gain experienced by the preterm neonates receiving the moderate-pressure massage therapy may have been mediated by increased vagal activity and gastric motility inasmuch as weight gain was significantly related to gastric motility and vagal tone during the massage. These findings were consistent with another study in which vagal tone was significantly higher after massage than before massage (H. K. Lee, 2005).

Infant massage has also been used with older infants for different reasons. In one study on infants ages 2 to 6 months, mother–infant interactions improved after 4 weeks of massage (H. K. Lee, 2006), including increased maternal responsiveness and infant responsiveness, which may have related to the increased alertness that typically accompanies massage therapy (Field, Diego, & Hernandez-Reif, 2007). In another study on normal 8-month-old infants, the infants who received daily massages for 1 month were less likely to snore during sleep, required less feeding when they woke up at night, and appeared more alert during the day (Kelmanson & Adulas, 2006). Infants who have been orphaned and are living in orphanages have also been noted to experience less illness, including 50% less diarrhea, following 2 months of weekly massage (Jump, Fargo, & Akers, 2006).

In a study on Dominican preschool children infected with HIV, the children received a massage or a friendly control visit twice weekly for 12 weeks (Shor-Posner et al., 2006). Despite similar immune parameters at baseline in the two groups, after 12 weeks, the control group exhibited a decline in CD4 cell count (the cells killed by HIV cells), and these cells increased in the massage children as well as natural killer cells (cells that have been noted to kill HIV cells). In another report by the same group, the CD4 count decline was greater in the control children (Shor-Posner, Miguez, Hernandez-Reif, Perez-Then, & Fletcher, 2004).

ACUPUNCTURE

Acupuncture is rarely used with children, probably because of children's aversion to needles. However, acupuncture was used in at least three studies, including one with postsurgery vomiting, one with enuresis, and one with cerebral palsy. In the study on postsurgery vomiting, the effectiveness of laser acupuncture was compared with a drug that prevents postoperative nausea and vomiting in children after anesthesia (Butkovic, Toljan, Matolic, Kralik, & Radesic, 2005). The incidence of vomiting was higher in the control group in the first 2 hours postoperatively compared with the drug group and the acupuncture group. The acupuncture and drug groups did not differ in the occurrence and timing of vomiting.

In a meta-analysis on the use of acupuncture for nocturnal enuresis in children, Bower, Diao, Tang, and Yeung (2005) observed that acupuncture was useful for this condition in several studies. The authors noted, however, that the quality of the studies was questionable, and some forms of acupuncture were seemingly effective whereas others were not. It was also difficult to identify which parameters of acupuncture were actually leading to the effects.

In the study on children with spastic cerebral palsy, Duncan, Barton, Edmonds, and Blashill (2004) compared weekly osteopathic manipulation and acupuncture following a 6-month treatment. The most frequent gains were seen in the use of arms or legs (61% and 68%) in the osteopathic group and more restful sleep (39% and 68%) in the acupuncture group. Improved mood and bowel function were also reported for both groups.

YOGA

Yoga has been effective for improving cognitive function and for reducing irritable bowel syndrome in children. In a cognitive study by Manjunath and Telles (2004), the spatial memory scores for children who attended a yoga camp improved by 43% compared with children who attended a fine arts camp and those in a control group who did not attend camp. It is difficult to know what aspect of the yoga camp led to these improved spatial memory scores, given that the camp sessions included physical postures, yoga breathing, meditation, and guided relaxation.

In a study on the use of yoga for adolescents with irritable bowel syndrome, Kuttner et al. (2006) randomly assigned adolescents to either a yoga group or a wait-list control group. The yoga group received a 1-hour instructional session, demonstration, and practice followed by 4 weeks of daily home practice guided by a video. The adolescents in the yoga group reported lower levels of functional disability, less use of emotion-focused avoidance, and lower anxiety following the intervention. They also had significantly lower scores for gastrointestinal symptoms.

PILATES

Only one study could be found on the use of Pilates with children. In a study of 11-year-old girls by Jago, Jonker, Missaghian, and Baranowski (2006),

Pilates classes were given for 1 hour per day, 5 days a week, for 4 weeks. The Pilates group experienced larger reductions in the body mass index percentile compared with a nonexercise control group, even though they were not obese before the study.

EXERCISE

Exercise has received the most research of all pediatric CAM therapies. Statistics indicate that 39% of boys and 58% of girls ages 7 to 18 years do not achieve the recommended levels of exercise—that is, a minimum of 1 hour each day in a physical activity of at least moderate intensity (Horgan, 2005). Most of the exercise studies have targeted overweight children. According to Atlantis, Barnes, and Singh's (2006) meta-analysis of randomized trials on exercise in overweight and obese children and adolescents, overweight prevalence among children and adolescents is increasing, which is problematic because adult obesity can potentially cause a decline in life expectancy. In the meta-analysis, percentage of body fat and total body weight were lower in the exercise group. These effects were noted for studies that featured 3 hours per week of exercise.

Similar results were noted in an empirical study on exercise versus health education with overweight children (Taylor, Mazzone, & Wrotniak, 2005). An 8-week exercise intervention, scheduled twice weekly, led to a significant improvement in body mass index, waist and hip girth, blood pressure, resting heart rate, immediate postexercise heart rate, and 5-minute recovery heart rate at posttest. In a similar study, overweight middle school children with a body mass index above the 95th percentile for age were randomized to a treatment group that attended lifestyle-focused gym classes or a control group that attended standard gym classes for 9 months (Carrel et al., 2005). Compared with the control group, the treatment group demonstrated a greater loss of body fat, a greater increase in cardiovascular fitness, and a greater improvement in fasting insulin levels. This last study seems to indicate that education added value to simply exercising.

When change in diet is added to exercise training, an even greater effect has been noted. In Ribeiro et al.'s (2005) study on obese children, diet plus exercise training reduced body weight and decreased blood pressure levels.

Ventilatory efficiency has also improved in overweight children when they have participated in an aerobic exercise training program. In a study by Kaufman, Kelly, Kaiser, Steinberger, and Dengel (2007), overweight children (body mass index greater than 85th percentile) performed a graded cycle exercise test at baseline and were randomly assigned to 8 weeks of stationary cycling or to a nonexercising control group. After 8 weeks, significant improvements occurred in the exercise group compared with the control group for oxygen uptake at the ventilatory threshold.

Many of the studies on exercise and overweight children have been poorly controlled and have not stratified the independent effects of exercise versus dietary modification. Nonetheless, the well-controlled studies have evaluated the effects of exercise on body composition, cardiovascular fitness, muscular strength, and vascular function. Although exercise does not consistently decrease body weight or body mass index, it has been associated with beneficial changes in fat and lean body mass, cardiovascular fitness, and muscle strength.

Given that obesity is a risk factor for diabetes, it is not surprising that diabetes might also benefit from physical exercise. Several studies have highlighted the central role of physical exercise in the management of both Type 1 and Type 2 diabetes in children and adolescents (e.g., Giannini, de Giorgis, Mohn, & Chiarelli, 2007). In one study on children with Type 1 diabetes, 75-minute exercise sessions consisted of four 15-minute periods of walking on a treadmill to a target heart rate of 140 beats per minute and three 5-minute rest periods (Tansey et al., 2006). Plasma glucose concentration dropped at least 25% from baseline in most of the children (83%).

Children with asthma have also benefited from exercise. In a study by Basaran et al. (2006), grade-school-age children with mild to moderate asthma were given an intensive basketball training program for 8 weeks. Peak expiratory flow values improved in the exercise group, and the exercise group performed better on physical work capacity on a cycle ergometer task and in the 6-minute walk test, whereas no improvement was detected in the control group. Medication scores also improved in both groups, but symptoms scores only improved in the exercise group.

Other benefits have been reported for exercise in children, including a reduction in triglycerides, an increase in insulin-like growth factor 1, and an increase in bone mineral density. In a study on aerobic exercise and lipids in children and adolescents, triglycerides decreased by 12% (Kelley & Kelley, 2007). Decreases in low-density lipoprotein cholesterol were associated with increased training intensity and older age. In another study, insulin-like growth factor-1 concentrations were increased after 2 hours of exercise (Turgut, Kaptanoglu, Turgut, Genç, & Tekintürk, 2003).

Evidence increasingly suggests that regular weight-bearing exercise is an effective strategy for enhancing bone growth in children and adolescents. In their review, Hind and Burrows (2007) found that exercise such as games, dance, resistance training, and jumping, over time periods that ranged from 3 to 48 months, were effective. All of the trials in young children reported positive effects of exercise on bone growth. Unfortunately, it is unclear from these studies which of the exercise programs was more effective. In addition, many of the studies were uncontrolled and had low compliance rates and self-selection problems. Quantitative dose–response studies using larger sample sizes and measures of bone growth parameters and bone mineral density are needed to provide greater insight into the effects of exercise on bone growth.

Finally, depression in children has been responsive to exercise. In a meta-analysis of several trials, decreases were noted in depression for the exercise group (Larun, Nordheim, Ekeland, Hagen, & Heian, 2006). The methodological quality of these studies, however, was somewhat low, and the studies were heterogeneous with regard to the population, intervention, and measurement instruments used.

Underlying mechanisms for the effects of exercise per se are unknown, although a leading candidate is increased vagal activity. In at least one study, by Nagai, Hamada, Kimura, and Moritani (2004), a large sample of elementary school children participated in a 12-month school-based aerobic exercise training program (for 20 minutes per day, 5 days per week) with the goal of raising their exercise heart rate to 130 to 140 beats per minute. From the low-power heart rate variability group, 100 children were chosen as the experimental sample and were compared with height- and weight-matched controls. In the experimental group, the high-frequency component of heart rate variability (vagal activity) was increased after the training period, whereas only low-frequency power was increased in the control group. These data (and data from adult studies) suggest that vagal activity (the high-frequency component of heart rate variability) increases with exercise.

Increased vagal activity may contribute to the weight reduction noted in obese children because the vagus stimulates the gastrointestinal tract, thus increasing gastric motility and leading to more efficient food absorption. The vagus also has pathways to the heart, slowing the heart, which may contribute to enhanced alertness and increased vagal activity. This mechanism has been known to lead to reduced depression or at least reduced depressed behavior (Field, Diego, & Hernandez-Reif, 2007). Vagal activity has also been known to increase as depression decreases. Vagal activity has been similarly implicated as a potential mediating mechanism for the effects of massage therapy following the stimulation of moderate pressure receptors. Exercise would also be expected to lead to the stimulation of pressure receptors and could thereby lead to increased vagal activity. The many positive effects of exercise have similarly been seen following massage therapy.

MUSIC THERAPY

Music therapy has been used with children before and after medical procedures and in conditions such as autism and cancer. Several studies have been conducted using music with preterm infants and have shown significant benefits. For example, in one study by Lai et al. (2006), preterm infants had lullaby music played during *kangaroo care* (during which the parents carry the baby underneath their clothing in a chest-to-chest position) for 60 minutes per day for 3 consecutive days. The infants in the treatment group spent more time in quiet sleep states and less time crying. The music also resulted in significantly lower parental anxiety in the treatment group. In another study with preterm infants, Arnon et al. (2006) compared live music therapy, played over 3 consecutive days, with recorded music. Live music therapy led to significantly reduced heart rate and improved behavioral scores.

Music has also been used effectively to induce sleep and sedation in infants and toddlers undergoing electroencephalogram (EEG) testing (Loewy, Hallan, Friedman, & Martinez, 2006). This study compared the effects of chloral hydrate and music therapy. The results indicated that music therapy was more cost-effective and risk free than pharmacological sedation.

Music therapy has also been effective with children and adolescents with psychopathology. In Gold, Voracek, and Wigram's (2004) meta-analysis on 11 studies, music therapy had a medium to large positive effect on clinically relevant outcomes. The effects tended to be greater for behavioral and developmental disorders than for emotional disorders and greater for behavioral and developmental outcomes than for social skills and self-concept.

Kern and Aldridge (2006) used music as an intervention with children with autism. The music facilitated the children's play on the playground and their involvement with peers because they were attracted to the sounds and had the opportunity to use the instruments.

Music therapy has also been used for children following surgery. Hatem, Lira, and Mattos (2006) evaluated the effects of music on children in a pediatric cardiac intensive care unit following heart surgery. After the music intervention, pain scale scores, heart rate, and respiratory rate decreased. Music therapy also has reduced anxiety and increased the comfort of hospitalized children with cancer (Barrera, Rykov, & Doyle, 2002). The children rated their feelings as being more positive using a schematic faces mood scale following the music therapy.

RELAXATION THERAPY AND IMAGERY

Only one study could be found in the recent literature on relaxation therapy and guided imagery with children. In Ball, Shapiro, Monheim, and Weydert (2003), children with recurrent abdominal pain were trained in relaxation and guided imagery during four weekly 50-minute sessions. The children experienced a 67% decrease in pain during relaxation and imagery.

HYPNOSIS

Hypnosis has been performed with children for medical conditions, including headaches, insomnia, and asthma, and has also been used before and during invasive procedures. In a study on headaches by Kohen and Zajac (2007), children who learned self-hypnosis for recurrent headaches reported fewer headaches (from 4.5 per week to 1.4 per week), a reduction in intensity on an intensity scale (from 10.3 to 4.7), and a reduction in average duration (from 23.6 hours to 3.0 hours). Self-hypnosis has also been taught to children and adolescents for the treatment of insomnia (Anbar & Slothower, 2006). Following two hypnosis sessions, 90% of the children and adolescents reported a reduction in sleep onset time, 52% reported resolution of night awakenings, and 38% reported improvement in sleep. In addition, 87% reported improvement or resolution of the somatic complaints following hypnosis (chest pain, dyspnea, functional abdominal pain, habit cough, headaches, and vocal cord dysfunction). Hypnosis was also offered to children and adolescents who were treated at a pediatric pulmonary center (Anbar, 2002). Following hypnosis, there was improvement in 80% of the patients with persistent asthma, chest pain or pressure, habit cough, hyperventilation, shortness of breath, sighing, and vocal cord dysfunction. In some cases, the symptoms resolved immediately after hypnotherapy was first practiced, and in others, this improvement did not occur until after a few weeks of hypnosis.

Hypnosis has been compared with a local anesthetic for the management of pediatric procedure-related pain. In a study by Liossi, White, and Hatira (2006) on relief of lumbar puncture–induced pain and anxiety in pediatric cancer patients, the children were randomized to one of three groups: local anesthetic (EMLA, an analgesic cream), EMLA plus hypnosis, and EMLA plus attention. The patients in the EMLA plus hypnosis group reported less anticipatory anxiety and less procedure-related pain and anxiety, and they experienced less behavioral distress during the procedure than in the other two groups.

In another study, hypnosis was used as premedication and was compared with a sedative premedication (Calipel, Lucas-Polomeni, Wodey, & Ecoffey, 2005). In the hypnosis group, fewer of the children were anxious during the start of anesthesia, and behavior problems were reduced to half in that group on Day 1 and Day 7 following the procedure.

BIOFEEDBACK

During the past few decades, EEG biofeedback has been developed as a nonpharmacological treatment for ADHD. A series of case-controlled group studies conducted by Monastra and colleagues (Monastra, 2005; Monastra et al., 2005) examined the effects of EEG biofeedback. Clinical improvement was reported in approximately 75% of children in each of the research studies. On the basis of reviews of the literature, the short-term effects (i.e., decreases in inattention, hyperactivity, and impulsivity) suggest comparability of hypnosis with stimulant medications at the behavioral and neuropsychological level (Holtmann & Stadler, 2006).

In one study on children receiving Ritalin for ADHD, a subsample also received EEG biofeedback (Monastra, Monastra, & George, 2002). The children improved on the Attention Deficit Disorders Evaluation Scale and on the Test of Variables of Attention Scale while using Ritalin. However, only those who had received EEG biofeedback sustained their gains when tested without Ritalin.

In a similar study in Germany, 3 months of EEG biofeedback were provided to children with ADHD contingent on the production of cortical sensory motor rhythms of alpha and beta activity when given stimulant medication (Fuchs, Birbaumer, Lutzenberger, Gruzelier, & Kaiser, 2003). Both the EEG biofeedback and the stimulant medications were associated with improvements on all of the scales of the Test of Variables of Attention, and the children's behaviors were rated as improved by their teachers and parents on the Conners Behavior Rating Scale.

Biofeedback has also been used for dysfunction in voiding and constipation. In a study by Yagci et al. (2005) on voiding dysfunction, the effects of biofeedback were measured in a large group of children in Turkey. The children received biofeedback at 3- to 4-week intervals over a period of 6 months and were evaluated again at 2 years. Improvement was noted on all parameters, ranging from 59% to 88% at 6 months. These improvements continued at the 2-year follow-up.

A study was conducted using biofeedback with children with chronic constipation (Sunic-Omejc et al., 2002). After a 1-month treatment period, the prevalence of abnormal defecation dynamics was significantly lower in the group that received biofeedback therapy.

Finally, again in Turkey, Dursun, Dursun, and Alican (2004) used biofeedback with children with cerebral palsy to determine its effects on gait function. The children who received biofeedback also received a conventional exercise program and were compared with children in a control group who received only the exercise program. The biofeedback group showed significant improvements on the tonus of their plantar flexor muscles and active range of motion of their ankle joints. Gait function also was significantly improved in both groups, but to a greater degree in the biofeedback group.

REFERRING CHILDREN FOR COMPLEMENTARY AND ALTERNATIVE MEDICINE THERAPIES

Because CAM therapies are rarely provided for children and adolescents, clinicians may find that making CAM therapy referrals is problematic for their young clients. With the exception of children's yoga classes, there are few other CAM therapies for children. Even exercise programs (physical education) are disappearing from schools. Parents, however, can provide many of these therapies—for example, daily massages—or can engage their children in exercise programs such as Pilates and fast walking or at least arrange and supervise some form of exercise. Professional guidance and referrals would be needed for the more psychological therapies such as hypnosis and biofeedback, and perhaps then only for the more difficult pediatric conditions, such as obesity, ADHD, and migraine headaches, that have not responded to other therapies. Like adults, children can benefit psychologically and physically from CAM therapies.

APPENDIX A: THERAPIES THAT HAVE BEEN EFFECTIVE FOR DIFFERENT CONDITIONS AND PROCEDURES

Condition or procedure	Massage therapy	Acupuncture	Tai Chi	Yoga	Pilates	Exercise	Music therapy	Aromatherapy	PMR	Imagery	Meditation	Hypnosis	Biofeedback
Aerobic capacity			√	√									
Aggression	√							√	√				
Alertness	√							√					
Alzheimer's disease		√											
Angina				√									
Anorexia nervosa	√												
Anxiety	√	√	√	√				√	√	√	√	√	
Arteriosclerosis	√					√							
Arthritis	√	√	√	√				√	√	√			
Asthma	√			√						√			√
Attention-deficit disorder	√		√										
Attentiveness			√										
Back pain	√	√		√	√		√		√				
Balance			√										
Blood pressure	√		√	√			√	√	√	√			
Body mass index			√										
Breast cancer	√		√	√					√				
Bulimia	√												
Burns	√												
Cancer	√			√		√	√	√	√	√	√		
Cancer pain												√	
Carpal tunnel syndrome	√												√
Cerebral palsy	√												
Chemotherapy							√			√			
Chemotherapy-induced nausea		√							√	√			
Chemotherapy-induced vomiting		√							√	√			
Cholesterol			√	√		√							
Chronic fatigue syndrome	√												

(*continues*)

149

Condition or procedure	Massage therapy	Acupuncture	Tai Chi	Yoga	Pilates	Exercise	Music therapy	Aromatherapy	PMR	Imagery	Meditation	Hypnosis	Biofeedback
Chronic obstructive pulmonary disease	√					√			√	√			
Cognitive performance	√			√					√				
Colitis		√											
Colonoscopy							√						
Coronary artery bypass surgery									√				
Coronary artery disease				√									√
Cortisol	√			√			√	√	√		√		
Dementia							√						
Dental pain	√							√					
Depression	√		√	√		√	√			√	√		√
Dermatitis	√			√						√			√
Diabetes	√			√		√							√
Down syndrome	√												
Dysmenorrhea								√					
Electroencephalogram (EEG)	√		√	√			√	√			√		
Enhanced alertness	√												
Enhanced attentiveness	√												
Epilepsy		√					√						
Fatigue	√			√									
Fibromyalgia	√	√				√				√	√		√
Flexibility			√										
Gait			√										
Glucose	√			√									
Headaches (migraine)	√	√		√					√			√	√
Heart rate	√		√	√				√	√				
HIV	√		√										
Hypertension	√		√	√		√		√	√				√
Immune function	√	√									√		
Insomnia	√			√				√	√	√			
Irritable bowel syndrome									√		√	√	
Job stress	√												
Labor pain	√	√					√						
Menopausal syndrome								√					
Menstrual cramps	√							√					
Mood	√							√					
Multiple sclerosis	√	√		√			√						
Muscle strength			√										
Musculoskeletal pain	√												
Musculoskeletal problems	√												
Natural killer cells	√						√						
Neck pain	√	√											
Nerve conduction velocity				√									

Condition or procedure	Massage therapy	Acupuncture	Tai Chi	Yoga	Pilates	Exercise	Music therapy	Aromatherapy	PMR	Imagery	Meditation	Hypnosis	Biofeedback
Obesity						√		√		√			
Osteoporosis			√			√							
Oxygen consumption	√			√									
Pain	√											√	
Parkinson's	√	√	√				√			√			
Performance	√					√	√			√			√
Physical condition				√									
Physical fitness					√								√
Postmenopausal stress		√											
Postoperative care							√						
Postoperative nausea	√	√											
Postoperative pain	√	√						√	√			√	
Postoperative vomiting	√												
Posttraumatic stress disorder	√									√			
Pregnancy stress	√			√									
Pregnancy-related nausea		√											
Pregnancy-related vomiting		√											
Premenstrual syndrome	√												
Preoperative anxiety												√	
Preoperative nausea												√	
Preoperative pain												√	
Preterm delivery	√												
Psoriasis							√			√			
Relaxation	√		√	√					√				
Running performance				√									
Schizophrenia							√						
Sexual abuse	√												
Sleep disturbance	√			√			√	√					
Sleep problems	√	√	√				√						
Smoking	√	√				√		√		√			
Soreness	√												
Spinal cord injuries	√												
Stress	√					√	√	√	√	√	√		√
Stress hormones	√												
Stroke		√					√			√			√
TMJ		√											√
Vagal activity	√		√	√					√		√		
Weight reduction				√	√					√			
Wrinkling								√					

Note. PMR = progressive muscle relaxation; TMJ = temporomandibular joint disorder.

APPENDIX B: TRAINING
AND CREDENTIALS OF THERAPISTS

Training and credentials are important components of professionalism. Reliable and credible credentials help the public and consumers know that individuals offering the therapy to the public are qualified and competent. Knowing that a therapist meets the standards established for his or her profession should help clients feel more confident and comfortable. This appendix includes information on training and credentials for the different complementary and alternative therapies discussed in this volume.

MASSAGE THERAPY

Thirty-six states and the District of Columbia regulate massage therapists, who must meet certain standards established by the state. Each state law has different requirements, so a massage therapist may be referred to as *licensed, state certified,* or *registered.* In most cases, only individuals who have the state designation may perform massage and use a title indicating that they do massage.

As is the case with many other health care professions, there is a national certification exam for massage therapists. It is administered by the National Certification Board of Therapeutic Massage and Bodywork. Individuals who meet standards of education, training, and/or experience and pass the national certification examination are entitled to use the designation "Nationally Certified in Therapeutic Massage and Bodywork" and its initials, "NCTMB." National certification protects the consumer, the profession, and employers by ensuring that individuals who obtain this credential possess core skills, abilities, knowledge, and attributes to practice safely and competently.

A graduation certificate or diploma from a training program is another form of credential. What is important is the extent and quality of the training someone completes to earn the certificate or diploma, but this can vary widely among massage schools. Standards for education and training can assist the consumer in knowing whether a training program offers adequate preparation. The American Massage Therapy Association recommends a minimum of 500 hours of in-class training, including a specific number of hours in anatomy and physiology, the theory and practice of massage therapy, and elective topics.

One way of knowing whether a training program provides a nationally recognized standard level of education is to see whether it is accredited by a credible agency—that is, that the program follows the guidelines of the U.S. Department of Education and requires an extensive evaluation report, a site inspection by a team of experts, and an evaluation by an independent board or commission. The American Massage Therapy Association established the Commission on Massage Training Accreditation, an independent accreditation agency, to provide a system for ensuring that training programs meet such standards. Training programs that are accredited by the commission offer a minimum of 500 in-class hours of training in required subjects and have the faculty, staff, equipment, classrooms, and other attributes needed to provide adequate training in massage therapy.

ACUPUNCTURE

The National Council of Colleges of Acupuncture and Oriental Medicine has established three routes of eligibility for certification in acupuncture: formal education, apprenticeship, and a combination of formal education and apprenticeship. Individuals may qualify to take the examination by meeting all of the requirements specified under any one of the three routes.

For certification in acupuncture and Oriental medicine, official documentation demonstrating completion of a clean needle technique course is needed. Completion of an apprenticeship program with a minimum of 4,000 contact hours with no fewer than 3 years in acupuncture is also required.

It is becoming more common for medical doctors, such as anesthesiologists and neurologists, to be trained in acupuncture. Medical doctors must have 200 to 300 hours of acupuncture training in a program approved by the American Board of Medical Acupuncture.

TAI CHI

The core training for Tai Chi involves two primary features. The first is the *solo form*, a slow sequence of movements that emphasize a straight spine, abdominal breathing, and a natural range of motion. The second comprises the different styles of pushing hands for training movement principles of the form in a more practical way.

In the United States, the practice of Tai Chi is not regulated by the states or the federal government. Teacher training program requirements can vary from 50 to 1,000 hours depending on the school, and licensing is not required.

YOGA

The American Fitness Professionals and Associates (AFPA) Yoga Fitness Instructor Certification program is designed to instruct beginner and intermediate yoga students. This program offers instruction on how to live the yogic lifestyle, enhancing personal health and centeredness through yoga. The Yoga Fitness Instructor Certification program is designed to educate participants about various yoga techniques and how to incorporate them into an individual and group setting.

The following are the minimum prerequisites: one must (a) be at least 18 years of age and have a high school diploma or equivalent; (b) have basic understanding of anatomy, physiology, yogic philosophy, and *asanas* (postures); and (c) have training in cardiopulmonary resuscitation, which is not required to take the examination but is required to obtain liability insurance. The requirements for AFPA Yoga Fitness Instructor Certification (Level I) are to (a) complete the AFPA Yoga Fitness Level I certification exam, (b) complete the yoga practice sessions, (c) complete the Class Participation Log Sheet (required to participate in 10 yoga style classes), and (d) complete the practical demonstration of a conditioning program of one's choice.

The AFPA Yoga Fitness Instructor Certification program offers health and fitness teachers advice on structuring their yoga classes and shows instructors how to get more from their routines. Emphasis is placed on the importance of asanas, joint mobility, and muscular strength. In addition, the program includes a regimen of joint-freeing exercises and describes *body reading*, a technique that allows practitioners to detect muscular imbalances. Instructors also learn how to assess individual body imbalances and adapt classes around these imbalances and individuals' strengths, flexibility, and range of motion.

In the United States, a potential yoga instructor has the option to train for 2 or more years or to be certified after only taking a weekend-long course. As a result, there is a wide range of training from teacher to teacher.

PILATES

Broadly speaking, Pilates Instructor Certification can be divided into two parts: Pilates mat certification and comprehensive Pilates certification, which covers all of the Pilates equipment. Beyond these two basics, many levels of advanced training are available for those who wish to specialize in the sport-specific or rehabilitative aspects of Pilates. Full certification on Pilates equipment is much more elaborate than mat instructor certification. A prospective student is usually required to have completed at least a year of Pilates study, including a number of private lessons. Successful completion of mat teacher training is often expected as well. At this level, the student undertakes a basic education in anatomy and physiology, the history of Joseph Pilates, and the evolution of the Pilates method as well as in-depth instruction on the exercises for different apparatuses and their modifications.

Combining Pilates with other exercise methods and fitness equipment is a growing trend. One can now get certified in Pilates/yoga (sometimes referred to as *Piyo*), Pilates on the ball, Pilates with exercise bands, and more. These types of certification programs are often offered as weekend programs with few prerequisites. A minimum of mat instructor certification is highly recommended before engaging in crossover teaching.

MUSIC THERAPY

In the United States, a music therapist holds a bachelor's degree in music therapy from a college or university program approved by the American Music Therapy Association. After earning a bachelor's degree, a music therapist can then take the Certification Board for Music Therapists exam, which is required to practice professionally. When a music therapist passes the exam, he or she receives the credential of "MT–BC" (music therapist—board certified).

AROMATHERAPY

Aromatherapy is a natural healing method that uses essential oils that are thought to have beneficial effects. These oils can be ingested, inhaled, or absorbed through the skin. Although aromatherapists are not required to earn degrees in the subject, some formal training is essential for learning how the different oils affect clients. Students enrolled in an aromatherapy program learn to distill essential oils and work with chemicals. Aromatherapists must have a well-developed sense of smell and be able to distinguish among many different fragrances.

Although some countries require practitioners to have an aromatherapy license, there is no required training or licensing in the United States or the United Kingdom. Some credentials an aromatherapist may have are formal aromatherapy training from an established school and a state-issued license or certification on bodywork such as massage.

PROGRESSIVE MUSCLE RELAXATION

No licensing or certification is required for teaching progressive muscle relaxation, but many health care professionals have had training in this technique as part of their formal education.

MEDITATION

Because there are many different forms of meditation and just as many opinions about training requirements, there is no formal certification or licensing process for meditation instructors. Some spiritual traditions, such as Buddhism, do have requirements for extensive formal training for new teachers, and those vary widely depending on the institution.

HYPNOSIS

A person who is not a health care professional can be certified as a hypnotist at a number of schools, which may require 60 to more than 200 hours of training. In the United States, certified, experienced practitioners can be located through the National Board of Certified Clinical Hypnotherapists (NBCCH). Although certification with the NBCCH is not a requirement for practicing hypnosis, the NBCCH was formed by hypnotherapists to improve the standards and integrity of the hypnosis profession.

Mental health practitioners must have earned a graduate-level degree in any of the full spectrum of academic disciplines in mental health from a regionally accredited educational institution. Medical practitioners must hold an appropriate master's or doctorate degree. Categories include addictions and substance abuse counselors, chiropractors, marriage and family therapists, mental health counselors, pastoral counselors, psychiatric nurses, physicians, psychiatrists, psychologists, school counselors, and social workers.

All applicants must have acquired a total of 60 or more contact hours of classroom instruction. A single basic hypnosis course of at least 18 hours, which includes in-class supervised practice, is needed as part of the minimum 60-hour requirement. Application may be made prior to gaining the above hypnotherapy training as long as the applicant has acquired at least 30 hours of clinical hypnotherapy training and all other requirements are met. A certificate declaring board-eligible status is provided during the waiting period.

BIOFEEDBACK

Candidates are required to hold a bachelor's degree or higher from a regionally accredited academic institution in a health care field approved by the Biofeedback Certificate Institute of America. Licensed registered nurses are accepted with an associate degree. Institute-approved health care fields include psychology, nursing (including 2-year registered nurses with license, nonlicensed vocational nurses or licensed practical nurses), physical therapy, respiratory therapy, occupational therapy, social work, counseling, rehabilitation, chiropractic, recreational therapy, dental hygiene, physician's assistant (with certification or license), exercise physiology, speech pathology, and sports medicine. The following fields require a master's degree: music therapy and counseling education (MEd in counseling). Appropriately credentialed doctors of medicine and dentistry are also accepted. Degrees in health care fields other than those listed above must be submitted to the Certification Review Committee.

APPENDIX C: RESOURCES FOR COMPLEMENTARY AND ALTERNATIVE MEDICINE

GENERAL WEB SITES

Acupuncture: http://nccam.nih.gov/health/acupuncture/index.htm

CAM on PubMed: http://www.nlm.nih.gov/nccam/camonpubmed.html

Cancer Clinical Trials: http://www.nci.nih.gov/clinicaltrials

Food and Drug Administration: http://www.fda.gov

Healthfinder: http://www.healthfinder.gov

Medline Plus Complementary and Alternative Medicine:
    http://www.nlm.nih.gov/ medlineplus/alternativemedicine.html

National Cancer Institute: http://www.cancer.gov/

NCCAM Newsletter: http://nccam.nih.gov/news/newsletter/

NCCAM Research Grants: Information: http://nccam.nih.gov/research/

White House Commission on Complementary and Alternative Medicine Policy:
    http://www.whccamp.hhs.gov

DIRECTORY

Activity Therapies

National Coalition of Arts Therapies Associations
c/o Cynthia Briggs, Chairperson
2000 Century Plaza, Suite 108
Columbia, MD 21044

Acupressure

Acupressure Institute
1533 Shattuck Avenue
Berkeley, CA 94709
Phone: 800-442-2232 (outside California) or 510-845-1059
Fax: 510-845-1496
Web site: http://www.acupressure.com
E-mail: info@acupressure.com

Acupuncture

American Academy of Medical
    Acupuncture
5820 Wilshire Boulevard, Suite 500
Los Angeles, CA 90036
Phone: 323-937-5514
Web site: http://
    www.medicalacupuncture.org

American Oriental Body Work
    Association
50 Maple Place
Manhasset, NY 11030-1927

National Certification Commission
    for Acupuncture and Oriental
    Medicine
11 Canal Center Plaza, Suite 300
Alexandria, VA 22314
Phone: 703-548-9004
Web site: http://www.nccaom.org

Traditional Chinese Medicine and
    Acupuncture:
American Association of Acupuncture
    and Oriental Medicine
4101 Lake Boone Trail, Suite 201
Raleigh, NC 27607

Alexander Technique

North American Society of Teachers of the
    Alexander Technique
P.O. Box 3992
Champaigne, IL 61826-3992

Aromatherapy

Aromatherapy Institute and Research
P.O. Box 2354
Fair Oaks, CA 95628

Aroma Vera
5310 Beethoven Street
Los Angeles, CA 90066
Phone: 800-669-9514 or 310-574-6920
Fax: 310-306-5873
Web site: http://www.aromavera.com
E-mail: cservice@aromavera.com

Ellon Bach U.S.A., Inc. (Bach Flower
    Remedies)
644 Merrick Road
Lynbrook, NY 11563

Flower Essence Society
P.O. Box 459
Nevada City, CA 95959

National Association of Holistic
    Aromatherapy
P.O. Box 17622
Boulder, CO 80308-7622

Ayurvedic Medicine

Ayurvedic Institute
P.O. Box 23445
Albuquerque, NM 87192-1445
Phone: 505-291-9698
Fax: 505-294-7572
Web site: http://www.ayurveda.com
E-mail: wwerner@ayurveda.com

Himalayan International Institute
    of Yoga Science and Physiology of
    the U.S.A.
RR1, Box 400
Honesdale, PA 18431

Complementary and Alternative Medicine

National Center for Complementary
    and Alternative Medicine
P.O. Box 7923
Gaithersburg, MD 20898
Phone: 888-644-6226
Fax: 866-464-3616
TTY: 866-464-3615
Web site: http://nccam.nih.gov/
E-mail: info@nccam.nih.org

Day Spa Association
310-17th Street
Union City, NJ 07087
Phone: 201-865-2065

Fax: 201-865-3961
Web site:
    http://www.dayspaassociation.com
E-mail: info@dayspaassociation.com

International Medical Spa Association
310 Seventeenth Street
Union City, NJ 07087
Phone: 201-865-2065
Fax: 201-865-3961
Web site:
    http://www.medicalspaassociation.org
E-mail: info@medicalspaassociation.org

International Spa Association
2365 Harrodsburg Road, Suite A325
Lexington, KY 40504
Phone: 888-651-ISPA (651-4772) or
   859-226-4326 (international)

Fax: 859-226-4445
Web site:
   http://www.experienceispa.com and
   http://www.ispaconference.com
E-mail: ispa@ispastaff.com

Exercise

International College of Applied Kinesiology, U.S.A.
6405 Metcalf Avenue, Suite 503
Shawnee Mission, KS 66202-3929
Phone: 913-384-5336
Fax: 913-384-5112
Web site: http://www.icakusa.com
E-mail: info@icakusa.com

Guided Imagery

Academy for Guided Imagery
P.O. Box 2070
Mill Valley, CA 94942
Phone: 800-726-2070
Web site: http://www.academyforguidedimagery.com/

Hypnosis

American Society of Clinical Hypnosis
140 North Bloomingdale Road
Bloomingdale, IL 60108
Phone: 630-980-4740
Web site: http://www.asch.net

National Guild of Hypnotists
P.O. Box 308
Merrimack, NH 03054-0308
Phone: 603-429-9438
Web site: http://www.ngh.net

International Medicine and Dental
   Hypnotherapy Association
4110 Edgeland, Suite 800
Royal Oak, MI 48073-2285
Phone: 800-257-5467
Web site: http://www.imdha.com/

Society for Clinical and Experimental
   Hypnosis
2201 Haeden Road, Suite 1
Indianapolis, IN 46268
Phone: 509-332-7555
Web site: http://www.sceh.us/

Martial Arts

Wushu Resources, U.S.A.
P.O. Box 210159
San Francisco, CA 94121

Massage

Associated Bodywork and Massage
    Professionals (ABMP)
1271 Sugarbrush Drive
Evergreen, CO 80439
Phone: 800-458-2267 or 303-674-8478
Fax: 800-667-8260
Web sites (multiple sites for various
    issues):
http://www.abmp.com (ABMP's main site)
http://www.massageandbodywork.com
    (an ABMP magazine)
http://www.massagetherapy.com
    (ABMP's consumer-related site)
http://www.bodysensemagazine.com
    (an ABMP publication)
E-mail: expectmore@abmp.com

American Massage Therapy
    Association
500 David Street, Suite 900
Evanston, IL 60201-4695

Meditation

Contemplative Outreach, Ltd.
P.O. Box 737
10 Park Place, Suite 2B
Butler, NJ 07405
Phone: 973-838-3384
Fax: 973-492-5795
Web site:
    http://www.centeringprayer.com/
    cntrgpryr.htm
E-mail: office@coutreach.org

Phone: 877-905-2700 or 847-864-0123
Fax: 847-864-1178
Web site: http://www.amtamassage.org
E-mail: info@amtamassage.org

National Certification Board for Ther-
    apeutic Massage and Bodywork
8201 Greensboro Drive, Suite 300
McLean, VA 22102
Phone: 800-296-0664 or 703-610-9015
Web site: http://www.ncbtmb.com

Touch Research Institute
Department of Pediatrics
University of Miami School of Medicine
P.O. Box 016820
Miami, FL 33101
Phone: 305-243-6781
Web site:
    http://www.miami.edu/touch-
    research/

Center for Mindfulness in Medicine,
    Health Care and Society
University of Massachusetts Medical Center
419 Belmond Avenue, 2nd Floor
Worcester, MA 01604
Web site: http://www.umassmed.edu/
    Content.aspx?id=41252

Insight Meditation Society
1230 Pleasant Street
Barre, MA 01005
Web site: http://dharma.org/ims/

Maharishi Vedic School
636 Michigan Avenue
Chicago, IL 60605
Phone: 312-431-0110 or 808-532-7686
Web site: http://www.maharishi.org

Polarity

American Polarity Association
4101 Lake Boone Trail, Suite 201
Raleigh, NC 27607

Psychotherapies

American Psychiatric Association
1000 Wilson Boulevard, Suite 1825
Arlington, VA 22209-3901
Phone: 703-907-7300
E-mail: apa@psych.org
Web site: http://www.psych.org

American Psychological Association
750 First Street NE
Washington, DC 20002
Phone: 202-336-5500
Web site: http://www.apa.org

National Association of Social
    Workers
750 First Street NW, Suite 700
Washington, DC 20002
Web site: http://www.socialworkers.org

Reflexology

International Institute of Reflexology
P.O. Box 12642
St. Petersburg, FL 33733

Rosen Method

Rosen Institute
825 Bancroft Way
Berkeley, CA 94710

Rubenfeld Synergy

The Rubenfeld Center
115 Waverly Place
New York, NY 10011

Shiatsu

American Oriental Body Work Association
50 Maple Place
Manhasset, NY 11030-1927

Tai Chi

A Taste of China
111 Shirley Street
Winchester, VA 22601

Trager Approach

Trager Institute
10 Old Mill Street
Mill Valley, CA 94941
Web site: http://www.trager.com/

Yoga

American Institute of Vedic Studies
P.O. Box 8357
Santa Fe, NM 87504-8357
Phone: 505-983-9385
Web site: http://www.vedanet.com
E-mail: info@vedanet.com

American Yoga Association
P.O. Box 19986
Sarasota, FL 34276
Web site: http://
    www.americanyogaassociation.org/

REFERENCES

Aftanas, L., & Golosheykin, S. (2003). Changes in cortical activity in altered states of consciousness: The study of meditation by high-resolution EEG. *Human Physiology, 29,* 143–151.

Aftanas, L., & Golosheykin, S. (2005). Impact of regular meditation practice on EEG activity at rest and during evoked negative emotions. *International Journal of Neuroscience, 115,* 893–909.

Aly, H., Moustafa, M. F., Hassanein, S. M., Massaro, A. N., Amer, H. A., & Patel, K. (2004). Physical activity combined with massage improves bone mineralization in premature infants: A randomized trial. *Journal of Perinatology, 24,* 305–309.

American Psychiatric Association. (2000). *Diagnostic and statistical manual of mental disorders* (4th ed., text revision). Washington, DC: Author.

Anbar, R. D. (2002). Hypnosis in pediatrics: Applications at a pediatric pulmonary center. *BMC Pediatrics, 3,* 11.

Anbar, R. D., & Slothower, M. P. (2006). Hypnosis for treatment of insomnia in school-age children: A retrospective chart review. *BMC Pediatrics, 16,* 23.

Ang, J. Y., Ray-Mazumder, S., Nachman, S. A., Rongkavilit, C., Asmar, B. R., & Ren, C. L. (2005). Use of complementary and alternative medicine by parents of children with HIV infection and asthma and well children. *Southern Medical Journal, 98,* 869–875.

Arakawa, S. (1995). Use of relaxation to reduce side effects of chemotherapy in Japanese patients. *Cancer Nursing, 18,* 60–66.

Arent, S. M., Landers, D. M., & Etnier, J. F. (2000). The effects of exercise on mood in older adults: A meta-analytic review. *Journal of Aging and Physical Activity, 8,* 407.

Arias, A., Steinberg, K., Banga, A., & Trestman, R. (2006). Systematic review of the efficacy of meditation techniques as treatments for medical illness. *Journal of Alternative and Complementary Medicine, 12,* 817–832.

Arnon, S., Shapsa, A., Forman, L., Regev, R., Bauer, S., Litmanovitz, I., & Dolfin, T. (2006). Live music is beneficial to preterm infants in the neonatal intensive care unit environment. *Birth, 33,* 131–136.

Arranz, L., Guayerbas, N., Siboni, L., & De la Fuente, M. (2007). Effect of acupuncture treatment on the immune function impairment found in anxious women. *American Journal of Chinese Medicine, 35,* 35–51.

Ashida, S. (2000). The effects of reminiscence music therapy sessions on changes in depressive symptoms in elderly persons with dementia. *Journal of Music Therapy, 37*, 170–182.

Atlantis, E., Barnes, E. H., & Singh, M. A. (2006). Efficacy of exercise for treating overweight in children and adolescents: A systematic review. *International Journal of Obesity, 30*, 1027–1040.

Avants, S. K., Margolin, A., Chang, P., Kosten, T. R., & Birch, S. (1995). Acupuncture for the treatment of cocaine addiction: Investigation of a needle puncture control. *Journal of Substance Abuse Treatment, 12*, 195–205.

Baird, C. L., & Sands, L. (2004). A pilot study of the effectiveness of guided imagery with progressive muscle relaxation to reduce chronic pain and mobility difficulties of osteoarthritis. *Pain Management Nursing, 5*, 97–104.

Bakke, A. C., Purtzer, M. Z., & Newton, P. (2002). The effect of hypnotic-guided imagery on psychological well-being and immune function in patients with prior breast cancer. *Journal of Psychosomatic Research, 53*, 1131–1137.

Ball, T. M., Shapiro, D. E., Monheim, C. J., & Weydert, J. A. (2003). A pilot study of the use of guided imagery for the treatment of recurrent abdominal pain in children. *Clinical Pediatrics, 42*, 527–532.

Balon, J. W., & Mior, S. A. (2004). Chiropractic care in asthma and allergy. *Annals of Allergy, Asthma and Immunology, 93*(Suppl. 1), 55–60.

Barrera, M. E., Rykov, M. H., & Doyle, S. L. (2002). The effects of interactive music therapy on hospitalized children with cancer: A pilot study. *Psychooncology, 11*, 379–388.

Basaran, S., Guler-Uysal, F., Ergen, N., Seydaoglu, G., Bingol-Karakoç G., & Ufuk Altintas, D. (2006). Effects of physical exercise on quality of life, exercise capacity and pulmonary function in children with asthma. *Journal of Rehabilitative Medicine, 38*, 130–135.

Batty, M., Bonnington, S., Tang, B., Hawken, M., & Gruzelier, J. (2006). Relaxation strategies and enhancement of hypnotic susceptibility: EEG neurofeedback, progressive muscle relaxation and self-hypnosis. *Brain Research Bulletin, 71*, 83–90.

Bisson, E., Contant, B., Sveistrup, H., & Lajoie, Y. (2007). Functional balance and dual-task reaction times in older adults are improved by virtual reality and biofeedback training. *Cyberpsychology and Behavior, 10*, 16–23.

Blood, A., & Zatorre, R. (2001). Intensely pleasurable responses to music correlate with activity in brain regions implicated in reward and emotion. *Proceedings of the National Academy of Sciences, 98*, 11818–11823.

Bower, W. F., Diao, M., Tang, J. L., & Yeung, C. K. (2005). Acupuncture for nocturnal enuresis in children: A systematic review and exploration of rationale. *Neurourology and Urodynamics, 24*, 267–272.

Brand, R., Schlicht, W., Grossman, K., & Duhnsen, R. (2006). Effects of a physical exercise intervention on employees' perceptions quality of life: A randomized controlled trial. *Sozial- und Präventivmedizin, 51*, 14–23.

Braun, C. A., Bearinger, L. H., Halcón, L. L., & Pettingell, S. L. (2005). Adolescent use of complementary therapies. *Journal of Adolescent Health, 37,* 76.

Brazelton, T. B. (1973). *Neonatal Behavior Assessment Scale.* London: Spastics International Medical Publications.

Brismee, J., Paige, R., Chyu, M., Boatright, J., Hagar, J., McCaleb, J., et al. (2007). Group and home-based Tai Chi in elderly subjects with knee osteoarthritis: A randomized controlled trial. *Clinical Rehabilitation, 21,* 99–111.

Brooks, C. P., Woodruff, L. D., Wright, L. L., & Donatelli, R. (2005). The immediate effects of manual massage on power-grip performance after maximal exercise in healthy adults. *Journal of Alternative and Complementary Medicine, 11,* 1093–1101.

Browning, C. (2001). Music therapy in childbirth: Research in practice. *Music Therapy Perspectives, 19,* 74–81.

Burnett, K. M., Solterbeck, L. A., & Strapp, C. M. (2004). Scent and mood state following an anxiety-provoking task. *Psychological Reports, 95,* 707–722.

Burns, D. S. (2001). The effect of the Bonny method of guided imagery and music on the mood and life quality of cancer patients. *Journal of Music Therapy, 38,* 51–65.

Burns, D. S., Sledge, R. B., Fuller, L. A., Daggy, J. K., & Monahan, P. O. (2005). Cancer patients' interest and preferences for music therapy. *Journal of Music Therapy, 42,* 185–199.

Butkovic, D., Toljan, S., Matolic, M., Kralik, S., & Radesic, L. (2005). Comparison of laser acupuncture and metoclopramide in PONV prevention in children. *Paediatric Anaesthesia, 15,* 37–40.

Cady, S. H., & Jones, G. E. (1997). Massage therapy as a workplace intervention for reduction of stress. *Perceptual and Motor Skills, 84,* 157–158.

Cai, G., Qiao, Y., Li, P., Jiao, L., & Lu, L. (2001). Music therapy in treatment of cancer patients. *Chinese Mental Health Journal, 15,* 179–181.

Calipel, S., Lucas-Polomeni, M. M., Wodey, F., & Ecoffey, C. (2005). Premedication in children: Hypnosis versus midazolam. *Paediatric Anaesthesia, 15,* 275–281.

Cambron, J. A., Cramer, G. D., & Winterstein, J. (2007). Patient perceptions of chiropractic treatment for primary care disorders. *Journal of Manipulative and Physiological Therapeutics, 30,* 11–16.

Campenni, C. E., Crawler, E., & Meier, M. (2004). Role of suggestion in odor-induced mood change. *Psychology and Reproduction, 94,* 1127–1136.

Carlson, C., & Hoyle, R. (1993). Efficacy of abbreviated progressive muscle relaxation training: A quantitative review of behavioral medicine research. *Journal of Consulting and Clinical Psychology, 61,* 1059–1067.

Carlson, E., Speca, M., Patel, K., & Goodey, E. (2003). Mindfulness-based stress reduction in relation to quality of life, mood, symptoms of stress, and immune parameters in breast and prostate cancer outpatients. *Psychosomatic Medicine, 65,* 571–581.

Carlson, E., Speca, M., Patel, K., & Goodey, E. (2004). Mindfulness-based stress reduction in relation to quality of life, mood, symptoms of stress, and levels of cortisol, dehydroepiandrosterone sulfate (DHEAS) and melatonin in breast and prostate cancer outpatients. *Psychoneuroendocrinology, 29,* 448–474.

Carrel, A. L., Clark, R. R., Peterson, S. E., Nemeth, B. A., Sullivan, J., & Allen, D. B. (2005). Improvement of fitness, body composition, and insulin sensitivity in overweight children in a school-based exercise program: A randomized, controlled study. *Archives of Pediatrics and Adolescent Medicine, 159,* 963–968.

Carson, C., Cookson, B., Farrelly, H., & Riley, T. (1995). Susceptibility of methicillin-resistant *Staphylococcus aureus* to the essential oils of *Melaleuca alternifolia. Journal of Antimicrobial Chemotherapy, 35,* 421–424.

Carson, J., Carson, K., Porter, L., Keefe, F., Shaw, H., & Miller, J. (2007). Yoga for women with metastatic breast cancer: Results from a pilot study. *Journal of Pain Symptoms Management, 33,* 331–341.

Casiglia, E., Schiavon, L., Tikhonoff, V., Haxhi Nasto, H., Azzi, M., Rempelou, P., et al. (2007). Hypnosis prevents the cardiovascular response to cold pressor test. *American Journal of Clinical Hypnosis, 49,* 255–266.

Caspi, O., & Burlesson, K. (2005). Methodological challenges in meditation research. *Advances in Mind–Body Medicine, 21,* 4–11.

Castel, A., Perez, M., Sala, J., Padrol, A., & Rull, M. (2007). Effects of hypnotic suggestion on fibromyalgic pain: Comparison between hypnosis and relaxation. *European Journal of Pain, 11,* 463–468.

Ceniceros, S., & Brown, G. (1998). Acupuncture: A review of its history, theories and indications. *Southern Medical Journal, 91,* 1121–1125.

Chafin, S., Roy, M., Gerin, W., & Christenfeld N. (2004). Music can facilitate blood pressure recovery from stress. *British Journal of Health Psychology, 9,* 393–403.

Chan, K., Qin, L., Lau, M., Woo, J., Au, S., Chou, W., et al. (2004). A randomized, prospective study of the effects of Tai Chi Chuan exercise on bone mineral density in postmenopausal women. *Archives of Physical Medicine and Rehabilitation, 85,* 717–722.

Chang, M. Y., Wang, S. Y., & Chen, C. H. (2002). Effects of massage on pain and anxiety during labor: A randomized controlled trial in Taiwan. *Journal of Advanced Nursing, 38,* 68–73.

Chang, S., & Chen, C. (2005) . Effects of music therapy on women's physiologic measures, anxiety, and satisfaction during cesarean delivery. *Research in Nursing & Health, 28,* 453–461.

Chao, S. A., Chao, A., Wang, T., Chang, Y., Peng, H., Chang, S., et al. (2006). Pain relief by applying transcutaneous electrical nerve stimulation (TENS) on acupuncture points during the first stage of labor: A randomized double-blind placebo-controlled trial. *Pain, 127,* 214–220.

Chen, K., Chen, W., Wang, J., & Huang, M. (2005). Frail elders' view of Tai Chi. *Journal of Nursing Research, 13,* 11–20.

Chen, K. T., & Yang, R. S. (2004). Effects of exercise on lipid metabolism and musculoskeletal fitness in female athletes. *World Journal of Gastroenterology, 10,* 122–126.

Cheng, Y. J., Macera, C. A., Addy, C. L., Sy, F. S., Wieland, D., & Blair, S. N. (2003). Effects of physical activity on exercise tests and respiratory function. *British Journal of Sports Medicine, 37,* 521–528.

Cherkin, D. C., Eisenberg, D., Sherman, K. J., Barlow, W., Kaptchuk, T. J., Street, J., & Deyo, R. A. (2001). Randomized trial comparing traditional Chinese medical acupuncture, therapeutic massage, and self-care education for chronic low back pain. *Archives of Internal Medicine, 161,* 1081–1088.

Clark, C. J., Cochrane, L. M., Mackay, E., & Paton, B. (2000). Skeletal muscle strength and endurance in patients with mild COPD and the effects of weight training. *European Respiratory Journal, 15,* 92–97.

Clark, M., Isaacks-Downton, G., Wells, N., Readlin-Frazier, S., Eck, C., Hepworth, J., & Chakravarthy, B. (2006). Uses of preferred music to reduce emotional distress and symptom activity during radiation therapy. *Journal of Music Therapy, 43,* 247–265.

Cohen, I., Tagliaferri, M., & Tripathy, D. (2002). Traditional Chinese medicine in the treatment of breast cancer. *Seminars in Oncology, 29,* 563–574.

Cohen, L., Warneke, C., Fouladi, R., Rodriguez, M., & Chaoul-Reich, A. (2004). Psychological adjustment and sleep quality in a randomized trial of the effects of a Tibetan yoga intervention in patients with lymphoma. *Cancer, 15,* 2253–2260.

Cooke, M., Chaboyer, W., Schluter, P., & Hiratos, M. (2005). The effect of music on preoperative anxiety in day surgery. *Journal of Advances in Nursing, 52,* 47–55.

Cramer, E. H., Jones, P., Keenan, N. L., & Thompson, B. L. (2003). Is naturopathy as effective as conventional therapy for treatment of menopausal symptoms? *Journal of Alternative and Complementary Medicine, 9,* 529–538.

Crider, A. B., & Glaros, A. G. (1999). A meta-analysis of EMG biofeedback treatment of temporomandibular disorders. *Journal of Orofacial Pain, 13,* 29–37.

Crider, A., Glaros, A. G., & Gevirtz, R. N. (2005). Efficacy of biofeedback-based treatments for temporomandibular disorders. *Applied Psychophysiology and Biofeedback, 30,* 333–345.

Culos-Reed, S., Carlson, L., Daroux, L., & Hately-Aldous, S. (2006). A pilot study of yoga for breast cancer survivors: Physical and psychological benefits. *Psychoncology, 15,* 891–897.

Damodaran, A., Malathi, A., Patil, N., Shah, N., Suryavansihi, & Marathe, S. (2002). Therapeutic potential of yoga practices in modifying cardiovascular risk profile in middle aged men and women. *Journal of the Association of Physicians of India, 50,* 633–640.

Davidson, R., Kabat-Zinn, J., Schumacher, J., Rosenkranz, M., Muller, D., Santorelli, D., et al. (2003). Alterations in brain and immune function produced by mindfulness meditation. *Psychosomatic Medicine, 65,* 564–570.

Davis, M. P., & Darden, P. M. (2003). Use of complementary and alternative medicine by children in the United States. *Archives of Pediatrics and Adolescent Medicine, 157,* 393–396.

de L'Etoile, S. (2002). The effectiveness of music therapy in group psychotherapy for adults with mental illness. *Arts in Psychotherapy, 29,* 69–78.

Dechent, P., Merboldt, K. D., & Frahm, J. (2004). Is the human primary motor cortex involved in motor imagery? *Brain Research, 19,* 138–144.

Degan, M., Fabris, F., Vanin, F., Bevilacqua, M., Genova, V., Mazzucco, M., & Negrisolo, A. (2000). The effectiveness of foot reflexotherapy on chronic pain associated with a herniated disk. *Professioni Infermieristiche, 53,* 80–87.

Delloiagono de Paula, A., Campos de Carvalho, E., & Benita dos Santos, C. (2002). The use of the progressive muscle relaxation technique for pain relief in gynecology and obstetrics. *Revista Latino Americana de Enfermagem, 10,* 654–659.

DeVocht, J. W. (2006). History and overview of theories and methods of chiropractic: A counterpoint. *Clinical Orthopaedics and Related Research, 444,* 243–249.

Diego, M., & Field, T. (in press). Moderate pressure massage elicits a parasympathetic nervous system response. *International Journal of Neuroscience.*

Diego, M. A., Field, T., & Hernandez-Reif, M. (2005). Vagal activity, gastric motility, and weight gain in massaged preterm neonates. *Journal of Pediatrics, 147,* 50–55.

Diego, M. A., Field, T., Hernandez-Reif, M., Hart, S., Brucker, B., Field, T., & Burman, I. (2002). Spinal cord patients benefit from massage therapy. *International Journal of Neuroscience, 112,* 133–142.

Diego, M. A., Field, T., Sanders, C., & Hernandez-Reif, M. (2004). Massage therapy of moderate and light pressure and vibrator effects on EEG and heart rate. *International Journal of Neuroscience, 114,* 31–44.

Diego, M. A., Hernandez-Reif, M., Field, T., Friedman, L., & Shaw, K. (2001). HIV adolescents show improved immune function following massage therapy. *International Journal of Neuroscience, 106,* 35–45.

Diego, M., Jones, N. A., Field, T., Hernandez-Reif, M., Schanberg, S., Kuhn, C., et al. (1998). Aromatherapy positively affects mood, EEG patterns of alertness and math computations. *International Journal of Neuroscience, 96,* 217–224.

Dimeo, F., Bauer, M., Varahram, I., Proest, G., & Halter, U. (2001). Benefits from aerobic exercise in patients with major depression: A pilot study. *British Journal of Sports Medicine, 35,* 114–117.

Ditto, B., Eclache, M., & Goldman, N. (2006). Short-term autonomic and cardiovascular effects of mindfulness body scan meditation. *Annals of Behavioral Medicine, 32,* 227–234.

Dobrzynska, E., Cesarz, H., Rymaszewska, J., & Kiejna, A. (2006). Music therapy: History, definitions, and application. *Archives of Psychiatry and Psychotherapy, 8,* 47–52.

Donaldson, V. W. (2000). A clinical study of visualization on depressed white blood cell count in medical patients. *Applied Psychophysiology and Biofeedback, 25,* 117.

Donohue, B., Miller, A., Beisecker, M., Houser, D., Valdez, R., Tiller, S., & Taymar, T. (2006). Effects of brief yoga exercises and motivational preparatory interventions in distance runners: Results of a control trial. *British Journal of Sports Medicine, 40,* 60–63.

Donzelli, S., Di Domenica, E., Cova, A., Galletti, R., & Giunta, N. (2006). Two different techniques in the rehabilitation treatment of low back pain: A randomized controlled trial. *Europa Medicophysica, 42,* 205–210.

Drexler, A. R., Mur, E. J., & Günther, V. C. (2002). Efficacy of an EMG-biofeedback therapy in fibromyalgia patients: A comparative study of patients with and without abnormality in (MMPI) psychological scales. *Clinical and Experimental Rheumatology, 20,* 677–682.

Duncan, B., Barton, L., Edmonds, D., & Blashill, B. M. (2004). Parental perceptions of the therapeutic effect from osteopathic manipulation or acupuncture in children with spastic cerebral palsy. *Clinical Pediatrics (Philadelphia), 43,* 349–353.

Dursun, E., Dursun, N., & Alican, D. (2004). Effects of biofeedback treatment on gait in children with cerebral palsy. *Disability and Rehabilitation, 26,* 116–120.

Egbert, L., Battit, G., Welch, C., & Bartlett, M. (1964). Reduction of postoperative pain by encouragement and instruction of patients. *New England Journal of Medicine, 270,* 825–827.

Egner, T., & Gruzelier, J. (2003). Ecological validity of neurofeedback: Modulation of slow wave EEG enhances performance. *NeuroReport, 14,* 1221–1224.

Elkin, I., Shea, T., Watkins, J. T., Imber, S. D., Sotsky, S. M., Collins, J. F., et al. (1989). National Institute of Mental Health Treatment of Depression Collaborative Research Program. *Archives of General Psychiatry, 46,* 971–982.

Epstein, G. N., Halper, J. P., Barrett, E. A., Birdsall, C., McGee, M., Baron, K. P., & Lowenstein, S. (2004). A pilot study of mind–body changes in adults with asthma who practice mental imagery. *Alternative Therapies in Health and Medicine, 10,* 66–71.

Ernst, E. (2003). Chiropractic manipulation for non-spinal pain: A systematic review. *New Zealand Medical Journal, 116,* U539.

Evans, D. (2002). The effectiveness of music as an intervention for hospital patients: A systematic review. *Journal of Advanced Nursing, 37,* 8–18.

Ezzo, J., Streitberger, K., & Schneider A. (2006). Cochrane systematic reviews examine P6 acupuncture-point stimulation for nausea and vomiting. *Journal of Alternative and Complementary Medicine, 12,* 489–495.

Faymonville, M., Laureys, S., Degueldre, C., DelFiore, G., Luxen, A., Franck, G., et al. (2000). Neural mechanisms of antinociceptive effects of hypnosis. *Anesthesiology, 92,* 1257–1267.

Federico, G., & Whitwell, G. (2001). Music therapy and pregnancy. *Journal of Prenatal and Perinatal Psychology and Health, 15,* 299–311.

Field, T. (Ed.). (2004). *Touch and massage in early child development.* New Brunswick, NJ: Johnson & Johnson Pediatric Institute.

Field, T., Deeds, O., Diego, M., Gauler, A., Sullivan, S., Wilson, D., & Nearing, G. (2008). *Massage therapy facilitates group interpersonal psychotherapy for prenatally depressed women.* Manuscript submitted for publication.

Field, T., Diego, M., Cullen, C., Hartshorn, K., Gruskin, A., Hernandez-Reif, M., & Sunshine, W. (2004). Carpal tunnel syndrome symptoms are lessened following massage therapy. *Journal of Bodywork and Movement Therapies, 8,* 9–14.

Field, T., Diego, M., Cullen, C., Hernandez-Reif, M., Sunshine, W., & Douglas, S. (2002). Fibromyalgia pain and substance P decreases and sleep improves following massage therapy. *Journal of Clinical Rheumatology, 8,* 72–76.

Field, T., Diego, M., & Hernandez-Reif, M. (2007). Massage therapy research. *Developmental Review, 27,* 75–89.

Field, T., Diego, M., Hernandez-Reif, M., Cisneros, W., Feijo, L., Vera, Y., et al. (2005). Lavender fragrance cleansing gel effects on relaxation. *International Journal of Neuroscience, 115,* 207–222.

Field, T., Diego, M., Hernandez-Reif, M., Deeds, O., & Figuereido, B. (2006). Moderate versus light pressure massage therapy leads to greater gain in preterm infants. *Infant Behavior and Development, 29,* 574–578.

Field, T., Diego, M., Hernandez-Reif, M., Deeds, O., & Figuereido, B. (2008). *Pregnancy massage reduces prematurity, low birthweight and postpartum depression.* Manuscript under review.

Field, T., Diego, M., Hernandez-Reif, M., Schanberg, S., & Kuhn, C. (2004). Massage therapy effects on depressed pregnant women. *Journal of Psychosomatic Obstetrics & Gynecology, 25,* 115–122.

Field, T., Hernandez-Reif, M., Diego, M., & Fraser, M. (2007). Lower back pain and sleep disturbance are reduced following massage therapy. *Journal of Bodywork and Movement Therapies, 11,* 141–145.

Field, T., Hernandez-Reif, M., Hart, S., Quintino, O., Drose, L., Field, T., et al. (1997). Sexual abuse effects are lessened by massage therapy. *Journal of Bodywork and Movement Therapies, 1,* 65–69.

Field, T., Hernandez-Reif, M., Hart, S., Theakston, H., Schanberg, S., Kuhn, C., & Burman, I. (1999). Pregnant women benefit from massage therapy. *Journal of Psychosomatic Obstetrics and Gynecology, 20,* 31–38.

Field, T., Hernandez-Reif, M., Quintino, O., Schanberg, S., & Kuhn, C. (1998). Elder retired volunteers benefit from giving massage therapy to infants. *Journal of Applied Gerontology, 17,* 229–239.

Field, T., Hernandez-Reif, M., Taylor, S., Quintino, O., & Burman, I. (1997). Labor pain is reduced by massage therapy. *Journal of Psychosomatic Obstetrics and Gynecology, 18,* 286– 291.

Field, T., Ironson, G., Scafidi, F., Nawrocki, T., Goncalves, A., Burman, I., et al. (1996). Massage therapy reduces anxiety and enhances EEG pattern of alertness and math computations. *International Journal of Neuroscience, 86,* 197–205.

Field, T., Martinez, A., Nawrocki, T., Pickens, J., Fox, N., & Schanberg, S. (1998). Music shifts frontal EEG in depressed adolescents. *Adolescence, 33,* 109–116.

Field, T., Peck, M., Hernandez-Reif, M., Krugman, S., Burman, I., & Ozment-Schenck, L. (2000). Postburn itching, pain, and psychological symptoms are reduced with massage therapy. *Journal of Burn Care and Rehabilitation, 21,* 189–193.

Field, T., Peck, M., Krugman, S., Tuchel, T., Schanberg, S., Kuhn, C., & Burman, I. (1998). Burn injuries benefit from massage therapy. *Journal of Burn Care and Rehabilitation, 19,* 241–244.

Field, T., Schanberg, S., Kuhn, C., Field, T., Fierro, K., Henteleff, T., et al. (1998). Bulimic adolescents benefit from massage therapy. *Adolescence, 33,* 555–563.

Field, T., Sunshine, W., Hernandez-Reif, M., Quintino, O., Schanberg, S., Kuhn, C., & Burman, I. (1997). Chronic fatigue syndrome: Massage therapy effects on depression and somatic symptoms in chronic fatigue syndrome. *Journal of Chronic Fatigue Syndrome, 3,* 43–51.

Forbes, D., Phelps, A., & McHugh, T. (2001). Treatment of combat-related nightmares using imagery rehearsal: A pilot study. *Journal of Traumatic Stress, 14,* 433–442.

Forchuk, C., Baruth, P., Prendergast, M., Holliday, R., Bareham, R., Brimner, S., et al. (2004). Postoperative arm massage: A support for women with lymph node dissection. *Cancer Nursing, 27,* 25–33.

Fors, E. A., & Gotestam, K. G. (2000). Patient education, guided imagery and pain related talk in fibromyalgia coping. *European Journal of Psychiatry, 14,* 233–240.

Fors, E. A., Sexton, H., & Gotestam, K. G. (2002). The effect of guided imagery and amitriptyline on daily fibromyalgia pain: A prospective, randomized, controlled trial. *Journal of Psychiatric Research, 36,* 179–187.

Foster, J., & Sweeney, B. (1987). The mechanisms of acupuncture analgesia. *British Journal of Hospital Medicine, 38,* 308–312.

Foster, K. A., Liskin, J., Cen, S., Abbott, A., Armisen, V., Globe, D., et al. (2004). The Trager approach in the treatment of chronic headache: A pilot study. *Alternative Therapies in Health and Medicine, 10,* 40–46.

Frank, E., Kupfer, D. J., Perel, J. M., Cornes, C., Jarrett, D. B., Mallinger, A. G., et al. (1990). Three-year outcomes for maintenance therapies in recurrent depression. *Archives of General Psychiatry, 47,* 1093–1099.

Freeman, L. (2004). *Mosby's complementary and alternative medicine: A research-based approach.* St. Louis, MO: Mosby.

Freire, A., Sugai, G., Chrispin, F., Togeiro, S., Yamamura, Y., Mello, L., & Tufik, S. (2007). Treatment of moderate obstructive sleep apnea syndrome with acupuncture: A randomized, placebo-controlled pilot trial. *Sleep Medicine, 8,* 43–50.

Fuchs, T., Birbaumer, N., Lutzenberger, W., Gruzelier, J. H., & Kaiser, J. (2003). Neurofeedback treatment for attention-deficit/hyperactivity disorder in children: A comparison with methylphenidate. *Applied Psychophysiology and Biofeedback, 28,* 1–12.

Furlan, A., van Tulder, M., Cherkin, D., Tsukayama, H., Lao, L., Koes, B., et al. (2005). Acupuncture and dry needling for low back pain: An updated systematic review within the framework of the Cochrane Collaboration. *Spine, 30,* 944–963.

Galantino, M., Shepard, K., Krafft, L., Laperriere, A., Ducette, J., Sorbello, A., et al. (2005). The effects of group aerobic exercise and Tai Chi on functional outcomes and quality of life for persons living with acquired immunodeficiency syndrome. *Journal of Alternative and Complementary Medicine, 11,* 1085–1092.

Garfinkel, M. S., Schumacher, H. R., Jr., Husain, A., Levy, M., & Reshetar, R. A. (1994). Evaluation of a yoga based regimen for treatment of osteoarthritis of the hands. *Journal of Rheumatology, 21*, 2341–2343.

Gemmell, C., & Leathem, J. (2006). A study investigating the effects of Tai Chi Chuan: Individuals with traumatic brain injuries compared to controls. *Brain Injury, 20*, 151–156.

Genest, J. J., Jr., McNamara, J. R., Upson, B., Salem, D. N., Ordovas, J. M., Schaefer, E. J., & Malinow, M. R. (1991). Prevalence of familial hyperhomocyst(e)inemia in men with premature coronary artery disease. *Arteriosclerosis and Thrombosis, 11*, 1129–1136.

Ghonchech, S., & Smith, J. (2004). Progressive muscle relaxation, yoga stretching and ABC relaxation theory. *Journal of Clinical Psychology, 60*, 131–136.

Giannini, C., de Giorgis, T., Mohn, A., & Chiarelli, F. (2007). Role of physical exercise in children and adolescents with diabetes mellitus. *Journal of Pediatric Endocrinology and Metabolism, 20*, 173–184.

Giaquinto, S., Cacciato, A., Miansi, S., Sostero, E., & Amanda, S. (2006). Effects of music-based therapy on distress following knee arthroplasty. *British Journal of Nursing, 15*, 576–579.

Giardino, N. D., Chan, L., & Borson, S. (2004). Combined heart rate variability and pulse oximetry biofeedback for chronic obstructive pulmonary disease: Preliminary findings. *Applied Psychophysiology and Biofeedback, 29*, 121–133.

Ginandes, C., Brooks, P., Sando, W., Jones, C., & Aker, J. (2003). Can medical hypnosis accelerate post-surgical wound healing? Results of a clinical trial. *American Journal of Clinical Hypnosis, 45*, 333–351.

Gold, C., Voracek, M., & Wigram, T. (2004). Effects of music therapy for children and adolescents with psychopathology: A meta-analysis. *Journal of Child Psychology and Psychiatry, 45*, 1054–1063.

Gruzelier, J., Egner, T., & Vernon, D. (2006). Validating the efficacy of neurofeedback for optimizing performance. *Progress in Brain Research, 159*, 421–431.

Guetin, S., Coudeyre, E., Picot, M. C., Ginies, P., Graber-Duvernay, B., Ratsimba, D., et al. (2005). Effect of music therapy among hospitalized patients with chronic low back pain: A controlled, randomized trial. *Annales de Readaptation et de Medecine Physique, 48*, 217–224.

Gurevich, M. I., Duckworth, D., Imhof, J. E., & Katz, J. L. (1996). Is auricular acupuncture beneficial in the inpatient treatment of substance-abusing patients? A pilot study. *Journal of Substance Abuse Treatment, 13*, 165–171.

Haas, M., Sharma, R., & Stano, M. (2005). Cost-effectiveness of medical and chiropractic care for acute and chronic low back pain. *Journal of Manipulative and Physiological Therapeutics, 28*, 555–563.

Hale, B. D., & Whitehouse, A. (1998). The effects of imagery-manipulated appraisal on intensity and direction of competitive anxiety. *Sport Psychologist, 12*, 40–51.

Hammond, D. C. (2005). Neurofeedback with anxiety and affective disorders. *Child and Adolescent Psychiatric Clinics of North America, 14*, 105–123.

Hammond, D. C. (2007). Review of the efficacy of clinical hypnosis with headaches and migraines. *International Journal of Clinical and Experimental Hypnosis, 55*, 207–219.

Han, S., Hur, M., Buckle, J., Choi, J., & Lee, M. (2006). Effects of aromatherapy on symptoms of dysmenorrhea in college students: A randomized placebo-controlled clinical trial. *Journal of Alternative and Complementary Medicine, 12*, 535–541.

Han, S. H., Yang, B. S., & Kim, H. J. (2003). Effectiveness of aromatherapy massage on abdominal obesity among middle aged women. *Taehan Kanho Hakhoe Chi, 33*, 839–846.

Haneishi, E. (2001). Effects of a music therapy voice protocol on speech intelligibility, vocal acoustic measures, and mood of individuals with Parkinson's disease. *Journal of Music Therapy, 38*, 273–290.

Hanson, E., Kalish, L. A., Bunce, E., Curtis, C., McDaniel, S., Ware, J., & Petry, J. (2007). Use of complementary and alternative medicine among children diagnosed with autism spectrum disorder. *Journal of Autism and Developmental Disorders, 37*, 628–636.

Hantoushzadeh, S., Alhusseini, N., & Lebaschi, A. (2007). The effects of acupuncture during labor on nulliparous women: A randomized control trial. *Australian Journal of Obstetrics and Gynecology, 47*, 26–30.

Harinath, K., Malhotra, A. S., Pal, K., Prasad, R., Kumar, R., Kain, T. C., et al. (2004). Effects of Hatha yoga and Omkar meditation on cardiorespiratory performance, psychologic profile, and melatonin secretion. *Journal of Alternative and Complementary Medicine, 10*, 261–268.

Harper, T., Coeytaux, R., Chen, W., Campbell, K., Kaufman, J., Moise, K., & Thorp, J. (2006). A randomized controlled trial of acupuncture for initiation of labor in nulliparous women. *Journal of Maternal-Fetal & Neonatal Medicine, 19*, 465–470.

Harrington, J. W., Rosen, L., Garnecho, A., & Patrick, P. A. (2006). Parental perceptions and use of complementary and alternative medicine practices for children with autistic spectrum disorders in private practice. *Journal of Developmental and Behavioral Pediatrics, 27*, S156–S161.

Harris, A. H., Cronkite, R., & Moos, R. (2006). Physical activity, exercise coping, and depression in a 10-year cohort study of depressed patients. *Journal of Affective Disorders, 93*, 79–85.

Hart, S., Field, T., Hernandez-Reif, M., Nearing, G., Shaw, S., Schanberg, S., & Kuhn, C. (2001). Anorexia nervosa symptoms are reduced by massage therapy. *Eating Disorders, 9*, 289–299.

Harvey, K., Kemps, E., & Tiggemann, M. (2005). The nature of imagery processes underlying food cravings. *British Journal of Health Psychology, 10*, 49–56.

Hasegawa, Y., Kubota, N., Inagaki, T., & Shinagawa, N. (2001). Music therapy induced alternations in natural killer cell count and function. *Nippon Ronen Igakkai Zasshi, 38*, 201–204.

Hassett, A. L., Radvanski, D. C., Vaschillo, E. G., Vaschillo, B., Sigal, L. H., Karavidas, M. K., et al. (2007). A pilot study of the efficacy of heart rate variability

(HRV) biofeedback in patients with fibromyalgia. *Applied Psychophysiology and Biofeedback, 32,* 1–10.

Hasson, D., Arnetz, B., Jelveus, L., & Edelstam, B. (2004). A randomized clinical trial of the treatment effects of massage compared to relaxation tape recordings on diffuse long-term pain. *Psychotherapy and Psychosomatics, 73,* 17–24.

Hatem, T. P., Lira, P. I., & Mattos, S. S. (2006). The therapeutic effects of music in children following cardiac surgery. *Journal of Pediatrics, 82,* 186–192.

Haun, M., Mainous, R. O., & Looney, S. W. (2001). Effect of music on anxiety of women awaiting breast biopsy. *Behavioral Medicine, 27,* 127–132.

Helsel, D. G., Mochel, M., & Bauer, R. (2004). Shamanisms in a Hmong American community. *Journal of Alternative and Complementary Medicine, 10,* 933–938.

Herman, C., & Blanchard, E. (1998). Psychophysiological reactivity in migraine patients and healthy controls. *Journal of Psychosomatic Research, 44,* 229–240.

Hernandez-Reif, M., Field, T., Dieter, J., Swerdlow, B., & Diego, M. (1998). Migraine headaches are reduced by massage therapy. *International Journal of Neuroscience, 96,* 1–11.

Hernandez-Reif, M., Field, T., & Hart, S. (1999). Smoking cravings are reduced by self-massage. *Preventive Medicine, 28,* 28–32.

Hernandez-Reif, M., Field, T., Ironson, G., Beutler, J., Vera, Y., Hurley, J., et al. (2005). Natural killer cells and lymphocytes increase in women with breast cancer following massage therapy. *International Journal of Neuroscience, 115,* 495–510.

Hernandez-Reif, M., Field, T., Krasnegor, J., & Theakston, H. (2001). Lower back pain is reduced and range of motion increased after massage therapy. *International Journal of Neuroscience, 106,* 131–145.

Hernandez-Reif, M., Field, T., Krasnegor, J., Theakston, H., Hossain, Z., & Burman, I. (2000). High blood pressure and associated symptoms were reduced by massage therapy. *Journal of Bodywork and Movement Therapies, 4,* 31–38.

Hernandez-Reif, M., Field, T., Largie, S., Cullen, C., Beutler, J., Sanders, C., et al. (2002). Parkinson's disease symptoms are reduced by massage therapy and progressive muscle exercises. *Journal of Bodywork and Movement Therapies, 6,* 177–182.

Hernandez-Reif, M., Field, T., & Theakston, H. (1998). Multiple sclerosis patients benefit from massage therapy. *Journal of Bodywork and Movement Therapies, 2,* 168–174.

Hernandez-Reif, M., Field, T., & Thimas, E. (2001). Attention deficit hyperactivity disorder: Benefits from Tai Chi. *Journal of Bodywork and Movement Therapies, 5,* 120–123.

Hernandez-Reif, M., Ironson, G., Field, T., Katz, G., Diego, M., Weiss, S., et al. (2003). Breast cancer patients have improved immune functions following massage therapy. *Journal of Psychosomatic Research, 57,* 45–52.

Hernandez-Reif, M., Martinez, A., Field, T., Quintero, O., & Hart, S. (2000). Premenstrual syndrome symptoms are relieved by massage therapy. *Journal of Psychosomatic Obstetrics and Gynecology, 21,* 9–15.

Hernandez-Ruiz, E. (2005). Effect of music therapy on the anxiety levels and sleep patterns of abused women in shelters. *Journal of Music Therapy, 42*, 140–158.

Hilbert, J. E., Sforzo, G. A., & Swensen, T. (2003). The effects of massage on delayed onset muscle soreness. *British Journal of Sports Medicine, 37*, 72–75.

Hind, K., & Burrows, M. (2007). Weight-bearing exercise and bone mineral accrual in children and adolescents: A review of controlled trials. *Bone, 40*, 14–27.

Holmes, E. A., & Mathews, A. (2005). Mental imagery and emotion: A special relationship? *Emotion, 5*, 489–497.

Holtmann, M., & Stadler, C. (2006). Electroencephalographic biofeedback for the treatment of attention-deficit hyperactivity disorder in childhood and adolescence. *Expert Review of Neurotherapies, 6*, 533–540.

Homola, S. (2006). Chiropractic: History and overview of theories and methods. *Clinical Orthopaedics and Related Research, 444*, 236–242.

Hon, K. L., Ma, K. C., Wong, Y., Leung, T. F., & Fok, T. F. (2005). A survey of traditional Chinese medicine use in children with atopic dermatitis attending a pediatric dermatology clinic. *Dermatologic Therapy, 16*, 154–157.

Horgan, G. (2005). Healthier lifestyles series: 1. Exercise for children. *Journal of Family Health Care, 15*, 15–17.

Horton, J., Crawford, H., Harrington, G., & Downs, J. (2004). Increase of anterior corpus callosum size is associated positively with hypnotizability and the ability to control pain. *Brain, 127*, 1741–1747.

Howes, M. J., & Houghton, P. J. (2003). Plants used in Chinese and Indian traditional medicine for improvement of memory and cognitive function. *Pharmacology, Biochemistry and Behavior, 75*, 513–527.

Hsieh, L. L., Kuo, C. H., Yen, M. F., & Chen, T. H. (2004). A randomized controlled clinical trial for low back pain treated by acupressure and physical therapy. *Preventive Medicine, 39*, 168–176.

Hsu, W. C., & Lai, H. L. (2004). Effects of music on major depression in psychiatric inpatients. *Archives of Psychiatric Nursing, 18*, 193–199.

Hurvitz, E. A., Leonard, C., Ayyangar, R., & Nelson, V. S. (2003). Complementary and alternative medicine use in families of children with cerebral palsy. *Developmental Medicine and Child Neurology, 45*, 364–370.

Hurwitz, E. L., Morgenstern, H., Kominski, G. F., Yu, F., & Chiang, L. M. (2006). A randomized trial of chiropractic and medical care for patients with low back pain: Eighteen-month follow-up outcomes from the UCLA low back pain study. *Spine, 31*, 611–621.

Hwang, J. (2006). The effects of the inhalation method using essential oils on blood pressure and stress responses of clients with essential hypertension. *Taehan Kanho Hakhoe Chi, 36*, 1123–1134.

Imura, M., Ushijima, H., & Misao, H. (2005). A clinical trial on the effect of aroma-massage among normal postpartum mothers: Maternity blues, anxiety, moods, feelings toward baby, and salivary cortisol. *Japanese Journal of Aromatherapy, 5*, 128–131.

Inoue, M., Kitakoji, H., Ishizaki, N., Tawa, M., Yano, T., Katsumi, Y., & Kawakita, K. (2006). Relief of low back pain immediately after acupuncture treatment: A randomized, placebo controlled trial. *Acupuncture Medicine, 24,* 103–108.

Ironson, G., Field, T., Scafidi, F., Hashimoto, M., Kumar, M., Kumar, A., et al. (1996). Massage therapy is associated with enhancement of the immune system's cytotoxic capacity. *International Journal of Neuroscience, 84,* 205–217.

Irwin, M., Pike, J., Cole, J., & Oxman, M. (2003). Effects of a behavioral intervention, Tai Chi Chih, on varicella-zoster virus specific immunity and health functioning in older adults. *Psychosomatic Medicine, 65,* 824–830.

Itai, T., Amayasu, H., Kuribayashi, M., Kawamura, N., Okada, M., Momose, A., et al. (2000). Psychological effects of aromatherapy on chronic hemodialysis patients. *Psychiatry and Clinical Neuroscience, 54,* 393–397.

Jago, R., Jonker, M. L., Missaghian, M., & Baranowski, T. (2006). Effect of 4 weeks of Pilates on the body composition of young girls. *Preventative Medicine, 42,* 177–180.

Jain, S., Shapiro, S., Swanick, S., Roesch, S., Mills, P., Bell, I., & Schwarts, G. (2007). A randomized controlled trial of mindfulness meditation versus relaxation training: Effects on distress, positive state of mind, rumination and distraction. *Annals of Behavioral Medicine, 33,* 11–21.

Jin, P. (1989). Changes in heart rate, noradrenaline, cortisol and mood during Tai Chi. *Journal of Psychosomatic Research, 33,* 197–206.

Jin, P. (1992). Efficacy of Tai Chi, brisk walking, medication, and reading in reducing mental and emotional stress. *Journal of Psychosomatic Research, 36,* 361–370.

John, P., Sharma, N., Sharma, C., & Kankane, A. (2007). Effectiveness of yoga therapy in the treatment of migraine without aura: A randomized controlled trial. *Headache, 47,* 654–661.

Jones, N. A., & Field, T. (1999). Massage and music therapies attenuate frontal EEG asymmetry in depressed adolescents. *Adolescence, 34,* 529–534.

Jones, J. (2006). The use of control groups in music therapy research: A content analysis of articles in the *Journal of Music Therapy. Journal of Music Therapy, 43,* 334–355.

Joos, S., Wildau, N., Kohnen, R., Szecsenyi, J., Schuppan, D., Willich, S., et al. (2006). Acupuncture and moxibustion in the treatment of ulcerative colitis: A randomized controlled study. *Scandinavian Journal of Gastroenterology, 41,* 1056–1063.

Jump, V. K., Fargo, J. D., & Akers, J. F. (2006). Impact of massage therapy on health outcomes among orphaned infants in Ecuador: Results of a randomized clinical trial. *Family Community Health, 29,* 314–319.

Kabat-Zinn, J. (1990). *Full catastrophe living: Using the wisdom of your body and mind to face stress, pain, and illness.* New York: Dell.

Kabat-Zinn, J. (2003). Mindfulness-based interventions in context: Past, present and future. *Clinical Psychology: Science and Practice, 10,* 144–158.

Kamei, T., Toriumi, Y., Kimura, H., Ohno, S., Kumano, H., & Kimura, K. (2000). Decrease in serum cortisol during yoga exercise is correlated with alpha wave activation. *Perceptual and Motor Skills, 90,* 1027–1032.

Karavidas, M. K., Lehrer, P. M., Vaschillo, E., Vaschillo, B., Marin, H., Buyske, S., et al. (2007). Preliminary results of an open label study of heart rate variability biofeedback for the treatment of major depression. *Applied Psychophysiology and Biofeedback, 32,* 19–30.

Karst, M., Winterhalter, M., Munte, S., Francki, B., Hondronikos, A., Eckardt, A., et al. (2007). Auricular acupuncture for dental anxiety: A randomized controlled trial. *Anesthesia & Analgesia, 104,* 295–300.

Katz, J., Wowk, A., Culp, D., & Wakeling, H. (1999). Pain and tension are reduced among hospital nurses after on-site massage treatments: A pilot study. *Journal of Perianesthesia Nursing, 14,* 128–133.

Kaufman, C., Kelly, A. S., Kaiser, D. R., Steinberger, J., & Dengel, D. R. (2007). Aerobic-exercise training improves ventilatory efficiency in overweight children. *Pediatric Exercise Science, 19,* 82–92.

Kaushik, R., Kaushik, R. M., Mahajan, S. K., & Rajesh, V. (2005). Biofeedback assisted diaphragmatic breathing and systematic relaxation versus propranolol in long term prophylaxis of migraine. *Complementary Therapies in Medicine, 13,* 165–174.

Keefer, L., & Blanchard, E. (2002). A one year follow-up of relaxation response meditation as a treatment for irritable bowel syndrome. *Behavior Research and Therapy, 40,* 541–546.

Kelley, G. A., & Kelley, K. S. (2007). Aerobic exercise and lipids and lipoproteins in children and adolescents: A meta-analysis of randomized controlled trials. *Atherosclerosis, 191,* 447–453.

Kelmanson, I. A., & Adulas, E. I. (2006). Massage therapy and sleep behavior in infants born with low birth weight. *Complementary Therapy in Clinical Practice, 12,* 200–205.

Kern, P., & Aldridge, D. (2006). Using embedded music therapy interventions to support outdoor play of young children with autism in an inclusive community-based child care program. *Journal of Music Therapy, 43,* 270–294.

Khalsa, S. B. (2004). Treatment of chronic insomnia with yoga: A preliminary study with sleep-wake diaries. *Applied Psychophysiology and Biofeedback, 29,* 269–278.

Kharti, P., Blumenthal, J. A., Babyak, M. A., Craighead, W. E., Herman, S., Baldewicz, T., et al. (2001). Effects of exercise training on cognitive functioning among depressed older men and women. *Journal of Aging and Physical Activity, 9,* 43–57.

Khumar, S. S., Kaur, P., & Kaur, S. (1993). Effectiveness of Shavasana on depression among university students. *Indian Journal of Clinical Psychology, 20,* 82–87.

Kiive, E., Maaroos, J., Shlik, J., Tõru, I., & Harro, J. (2004). Growth hormone, cortisol and prolactin responses to physical exercise: Higher prolactin response in depressed patients. *Progress in Neuro-Psychopharmacology and Biological Psychiatry, 28,* 1007–1013.

Kim, J., Wadjda, M., Cuff, G., Serota, D., Schlame, M., Axelrod, D., et al. (2006). Evaluation of aromatherapy in treating postoperative pain: Pilot study. *Pain Practice, 6,* 273–277.

Kim, M. J., Nam, E. S., & Paik, S. I. (2005). The effects of aromatherapy on pain, depression, and life satisfaction of arthritis patients. *Taehan Kanho Hakhoe Chi, 35*, 186–194.

Kim, M. S., Cho, K. S., Woo, H., & Kim, J. H. (2001). Effects of hand massage on anxiety in cataract surgery using local anesthesia. *Journal of Cataract and Refractive Surgery, 27*, 884–890.

Kimata, H. (2003). Listening to Mozart reduces allergic skin wheal responses and in vitro allergen-specific IgE production in atopic dermatitis patients with latex allergy. *Behavioral Medicine, 29*, 15–19.

Kjaer, T., Bertelsen, C., Piccini, P., Brooks, D., Alving, J., & Lou, H. (2002). Increased dopamine tone during meditation-induced change of consciousness. *Cognitive Brain Research, 13*, 255–259.

Klerman, G. L., Weissman, M. M., Rounsaville, B. J., & Chevron, E. (1984). *Interpersonal psychotherapy for depression.* New York: Basic Books.

Ko, G., Tsang, P., & Chan, H. (2006). A 10-week Tai-Chi program improved the blood pressure, lipid profile and SF-36 scores in Hong Kong Chinese women. *Medical Science Monitor, 12*, 196–199.

Koger, S., & Brotons, M. (2000). Music therapy for dementia symptoms. *Cochrane Database of Systematic Reviews, 3*, CD001121.

Kohen, D. P., & Zajac, R. (2007). Self-hypnosis training for headaches in children and adolescents. *Journal of Pediatrics, 150*, 635–639.

Kolasinski, S. L., Garfinkel, M., Tsai, A. G., Matz, W., Van Dyke, A., & Schumacher, H. R. (2005). Iyengar yoga for treating symptoms of osteoarthritis of the knees: A pilot study. *Journal of Alternative and Complementary Medicine, 11*, 689–693.

Kolich, M., Taboun, S. M., & Mohamed, A I. (2000). Low back muscle activity in an automobile seat with a lumbar massage system. *International Journal of Occupational Safety and Ergonomics, 6*, 113–128.

Koo, J., & Desai, R. (2003). Traditional Chinese medicine in dermatology. *Dermatologic Therapy, 16*, 98–105.

Krakow, B., Hollifield, M., Johnston, L., Koss, M., Schrader, R., Warner, T. D., et al. (2001). Imagery rehearsal therapy for chronic nightmares in sexual assault survivors with posttraumatic stress disorder: A randomized controlled trial. *JAMA, 286*, 584–588.

Kranitz, L., & Lehrer, P. (2004). Biofeedback applications in the treatment of cardiovascular diseases. *Cardiology in Review, 12*, 177–181.

Kristal, A., Littman, A., Benitez, D., & White, E. (2005). Yoga practice is associated with attenuated weight gain in healthy, middle-aged men and women. *Journal of Alternative and Complementary Medicine, 11*, 28–33.

Kubsch, S. M., Neveau, T., & Vandertie, K. (2000). Effect of cutaneous stimulation on pain reduction in emergency department patients. *Complementary Therapies in Nursing and Midwifery, 6*, 25–32.

Kuttner, L., Chambers., C. T., Hardial, J., Israel, D. M., Jacobson, K., & Evans, K. (2006). A randomized trial of yoga for adolescents with irritable bowel syndrome. *Pain Research and Management, 11*, 217–223.

Kwon, I. S., Kim, J., & Park, M. K. (2006). Effects of music therapy on pain, discomfort, and depression for patients with leg fractures. *Taehan Kanho Hakhoe Chi, 36*, 630–636.

Kwon, Y., Pittler, M., & Ernst, E. (2006). Acupuncture for peripheral joint osteoarthritis: A systematic review and meta-analysis. *Rheumatology, 45*, 1331–1337.

Laaksonen, D. E., Atalay, M., Niskanen, L. K., Mustonen, J., Sen, C. K., Lakka, T. A., & Uusitupa, M. I. (2000). Aerobic exercise and the lipid profile in Type 1 diabetic men: A randomized controlled trial. *Medicine & Science in Sports & Exercise, 32*, 1541–1548.

Lai, H. L., Chen, C. J., Peng, T. C., Chang, F. M., Hsieh, M. L., Huang, H. Y., & Chang, S. C. (2006). Randomized controlled trial of music during kangaroo care on maternal state anxiety and preterm infants' responses. *International Journal of Nursing Studies, 43*, 139–146.

Lai, H. L., & Good, M. (2005). Music improves sleep quality in older adults. *Journal of Advances in Nursing, 49*, 234–244.

Lan, C., Chen, S., & Lai, J. (2004). Relative exercise intensity of Tai Chi Chuan is similar in different ages and gender. *American Journal of Chinese Medicine, 32*, 151–160.

Lan, C., Chen, S., Lai, J., & Wong, M. (2001). Heart rate responses and oxygen consumption during Tai Chi Chuan practice. *American Journal of Chinese Medicine, 29*, 403–410.

Lan, C., Chou, S., Chen, S., Lai, J., & Wong, M. (2004). The aerobic capacity and ventilatory efficiency during exercise in Qigong and Tai Chi Chuan practitioners. *American Journal of Chinese Medicine, 32*, 141–150.

Lang, E., Benotsch, E., Fick, L., Lutgendorf, S., Berbaum, M. L., Berbaum, K. S., et al. (2000). Adjunctive non-pharmacological analgesia for invasive medical procedures: A randomised trial. *Lancet, 355*, 1486–1490.

Langevin, H. M., Badger, G. J., Povolny, B. K., Davis, R. T., Johnston, A. C., Sherman, K. J., et al. (2004). Yin scores and yang scores: A new method for quantitative diagnostic evaluation in traditional Chinese medicine research. *Journal of Alternative and Complementary Medicine, 10*, 389–395.

Larun, L., Nordheim, L. V., Ekeland, E., Hagen, K. B., & Heian, F. (2006). Exercise in prevention and treatment of anxiety and depression among children and young people. *Cochrane Database of Systematic Reviews, 3*, CD004691.

Lau, M., & McMain, S. (2005). Integrating mindfulness meditation with cognitive and behavioral therapies: The challenge of combining acceptance- and change-based strategies. *Canadian Journal of Psychiatry, 50*, 863–869.

Lau, M. A., Bishop, S. R., Segal, Z. V., Buis, T., Anderson, N. D., Carlson, L., et al. (2003). The Toronto Mindfulness Scale: Development and validation. *Journal of Clinical Psychology, 62*, 1445–1467.

Lawlor, D. A., & Hopker, S. W. (2001). The effectiveness of exercise as an intervention in the management of depression: Systematic review and meta-analysis of randomized controlled trials. *British Medical Journal, 322,* 763–767.

Lazar, S., Kerr, C., Wasserman, R., Gray, J., Greve, D., Treadway, M., et al. (2005). Meditation experience is associated with increased cortical thickness. *NeuroReport, 16,* 1893–1897.

Lazaroff, I., & Shimshoni, R. (2000). Effects of medical resonance therapy music on patients with psoriasis and neurodermatitis: A pilot study. *Integrative Physiological and Behavioral Science, 35,* 189–198.

LeDoux, J. (1996). Emotional networks and motor control: A fearful view. *Progress in Brain Research, 107,* 437–446.

Lee, D., Chan, K., Poom, C., Ko, C., Chan, K., Sin, K., et al. (2002). Relaxation music decreases the dose of patient-controlled sedation during colonoscopy: A prospective randomized controlled trial. *Gastrointestinal Endoscopy, 55,* 33–36.

Lee, H., Park, H., Park, J., Kim, M., Hong, M., Yang, J., et al. (2007). Acupuncture application for neurological disorders. *Neurological Research, 29,* 49–54.

Lee, H. K. (2005). The effect of infant massage on weight gain, physiological and behavioral responses in premature infants. *Taehan Kanho Hakhoe Chi, 35,* 1451–1460.

Lee, H. K. (2006). The effects of infant massage on weight, height, and mother–infant interaction. *Taehan Kanho Hakhoe Chi, 36,* 1331–1339.

Lee, S. H., Ahn, S. C., Lee, Y. J., Choi, T. K., Yook, K. H., & Suh, S. Y. (2007). Effectiveness of a meditation based stress management program as an adjunct to pharmacotherapy in patients with anxiety disorder. *Journal of Psychosomatic Research, 62,* 189–195.

Lehrer, P. M., Vaschillo, E., Vaschillo, B., Lu, S. E., Eckberg, D. L., Edelberg, R., et al. (2003). Heart rate variability biofeedback increases baroreflex gain and peak expiratory flow. *Psychosomatic Medicine, 65,* 796–805.

Lehrer, P. M., Vaschillo, E., Vaschillo, B., Lu, S. E., Scardella, A., Siddique, M., & Habib, R. H. (2004). Biofeedback treatment for asthma. *Chest, 126,* 352–361.

Lehrner, J., Marwinski, G., Lehr, S., Johren, P., & Deecke, L. (2005). Ambient odors of orange and lavender reduce anxiety and improve mood in a dental office. *Physiology and Behavior, 86,* 92–95.

Leivadi, S., Hernandez-Reif, M., Field, T., O'Rourke, M., D'Arienzo, S., Lewis, D., et al. (1999). Massage therapy and relaxation effects on university dance students. *Journal of Dance Medicine and Science, 3,* 108–112.

Leppämäki, S. J., Partonen, T. T., Hurme, J., Haukka, J. K., & Lönnqvist, J. K. (2002). Randomized trial of the efficacy of bright-light exposure and aerobic exercise on depressive symptoms and serum lipids. *Journal of Clinical Psychiatry, 63,* 316–321.

Leung, P. C. (2006). A practical way of research in Chinese medicine. *Annals of the Academy of Medicine Singapore, 35,* 770–772.

Lewinsohn, P. M., Allen, N. B., Seeley, J. R., & Gotlib, I. H. (1999). First onset versus recurrence of depression: Differential processes of psychosocial risk. *Journal of Abnormal Psychology, 108*, 483–489.

Lewith, G. T., Godfrey, A. D., & Prescott, P. (2005). A single-blinded, randomized pilot study evaluating the aroma of Lavandula Augustifolia as a treatment for mild insomnia. *Journal of Alternative and Complementary Medicine, 11*, 631–637.

Li, F., Fisher, K., Harmer, P., Irbe, D., Tearse, R., & Weimer, C. (2004). Tai Chi and self-rated quality of sleep and daytime sleepiness in older adults: A randomized controlled trial. *Journal of the American Geriatric Society, 5*, 892–900.

Li, F., Harmer, P., Fisher, K., McAuley, E., Chaumeton, N., Eckstrom, E., & Wilson, N. (2005). Tai Chi and fall reductions in older adults: A randomized controlled trial. *Journals of Gerontology Series A: Biological Sciences and Medical Sciences, 60*, 187–194.

Li, G., Jack, C., & Yang, E. (2006). An fMRI study of somatosensory-implicated acupuncture points in stable somatosensory stroke patients. *Journal of Magnetic Resonance Imaging, 24*, 1018–1024.

Li, K., Shan, B., Xu, J., Liu, H., Wang, W., Zhi, L., et al. (2006). Changes in fMRI in the human brain related to different durations of manual acupuncture needling. *Journal of Alternative and Complementary Medicine, 12*, 615–623.

Lin, M., Hwang, H., Wang, Y., Chang, S., & Wolf, S. (2006). Community-based Tai Chi and its effects on injurious falls, balance, gait and fear of falling in older people. *Physical Therapy, 86*, 1189–1201.

Linde, K., Witt, C., Streng, A., Weidenhammer, W., Wagenpfeil, S., Brinkhaus, B., et al. (2007). The impact of patient expectations on outcomes in four randomized controlled trials of acupuncture in patients with chronic pain. *Pain, 128*, 264–271.

Liossi, C., White, P., & Hatira, P. (2006). Randomized clinical trial of local anesthetic versus a combination of local anesthetic with self-hypnosis in the management of pediatric procedure-related pain. *Health Psychology, 25*, 307–315.

Lis-Balchin, M. (Ed.). (2006). *Aromatherapy science—A guide for healthcare professionals*. New York: Pharmaceutical Press.

Liu, Y., Mimura, K., Wang, L., & Ikuda, K. (2003). Physiological benefits of 24-style Taijiquan exercise in middle-aged women. *Journal of Physiological Anthropology and Applied Human Science, 22*, 219–225.

Loewy, J., Hallan, C., Friedman, E., & Martinez, C. (2006). Sleep/sedation in children undergoing EEG testing: A comparison of chloral hydrate and music therapy. *American Journal of Electroneurodiagnostic Technology, 46*, 343–355.

Lotman, D. G. (2003). The use of complementary and alternative health care practices among children. *Journal of Pediatric Health Care, 17*, 58–63.

Louie, S. W. (2004). The effects of guided imagery relaxation in people with COPD. *Occupational Therapy International, 11*, 145–159.

Lowe, G., Bland, R., Greenman, J., Kirkpatrick, N., & Lowe, G. (2001). Progressive muscle relaxation and secretory immunoglobulin A. *Psychological Reports, 88*, 912–914.

Lu, W., & Kuo, C. (2003). The effect of Tai Chi Chuan on the autonomic nervous modulation in older persons. *Medicine & Science in Sports & Exercise, 35,* 1972–1976.

Lu, W., & Kuo, C. (2006). Comparison of the effects of Tai Chi Chuan and Wai Tan Kung exercises on autonomic nervous system modulation and on hemodynamics in elder adults. *American Journal of Chinese Medicine, 34,* 959–968.

Lucini, D., Covacci, G., Milani, R., Mela, G., Maliani, A., & Pagani, M. (1997). A control study of the effects of mental relaxation on autonomic excitatory responses in healthy subjects. *Psychosomatic Medicine, 59,* 541–552.

Ma, S., & Teasdale, J. (2004). Mindfulness-based cognitive therapy for depression: Replication and exploration of differential relapse prevention effects. *Journal of Consulting and Clinical Psychology, 72,* 31–40.

Maciaszek, J., Osinski, W., Szeklicki, R., & Stemplewski, R. (2007). Effects of Tai Chi on body balance: Randomized controlled trial in men with osteopenia or osteoporosis. *American Journal of Chinese Medicine, 35,* 1–9.

Madanmohan, Udupa, K., Bhavanani, A. B., Shatapathy, C. C., & Sahai, A. (2004). Modulation of cardiovascular response to exercise by yoga training. *Indian Journal of Physiology and Pharmacology, 48,* 461–465.

Madeleine, P., Vedsted, P., Blangsted, A. K., Sjøgaard, G., & Søgaard, K. (2006). Effects of electromyographic and mechanomyographic biofeedback on upper trapezius muscle activity during standard computer work. *Ergonomics, 49,* 921–933.

Maiorana, A., Kegeles, S., Fernandez, P., Salazar, X., Cáceres, C., Sandoval, C., et al. (2007). Implementation and evaluation of an HIV/STD intervention in Peru. *Evaluation and Program Planning, 30,* 82–93.

Majumdar, M., Grossman, P., Dieyz-Waschkowski, B., Kersig, S., & Walach, H. (2002). Does mindfulness meditation contribute to health? Outcome evaluation of a German sample. *Journal of Alternative and Complementary Medicine, 8,* 719–730.

Malhotra, V., Singh, S., Tandon, O., & Sharma, S. (2005). The beneficial effect of yoga in diabetes. *Nepal Medical College Journal, 7,* 145–147.

Manchanda, S. C., Narang, R., Reddy, K. S., Sachdeva, U., Prabhakaran, D., Dharmanand, S., et al. (2000). Retardation of coronary atherosclerosis with yoga lifestyle intervention. *Journal of the Association of Physicians of India, 48,* 687–694.

Manjunath, N. K., & Telles, S. (2004). Spatial and verbal memory test scores following yoga and fine arts camps for school children. *Indian Journal of Physiology and Pharmacology, 48,* 353–356.

Manjunath, N. K., & Telles, S. (2005). Influence of yoga and Ayurveda on self-rated sleep in a geriatric population. *Indian Journal of Medical Research, 121,* 683–690.

Manocha, R. (2000). Why meditation? *Australian Family Physician, 29,* 1135–1138.

Manocha, R., Marks, G. B., Kenchington, P., Peters, D., & Salome, C. M. (2002). Sahaja yoga in the management of moderate to severe asthma: A randomised controlled trial. *Thorax, 57,* 110–115.

Martin, D., Sletten, C., Williams, B., & Berger, I. (2006). Improvement in fibromyalgia symptoms with acupuncture: Results of a randomized controlled trial. *Mayo Clinic Proceedings, 81*, 749–757.

Martyn-St James, M., & Carroll, S. (2006). Progressive high-intensity resistance training and bone mineral density changes among premenopausal women: Evidence of discordant site-specific skeletal effects. *Sports Medicine, 36*, 683–704.

Mason, O., & Hargreaves, I. (2001). A qualitative study of mindfulness-based cognitive therapy for depression. *British Journal of Medical Psychology, 74*, 197–212.

McCaffery, M., & Pasero, C. (1990). *Pain: Clinical manual* (2nd ed.). St. Louis, MO: Mosby.

McCallie, M., Blum, C., & Hood, J. (2006). Progressive muscle relaxation. *Journal of Human Behavior in the Social Environment, 13*, 51–66.

McCarney, R. W., Lasserson, T. J., Linde, K., & Brinkhaus B. (2004). An overview of two Cochrane systematic reviews of complementary treatments for chronic asthma: Acupuncture and homeopathy. *Respiratory Medicine, 98*, 687–696.

McCubbin, J., Wilson, J., Bruehl, S., Ibarra, P., Carlon, C., Norton, J., & Colclough, G. (1996). Relaxation training and opioid inhibition of blood pressure response to stress. *Journal of Consulting and Clinical Psychology, 64*, 593–601.

McGinnis, R. A., McGrady, A., Cox, S. A., & Grower-Dowling, K. A. (2005). Biofeedback-assisted relaxation in Type 2 diabetes. *Diabetes Care, 28*, 2145–2149.

McGlynn, F. D., Smitherman, T. A., & Gothard, K. D. (2004). Comment on the status of systematic desensitization. *Behavior Modification, 28*, 194–205.

Medlicott, M. S., & Harris, S. R. (2006). A systematic review of the effectiveness of exercise, manual therapy, electrotherapy, relaxation training, and biofeedback in the management of temporomandibular disorder. *Physical Therapy, 86*, 955–973.

Mehl-Madrona, L. E. (1999). Native American medicine in the treatment of chronic illness: Developing an integrated program and evaluating its effectiveness. *Alternative Therapies in Health and Medicine, 5*, 36–44.

Meister, I. G., Krings, T., Foltys, H., Boroojerdi, B., Müller, M., Töpper, R., & Thron, A. (2004). Playing piano in the mind: An fMRI study on music imagery and performance in pianists. *Brain Research, 19*, 219–228.

Melchart, D., Weidenhammer, W., Streng, A., Hoppe, A., Pfaffenrath, V., & Linde, K. (2006). Acupuncture for chronic headaches: An epidemiological study. *Headache, 46*, 632–641.

Melzack, R., & Wall, P. D. (1965, November 19). Pain mechanisms: A new theory. *Science, 150*, 971.

Menzies, V., Taylor, A. G., & Bourguignon, C. (2006). Effects of guided imagery on outcomes of pain, functional status, and self-efficacy in persons diagnosed with fibromyalgia. *Journal of Alternative and Complementary Medicine, 12*, 23–30.

Michalsen, A., Grossman, P., Acil, A., Langhorst, J., Ludtke, R., Esch, T., et al. (2005). Rapid stress reduction and anxiolysis among distressed women as a consequence of a three-month intensive yoga program. *Medicine and Science Monitoring, 11*, 555–561.

Middaugh, S. J., & Pawlick, K. (2002). Biofeedback and behavioral treatment of persistent pain in the older adult: A review and a study. *Applied Psychophysiology and Biofeedback, 27*, 185–202.

Miller, K., & Perry, P. (1990). Pain management-relaxation technique and postoperative pain in patients undergoing cardiac surgery. *Heart and Lung, 19*, 136–146.

Ming, J. L., Kuo, B. I., Lin, J. G., & Lin, L. C. (2002). The efficacy of acupressure to prevent nausea and vomiting in post-operative patients. *Journal of Advanced Nursing, 39*, 343–351.

Moffet, H. (2006). How might acupuncture work? A systematic review of physiologic rationales from clinical trials. BMC *Complementary and Alternative Medicine, 6*, 25.

Mollasiotis, A. (2002). A pilot study of the use of progressive muscle relaxation training in the management of post-chemotherapy nausea and vomiting. *European Journal of Cancer Care, 9*, 230–234.

Monastra, V. J. (2005). Electroencephalographic biofeedback (neurotherapy) as a treatment for attention deficit hyperactivity disorder: Rationale and empirical foundation. *Child and Adolescent Psychiatric Clinics of North America, 14*, 55–82.

Monastra, V. J., Lynn, S., Linden, M., Lubar, J. F., Gruzelier, J., & LaVaque, T. J. (2005). Electroencephalographic biofeedback in the treatment of attention deficit/hyperactivity disorder. *Applied Psychophysiology and Biofeedback, 30*, 95–114.

Monastra, V. J., Monastra, D. M., & George, S. (2002). The effects of stimulant therapy, EEG biofeedback, and parenting style on the primary symptoms of attention-deficit/hyperactivity disorder. *Applied Psychophysiology and Biofeedback, 27*, 231–249.

Money, M. (2001). Shamanism as a healing paradigm for complementary therapy. *Complementary Therapies in Nursing and Midwifery, 7*, 126–131.

Montgomery, G., David, D., Winkel, G., Silverstein, J. H., & Bovbjerg, D. H. (2002). The effectiveness of adjunctive hypnosis with surgical patients: A meta-analysis. *Anesthesia & Analgesia, 94*, 1639–1645.

Moore, L. E., & Kaplan, J. Z. (1983). Hypnotically accelerated burn wound healing. *American Journal of Clinical Hypnosis, 26*, 16–19.

Moore, N.C. (2000). A review of EEG biofeedback treatment of anxiety disorders. *Clinical EEG, 31*, 1–6.

Mori, H., Ohsawa, H., Tanaka, T. H., Taniwaki, E., Leisman, G., & Nishijo, K. (2004). Effect of massage on blood flow and muscle fatigue following isometric lumbar exercise. *Medical Science Monitor, 10*, 173–178.

Mori, M., Ikeda, N., Kato, Y., Minamino, M., & Watabe, K. (2002). Inhibition of elastase activity by essential oils in vitro. *Journal of Cosmetic Dermatology, 1*, 183–187.

Moss, M., Cook, J., Wesnes, K., & Duckett, P. (2003). Aromas of rosemary and lavender essential oils differentially affect cognition and mood in healthy adults. *International Journal of Neuroscience, 113*, 15–38.

Motivala, S., Sollers, J., Thayer, J., & Irwin, M. (2006). Tai Chi Chih acutely decreases sympathetic nervous system activity in older adults. *Journals of Gerontology Series A: Biological Sciences and Medical Sciences, 61*, 1177–1180.

Motomura, N., Sakurai, A., & Yotsuya, Y. (2001). Reduction of mental stress with lavender odorant. *Perception and Motor Skills, 93*, 713–718.

Munro, B. J., Steele, J. R., Campbell, T. E., & Wallace, G. G. (2004). Wearable textile biofeedback systems: Are they too intelligent for the wearer? *Studies in Health Technology and Informatics, 108*, 271–277.

Murray, J. (1995). Evidence for acupuncture's analgesic effectiveness and proposals for the physiological mechanisms involved. *Journal of Psychology, 129*, 443–461.

Mustian, K., Katula, J., & Zhao, H. (2006). A pilot study to assess the influence of Tai Chi Chuan on functional capacity among breast cancer survivors. *Journal of Supportive Oncology, 4*, 139–145.

Nagai, N., Hamada, T., Kimura, T., & Moritani, T. (2004). Moderate physical exercise increases cardiac autonomic nervous system activity in children with low heart rate variability. *Child's Nervous System, 20*, 209–214.

Nakao, M., Yano, E., Nomura, S., & Kuboki, T. (2003). Blood pressure-lowering effects of biofeedback treatment in hypertension: A meta-analysis of randomized controlled trials. *Hypertension Research, 26*, 37–46.

Narendran, S., Nagarathna, R., Narendran, V., Gunasheela, S., & Nagendra, H. R. (2005). Efficacy of yoga on pregnancy outcome. *Journal of Alternative and Complementary Medicine, 11*, 237–244.

National Center for Complementary and Alternative Medicine. (2007, October 24). *What is CAM?* Retrieved June 11, 2008, from http://nccam.nih.gov/health/whatiscam/

National Institutes of Health. (1994). *Proceedings NIH acupuncture research conference* (DHEW Publication No. 74-165). Bethesda, MD: Author.

Nauman, E. (2007). Native American medicine and cardiovascular disease. *Cardiology in Review, 15*, 35–41.

Nayak, S., Wheeler, B., Shiflett, S., & Agostinelli, S. (2000). Effects of music therapy on mood and social interaction among individuals with acute traumatic brain injury and stroke. *Rehabilitation Psychology, 45*, 274–283.

Nedstrand, E., Wyon, Y., Hammar, M., & Wijma, K. (2006). Psychological well-being improves in women with breast cancer after treatment with applied relaxation or electroacupuncture for vasomotor symptom. *Journal of Psychosomatic Obstetrics and Gynecology, 27*, 193–199.

Nelson, C. F., Metz, R. D., & LaBrot, T. (2005). Effects of a managed chiropractic benefit on the use of specific diagnostic and therapeutic procedures in the treatment of low back and neck pain. *Journal of Manipulative and Physiological Therapeutics, 28*, 564–569.

Nelson, J., & Harvey, A. G. (2002). The differential functions of imagery and verbal thought in insomnia. *Journal of Abnormal Psychology, 111*, 665–669.

Neri, I., Airola, G., Contu, G., Allais, G., Facchinetti, E., & Benedetto, C. (2004). Acupuncture plus moxibustion to resolve breech presentation: A randomized controlled study. *Journal of Maternal-Fetal & Neonatal Medicine, 15*, 247–252.

Nestoriuc, Y., & Martin, A. (2007). Efficacy of biofeedback for migraine: A meta-analysis. *Pain, 128*, 111–127.

Nickel, C., Lahmann, C., Muelhbacher, M., Pedrosa, F., Kaplan, P., Buschmann, W., et al. (2006). Pregnant women with bronchial asthma benefit from progressive muscle relaxation: A randomized, prospective, controlled trial. *Psychotherapy and Psychosomatics, 75*, 237–243.

Nilsson, U., Unosson, M., & Rawal, N. (2005). Stress reduction and analgesia in patients exposed to calming music postoperatively: A randomized controlled trial. *European Journal of Anaesthesiology, 22*, 96–102.

Nolan, R. P., Kamath, M. V., Floras, J. S., Stanley, J., Pang, C., Picton, P., & Young, Q. R. (2005). Heart rate variability biofeedback as a behavioral neurocardiac intervention to enhance vagal heart rate control. *American Heart Journal, 149*, 1137.

Norheim, A. J., Pederson, E. J., Fonnebo, V., & Berge, L. (2001). Acupressure treatment of morning sickness in pregnancy: A randomized, double-blind, placebo-controlled study. *Scandinavian Journal of Primary Health Care, 19*, 43–47.

Oaten, M., & Cheng, K. (2006). Longitudinal gains in self-regulation from regular physical exercise. *British Journal of Health Psychology, 11*, 717–733.

Oken, B., Kishiyama, S., Zajdel, D., Flegal, K., Dehen, C., Haas, M., et al. (2004). Randomized controlled trial of yoga and exercise in multiple sclerosis. *Neurology, 62*, 2058–2064.

Oken, B., Zajdel, D., Kishiyama, S., Flegal, K., Dehen, C., Haas, M., et al. (2006). Randomized, controlled, six-month trial of yoga in healthy seniors: Effects on cognition and quality of life. *Journal of Alternative and Complementary Medicine, 12*, 40–47.

Okura, T., Nakata, Y., & Tanaka, K. (2003). Effects of exercise intensity on physical fitness and risk factors for coronary heart disease. *Obesity Research, 11*, 1131–1139.

Olney, C. (2005). The effect of therapeutic back massage in hypertensive persons: A preliminary study. *Biological Research for Nursing, 7*, 98–105.

Onozawa, K., Glover, V., Adams, D., Modi, N., & Kumar, R. C. (2001). Infant massage improves mother–infant interaction for mothers with postnatal depression. *Journal of Affective Disorders, 63*, 201–207.

Orhan, F., Sekerel, B. E., Kocabas, C. N., Sackesen, C., Adalioglu, G., & Tuncer, A. (2003). Complementary and alternative medicine in children with asthma. *Annals of Allergy, Asthma and Immunology, 90*, 611–615.

Ostermann, T., & Schmid, W. (2006). Music therapy in the treatment of multiple sclerosis: A comprehensive literature review. *Expert Review of Neurotherapy, 6*, 469–477.

Otto, M., Norris, R., & Bauer-Wu, S. (2006). Mindfulness meditation for oncology patients: A discussion and critical review. *Integrated Cancer Therapy, 5*, 98–108.

Ovayolu, N., Ucan, O., Pehlivan, S., Pehlivan, Y., Buyukhatipoglu, H., Savas, M., & Gulsen, M. (2006). Listening to Turkish classical music decreases patients' anxiety, pain, dissatisfaction and the dose of sedative and analgesic drugs during colonoscopy: A prospective randomized controlled trial. *Clinical Research in Cardiology, 95*, 511–513.

Pacchetti, C., Mancini, F., Aglieri, R., Fundaro, C., Martignoni, E., & Nappi, G. (2000). Active music therapy in Parkinson's disease: An integrative method for motor and emotional rehabilitation. *Psychosomatic Medicine, 62*, 386–393.

Page, S. J., Levine, P., & Leonard, A. (2007). Mental practice in chronic stroke: Results of a randomized, placebo-controlled trial. *Stroke, 38*, 1293–1297.

Park, M. K., & Lee, E. S. (2004). The effect of aroma inhalation method on stress responses of nursing students. *Taehan Kanho Hakhoe Chi, 34*, 344–351.

Pawlow, L., & Jones, G. (2002). The impact of abbreviated progressive muscle relaxation on salivary cortisol. *Biological Psychology, 60*, 1–16.

Pawlow, L., & Jones, G. (2005). The impact of abbreviated progressive muscle relaxation on salivary cortisol and salivary immunoglobulin A (sIgA). *Applied Psychophysiology and Biofeedback, 30*, 375–387.

Penninx, B. W., Rejeski, W. J., Pandya, J., Miller, M. E., Di Bari, M., Applegate, W. B., & Pahor, M. (2002). Exercise and depressive symptoms: A comparison of aerobic and resistance exercise effects on emotional and physical function in older persons with high and low depressive symptomatology. *Journals of Gerontology Series B: Psychological Sciences and Social Sciences, 57*, 124–132.

Peper, E., Wilson, V. S., Gibney, K. H., Huber, K., Harvey, R., & Shumay, D. M. (2003). The integration of electromyography (SEMG) at the workstation: Assessment, treatment, and prevention of repetitive strain injury (RSI). *Applied Psychophysiology and Biofeedback, 28*, 167–182.

Perry, N., & Perry, E. (2006). Aromatherapy in the management of psychiatric disorders: Clinical and neuropharmacological perspective. *CNS Drugs, 20*, 257–280.

Pilkington, K., Kirkwood, G., Rampes, H., Fisher, P., & Richardson, J. (2005). Homeopathy for depression: A systematic review of the research evidence. *Journal of the Faculty of Homeopathy, 94*, 153–163.

Pilkington, K., Kirkwood, G., Rampes, H., Fisher, P., & Richardson, J. (2006). Homeopathy for anxiety and anxiety disorders: A systematic review of the research. *Journal of the Faculty of Homeopathy, 95*, 151–162.

Piotrowski, M. M., Paterson, C., Mitchinson, A., Kim, H. M., Kirsh, M., & Hinshaw, D. B. (2003). Massage as adjuvant therapy in the management of acute postoperative pain: A preliminary study in men. *Journal of the American College of Surgeons, 197*, 1037–1046.

Pippa, L., Manzoli, L., Corti, I., Congedo, G., Romanazzi, L., & Parruti, G. (2007). Functional capacity after traditional Chinese medicine (Qigong) training in patients with chronic atrial fibrillation: A randomized controlled trial. *Preventive Cardiology, 10,* 22–25.

Qin, L., Au, S., Choy, W., Leung, P., Neff, M., Lee, K., et al. (2002). Regular Tai Chi Chuan exercise may retard bone loss in postmenopausal women: A case-control study. *Archives of Physical Medicine and Rehabilitation, 83,* 1355–1359.

Qin, L., Choy, W., Leung, K., Au, P., Hung, S., Dambacher, W., & Chan, K. (2005). Beneficial effects of regular Tai Chi exercise on musculoskeletal system. *Journal of Bone and Mineral Metabolism, 23,* 186–190.

Quinn, C., Chandler, C., & Moraska, A. (2002). Massage therapy and frequency of chronic tension headaches. *American Journal of Public Health, 92,* 1657–1661.

Rainville, P., Duncan, G., Price, D., Carrier, B., & Bushnell, M. (1997). Pain affect encoded in human anterior cingulate but not somatosensory cortex. *Anesthesiology, 92,* 1257–1267.

Ramachandran, A., Rosengren, K., Yang, Y., & Hsiao-Wecksler, E. (2007). Effect of Tai Chi on gait and obstacle crossing behaviors in middle-aged adults. *Gait and Posture, 26,* 248–255.

Raschetti, R., Menniti-Ippolito, F., Forcella, E., & Bianchi, C. (2005). Complementary and alternative medicine in the scientific literature. *Journal of Alternative and Complementary Medicine, 11,* 209–212.

Ratcliffe, J., Thomas, K., MacPherson, H., & Brazier, J. (2006). A randomised controlled trial of acupuncture care for persistent low back pain: Cost effectiveness analysis. *British Medical Journal, 333,* 626–628.

Rausch, S., Gramling, S., & Auerbach, S. (2006). Effects of a single session of large-group meditation and progressive muscle relaxation training on stress reduction, reactivity, and recovery. *International Journal of Stress Management, 13,* 273–290.

Raymond, J., Sajid, I., Parkinson, L. A., & Gruzelier, J. (2005). Biofeedback and dance performance: A preliminary investigation. *Applied Psychophysiology and Biofeedback, 30,* 64–73.

Raymond, J., Varney, C., Parkinson, L. A., & Gruzelier, J. H. (2005). The effects of alpha/theta neurofeedback on personality and mood. *Brain Research, 23,* 287–292.

Reid, M. R., Mackinnon, L. T., & Drummond, P. D. (2001). The effects of stress management on symptoms of upper respiratory tract infection, secretory immunoglobulin A, and mood in young adults. *Journal of Psychosomatic Research, 51,* 721–728.

Remington, R. (2002). Calming music and hand massage with agitated elderly. *Nursing Research, 51,* 317–323.

Rho, K., Han, S., Kim, K., & Lee, M. (2006). Effects of aromatherapy massage on anxiety and self-esteem in Korean elderly women: A pilot study. *International Journal of Neuroscience, 116,* 1447–1455.

Ribeiro, M. M., Silva, A. G., Santos, N. S., Guazzelle, I., Matos, L. N., Trombetta, I. C., et al. (2005). Diet and exercise training restore blood pressure and vasodilatory responses during physiological maneuvers in obese children. *Circulation, 111,* 1915–1923.

Richards, K. C. (1998). Effect of a back massage and relaxation intervention on sleep in critically ill patients. *American Journal of Critical Care*, *7*, 288–299.

Richards, S. C., & Scott, D. L. (2002). Prescribed exercise in people with fibromyalgia: Parallel group randomised controlled trial. *British Medical Journal*, *27*, 185.

Riskin, J., & Frankel, F. (1994). A history of medical hypnosis. *Psychiatric Clinics of North America*, *17*, 601–609.

Rohan, K. (2003). Mindfulness-based cognitive therapy for depression: A new approach to preventing relapse and overcoming resistance in cognitive therapy. *Psychiatry: Interpersonal and Biological Processes*, *66*, 272–281.

Rooks, D. S., Silverman, C. B., & Kantrowitz, F. G. (2002). The effects of progressive strength training and aerobic exercise on muscle strength and cardiovascular fitness in women with fibromyalgia: A pilot study. *Arthritis and Rheumatism*, *47*, 22–28.

Rosen, H. (1960). Hypnosis: Applications and misapplications. *JAMA*, *172*, 683–687.

Ruan, W. J., Lai, M. D., & Zhou, J. G. (2006). Anticancer effects of Chinese herbal medicine, science or myth? *Journal of Zhejiang University. Science. B. 7*, 1006–1014.

Rydeard, R., Leger, A., & Smith, D. (2006). Pilates-based therapeutic exercise: Effects on subjects with nonspecific chronic low back pain and functional disability: A randomized controlled trial. *Journal of Orthopaedic and Sports Physical Therapy*, *36*, 472–484.

Saadat, H., Drummond-Lewis, J., Maranets, I., Kaplan, D., Saadat, A., Wang, S., & Kain, Z. (2006). Hypnosis reduces preoperative anxiety in adult patients. *Anesthesia & Analgesia*, *102*, 1394–1396.

Saeki, Y., & Mayumi, S. (2001). Physiological effects of inhaling fragrances. *International Journal of Aromatherapy*, *11*, 118–125.

Salzberg, C., Miller, A., & Johnson, L. (1995). Acupuncture: History, clinical uses, and proposed physiology. *Physical Medicine and Rehabilitation Clinics of North America*, *6*, 905–916.

Samdup, D. Z., Smith, R. G., & Il Song, S. (2006). The use of complementary and alternative medicine in children with chronic medical conditions. *American Journal of Physical Medicine and Rehabilitation*, *85*, 842–846.

Sanders, C., Diego, M., Fernandez, M., Field, T., Hernandez-Reif, M., & Roca A. (2002). EEG asymmetry responses to lavender and rosemary aromas in adults and infants. *International Journal of Neuroscience*, *112*, 1305–1320.

Sayette, M. A., & Parrott, D. J. (1999). Effects of olfactory stimuli on urge reduction in smokers. *Experimental and Clinical Psychopharmacology*, *7*, 151–159.

Schröder, S., Liepert, J., Remppis, A., & Greten, J. (2007). Acupuncture treatment improves nerve conduction in peripheral neuropathy. *European Journal of Neurology*, *14*, 276–281.

Schulz-Stubner, S., Krings, T., Meister, I., Rex, S., Thron, A., & Rossaint, R. (2004). Clinical hypnosis modulates functional magnetic resonance imaging signal intensities and pain perception in a thermal stimulation paradigm. *Regional Anesthesia and Pain Medicine, 29*, 549–556.

Segal, N., Hein, J., & Basford, J. (2004). The effects of Pilates training on flexibility and body composition: An observational study. *Archives of Physical Medicine and Rehabilitation, 85*, 1977–1981.

Segal, Z., Williams, J., & Teasdale, J. (2002). *Mindfulness-based cognitive therapy for depression*. New York: Guilford Press.

Seki, K., Chisaka, M., Eriguchi, M., Yanagie, H., Hisa, T., Osada, I., et al. (2005). An attempt to integrate Western and Chinese medicine: Rationale for applying Chinese medicine as chronotherapy against cancer. *Biomedicine and Pharmacotherapy, 1*, 132–140.

Sendelbach, S., Halm, M., Doran, K., Miller, E. H., & Gaillard, P. (2006). Effects of music therapy on physiological and psychological outcomes for patients undergoing cardiac surgery. *Annals of Thoracic Surgery, 81*, 205–206.

Sharma, S., & Kaur, J. (2006). Hypnosis and pain management. *Nursing Journal of India, 97*, 129–131.

Sheiman, U., Gross, M., Reuter, R., & Kellner, H. (2002). Improved procedure of colonoscopy under accompanying music therapy. *European Journal of Medical Research, 28*, 131–134.

Shenefelt, P. D. (2003). Biofeedback, cognitive–behavioral methods, and hypnosis in dermatology: Is it all in your mind? *Dermatological Therapy, 16*, 114–122.

Sherman, K. J., Cherkin, D. C., Erro, J., Miglioretti, D. L., & Deyo, R. A. (2005). Comparing yoga, exercise, and a self-care book for chronic low back pain: A randomized, controlled trial. *Annals of Internal Medicine, 143*, 849–856.

Shin, L. M., Orr, S. P., Carson, M. A., Rauch, S. L., Macklin, M. L., Lasko, N. B., et al. (2004). Regional cerebral blood flow in the amygdala and medial prefrontal cortex during traumatic imagery in male and female Vietnam veterans with PTSD. *Archives of General Psychiatry, 61*, 168–176.

Shin, Y. H., Kim, T. I., Shin, M. S., & Juon, H. S. (2004). Effect of acupressure on nausea and vomiting during chemotherapy cycle for Korean postoperative stomach cancer patients. *Cancer Nursing, 27*, 267–274.

Shor-Posner, G., Hernandez-Reif, M., Miguez, M. J., Fletcher, M., Quintero, N., Baez, J., et al. (2006). Impact of a massage therapy clinical trial on immune status in young Dominican children infected with HIV-1. *Journal of Alternative and Complementary Medicine, 12*, 511–516.

Shor-Posner, G., Miguez, M. J., Hernandez-Reif, M., Perez-Then, E., & Fletcher, M. (2004). Massage treatment in HIV-1 infected Dominican children: A preliminary report on the efficacy of massage therapy to preserve the immune system in children without antiretroviral medication. *Journal of Alternative and Complementary Medicine, 10*, 1093–1095.

Shulman, K. R., & Jones, G. E. (1996). The effectiveness of massage therapy intervention on reducing anxiety in the work place. *Journal of Applied Behavioral Science, 32*, 160–173.

Sibinga, E. M. S., Ottolini, M. C., Duggan, A. K., & Wilson, M. H. (2004). Parent–pediatrician communication about complementary and alternative medicine use for children. *Clinical Pediatrics, 43*, 367–373.

Sidorenko, V. (2000a). Clinical application of medical resonance therapy music in high-risk pregnancies. *Integrative Physiological and Behavioral Science, 35*, 199–207.

Sidorenko, V. (2000b). Effects of medical resonance therapy music in the complex treatment of epileptic patients. *Integrative Physiological and Behavioral Science, 35*, 212–217.

Siev-Ner, I., Gamus, D., Lerner-Geva, L., & Achiron, A. (2003). Reflexology treatment relieves symptoms of multiple sclerosis: A randomized controlled study. *Multiple Sclerosis, 9*, 356–361.

Sims, J. (1997). The mechanism of acupuncture analgesia: A review. *Complementary Therapies in Medicine, 5*, 102–111.

Singh, S., Malhotra, V., Singh, K., Madhu, S., & Tandon, O. (2004). Role of yoga in modifying certain cardiovascular functions in Type 2 diabetic patients. *Journal of the Association of Physicians of India, 52*, 203–206.

Sinha, D., & Efron, D. (2005). Complementary and alternative medicine use in children with attention deficit hyperactivity disorder. *Journal of Paediatrics and Child Health, 41*, 23–26.

Sloman, R. (2002). Relaxation and imagery for anxiety and depression control in community patients with advanced cancer. *Cancer Nursing, 25*, 432–435.

Smith, C., & Eckert, K. (2006). Prevalence of complementary and alternative medicine and use among children in South Australia. *Journal of Paediatrics and Child Health, 42*, 538–543.

Smith, M. C., Kemp, J., Hemphill, L., & Vojir, C. P. (2002). Outcomes of therapeutic massage for hospitalized cancer patients. *Journal of Nursing Scholarship, 34*, 257–262.

Smith, M. J., Ellenberg, S. S., Bell, L. M., & Rubin, D. M. (2008). Media coverage of the measles–mumps–rubella vaccine and autism controversy and its relationship to MMR immunization rates in the United States. *Pediatrics, 121*, e836–e843.

Smith, P., Mosscrop, D., Davies, S., Sloan, P., & Al-Ani, Z. (2007). The efficacy of acupuncture in the treatment of temporomandibular joint myofascial pain: A randomized controlled trial. *Journal of Dentistry, 35*, 259–267.

Smolen, D., Topp, R., & Singer, L. (2002). The effect of self-selected music during colonoscopy on anxiety, heart rate, and blood pressure. *Applied Nursing Research, 15*, 126–136.

Song, R., Lee, E., Lam, P., & Bae, S. (2003). Effects of Tai Chi exercise on pain, balance, muscle strength, and perceived difficulties in physical functioning in older women with osteoarthritis: A randomized clinical trial. *Journal of Rheumatology, 30*, 2039–2044.

Speca, M., Carlson, L., Goodey, E., & Angen, M. (2000). A randomized wait-list controlled clinical trial: The effect of a mindfulness meditation-based stress reduction program on mood and symptoms of stress in cancer outpatients. *Psychosomatic Medicine, 62,* 613–622.

Spies, G. (1979). Desensitization of test anxiety: Hypnosis compared with biofeedback. *American Journal of Clinical Hypnosis, 22,* 108–111.

Spinelli, M. G., & Endicott, J. (2003). Controlled clinical trial of interpersonal psychotherapy versus parenting education program for depressed pregnant women. *American Journal of Psychiatry, 160,* 555–562.

Stephenson, N. L., Weinrich, S. P., & Tavakoli, A. S. (2000). The effects of foot reflexology on anxiety and pain in patients with breast and lung cancer. *Oncology Nursing Forum, 27,* 67–72.

Streitberger, K., Ezzo, J., & Schneider, A. (2006). Acupuncture for nausea and vomiting: An update of clinical and experimental studies. *Autonomic Neuroscience, 129,* 107–117.

Streng, A., Linde, K., Hoppe, A., Pfaffenrath, V., Hammes, M., Wagenpfeil, S., et al. (2006). Effectiveness and tolerability of acupuncture compared with metoprolol in migraine prophylaxis. *Headache, 46,* 1492–1502.

Strüder, H. K., Hollman, W., Platen, P., Wöstmann, R., Ferrauti, A., & Weber, K. (1997). Effect of exercise intensity on free tryptophan to branched-chain amino acids ratio and plasma prolactin during endurance exercise. *Canadian Journal of Applied Physiology, 22,* 280–291.

Stuart, S., & Robertson, M. (2003). *Interpersonal psychotherapy: A clinician's guide.* London: Arnold.

Sunic-Omejc, M., Mihanovic, M., Bilic, A., Jurcic, D., Restek-Petrovic, B., Maric, N., et al. (2002). Efficiency of biofeedback therapy for chronic constipation in children. *Collegium Anthropologicum, 26,* 93–101.

Sunshine, W., Field, T., Schanberg, S., Quintino, O., Kilmer, T., Fierro, K., et al. (1996). Massage therapy and transcutaneous electrical stimulation effects on fibromyalgia. *Journal of Clinical Rheumatology, 2,* 18–22.

Suzuki, M., Kanamori, M., Watanabe, M., Nagasawa, S., Kojima, E., Ooshira, H., & Nakahara, D. (2004). Behavioral and endocrinological evaluation of music therapy for elderly patients with dementia. *Nursing and Health Sciences, 6,* 11–18.

Taggart, H., Arslanian, C., Bae, S., & Singh, K. (2003). Effects of Tai Chi exercise on fibromyalgia symptoms and health-related quality of life. *Orthopedic Nursing, 22,* 353–360.

Takahashi, T. (2006). Acupuncture for functional gastrointestinal disorders. *Journal of Gastroenterology, 41,* 408–417.

Takahashi, T., Murata, T., Hamada, T., Omori, M., Kosaka, H., Kikuchi, M., et al. (2005). Changes in EEG and autonomic nervous activity during meditation and their association with personality traits. *International Journal of Psychophysiology, 55,* 199–207.

Talwar, N., Crawford, M., Maratos, A., Nur, U., McDermott, O., & Proctor, S. (2006). Music therapy for inpatients with schizophrenia: Exploratory randomized controlled trials. *British Journal of Psychiatry, 189,* 405–409.

Tamir, R., Dickstein, R., & Huberman, M. (2007). Integration of motor imagery and physical practice in group treatment applied to subjects with Parkinson's disease. *Neurorehabilitation and Neural Repair, 21*, 68–75.

Tan, G., Hammond, D., & Joseph, G. (2005). Hypnosis and irritable bowel syndrome: A review of efficacy and mechanism of action. *American Journal of Clinical Hypnosis, 47*, 161–178.

Tansey, M. J., Tsalikian, E., Beck, R. W., Mauras, N., Buckingham, B. A., Weinzimer, S. A., et al. (2006). The effects of aerobic exercise on glucose and counterregulatory hormone concentrations in children with Type 1 diabetes. *Diabetes Care, 29*, 20–25.

Tavola, T., Gala, C., Conte, G., & Invernizzi, G. (1992). Traditional Chinese acupuncture in tension-type headache: A controlled study. *Pain, 48*, 325–329.

Taylor, M. J., Mazzone, M., & Wrotniak, B. H. (2005). Outcome of an exercise and educational intervention for children who are overweight. *Pediatric Physical Therapy, 17*, 180–188.

Taylor-Piliae, R., & Froelicher, E. (2004). Effectiveness of Tai Chi exercise in improving aerobic capacity: A meta-analysis. *Journal of Cardiovascular Nursing, 19*, 48–57.

Taylor-Piliae, R., Haskell, W., Waters, C., & Froelicher, E. (2006). Change in perceived psychosocial status following a 12-week Tai Chi exercise programme. *Journal of Advanced Nursing, 54*, 313–329.

Teague, A., Hahna, N., & McKinney, C. (2006). Group music therapy with women who have experienced intimate partner violence. *Music Therapy Perspectives, 24*, 80–86.

Teasdale, J. D., Segal, Z. V., & Williams, J. M. G. (1995). How does cognitive therapy prevent depressive relapse and why should attentional control (mindfulness) training help? *Behaviour Research and Therapy, 33*, 25–39.

Teasdale, J. D., Segal, Z. V., Williams, J. M., Ridgeway, V. A., Soulsby, J. M., & Lau, M. A. (2000). Prevention of relapse/recurrence in major depression by mindfulness-based cognitive therapy. *Journal of Consulting and Clinical Psychology, 68*, 615–623.

Telles, S., Mohapatra, R., & Naveen, K. (2005). Heart rate spectrum during Vipassana mindfulness meditation. *Journal of Indian Psychology, 23*, 1–5.

Telles, S., & Naveen, K. (2004). Changes in middle latency auditory evoked potentials during meditation. *Psychology and Reproduction, 94*, 398–400.

Telles, S., Reddy, S. K., & Nagendra, H. R. (2000). Oxygen consumption and respiration following two yoga relaxation techniques. *Applied Psychophysiology and Biofeedback, 25*, 221–227.

Thomas, R., & Peterson, D. (2003). A neurogenic theory of depression gains momentum. *Molecular Intervention, 3*, 441–444.

Thornton, E., Sykes, K., & Tang, W. (2004). Health benefits of Tai Chi exercise: Improved balance and blood pressure in middle-aged women. *Health Promotion International, 19*, 33–38.

Tornek, A., Field, T., Hernandez-Reif, M., Diego, M., & Jones, N. (2003). Music effects on EEG in intrusive and withdrawn mothers with depressive symptoms. *Psychiatry, 66*, 234–243.

Travis, F., & Arenander, A. (2006). Cross-sectional and longitudinal study effects of transcendental meditation practice on interhemispheric frontal asymmetry and frontal coherence. *International Journal of Neuroscience, 116*, 1519–1538.

Trinh, K., Graham, N., Gross, A., Goldsmith, C., Wang, E., Cameron, I., & Kay, T. (2007). Acupuncture for neck disorders. *Spine, 32*, 236–243.

Troosters, T., Gosselink, R., & Decramer, M. (2001). Exercise training in COPD: How to distinguish responders from nonresponders. *Journal of Cardiopulmonary Rehabilitation, 21*, 10.

Tryon, W. W. (2005). Possible mechanisms for why desensitization and exposure therapy work. *Clinical Psychology Review, 25*, 67–95.

Tsai, J., Wang, W., Chan, P., Lin, L., Wang, C., Tomlinson, B., et al. (2003). The beneficial effects of Tai Chi Chuan on blood pressure and lipid profile and anxiety status in a randomized controlled trial. *Journal of Alternative and Complementary Medicine, 9*, 747–754.

Tsang, W., & Hui-Chan, W. (2004a). Effect of 4- and 8-week intensive Tai Chi training on balance control in the elderly. *Medicine & Science in Sports & Exercise, 36*, 648–657.

Tsang, W., & Hui-Chan, W. (2004b). Effects of exercise on joint sense and balance in elderly men: Tai Chi versus golf. *Medicine & Science in Sports & Exercise, 36*, 658–667.

Tsay, S. L., Rong, J. R., & Lin, P. F. (2003). Acupoints massage in improving the quality of sleep and quality of life in patients with end-stage renal disease. *Journal of Advanced Nursing, 42*, 134–142.

Tse, M. M., Chan, M. F., & Benzie, I. F. (2005). The effect of music therapy on postoperative pain, heart rate, systolic blood pressure and analgesic use following anal surgery. *Journal of Pain and Palliative Care Pharmacotherapy, 19*, 21–29.

Tsuchiya, M., Sato, E., Inoue, M., & Asada, A. (2007). Acupuncture enhances generation of nitric oxide and increases local circulation. *Anesthesia & Analgesia, 104*, 30–37.

Turgut, G., Kaptanoglu, B., Turgut, S., Genç, O., & Tekintürk, S. (2003). Influence of acute exercise on urinary protein, creatinine, insulin-like growth factor-I (IGF-I) and IGF binding protein-3 concentrations in children. *Tohoku Journal of Experimental Medicine, 201*, 165–170.

Turner, S., Calhoun, K., & Adams, H. (Eds.). (1992). *Handbook of clinical behavior therapy.* New York: Wiley.

Uedo, N., Ishikawa, H., Morimoto, K., Ishihara, R., Narahara, H., Akedo, I., et al. (2004). Reduction in salivary cortisol level by music therapy during colonoscopy examination. *Hepatogastroenterology, 51*, 451–453.

Vainionpää, A., Korpelainen, R., Kaikkonen, H., Knip, M., Leppäluoto, J., & Jämsä T. (2007). Effect of impact exercise on physical performance and cardiovascular risk factors. *Medicine & Science in Sports & Exercise, 39*, 756–763.

Vainionpää, A., Korpelainen, R., Leppäluoto, J., & Jämsä, T. (2005). Effects of high-impact exercise on bone mineral density: A randomized controlled trial in premenopausal women. *Osteoporosis International, 16*, 191–197.

Van den Dolder, P. A., & Roberts, D. L. (2003). A trial into the effectiveness of soft tissue massage in the treatment of shoulder pain. *Australian Journal of Physiotherapy, 49*, 183–188.

Vasudeva, S., Claggett, A. L., Tietjen, G. E., & McGrady, A. V. (2003). Biofeedback-assisted relaxation in migraine headache: Relationship to cerebral blood flow velocity in the middle cerebral artery. *Headache, 43*, 245–250.

Verhagen, A., Immink, M., van der Meulen, A., & Bierma-Zeinstra, S. (2004). The efficacy of Tai Chi Chuan in older adults: A systematic review. *Family Practice, 21*, 107–113.

Vincent, S., & Thomson, J. (1928). The effect of hyper-respiratory on the blood-pressure in man. *Journal of Physiology, 66*, 307–315.

Walach, H., Jonas, W. B., Ives, J., van Wijk, R., & Weingärtner, O. (2005). Research on homeopathy: State of the art. *Journal of Alternative and Complementary Medicine, 11*, 813–829.

Waldon, E. (2001). The effects of group music therapy on mood states and cohesiveness in adult oncology patients. *Journal of Music Therapy, 38*, 212–238.

Wall, R. (2005). Tai Chi and mindfulness-based stress reduction in a Boston public middle school. *Journal of Pediatrics and Health Care, 19*, 230–237.

Wang, C., Collet, J., & Lau, J. (2004). The effects of Tai Chi on health outcomes in patients with chronic conditions: A systematic review. *Archives of Internal Medicine, 164*, 493–501.

Wang, H. L., & Keck, J. F. (2004). Foot and hand massage as an intervention for postoperative pain. *Pain Management and Nursing, 5*, 59–65.

Wang, Y., Taylor, L., Pearl, M., & Chang, L. (2004). Effects of Tai Chi exercise on physical and mental health of college students. *American Journal of Chinese Medicine, 32*, 453–459.

Watanabe, E., Fukuda, S., & Shirakawa, T. (2005). Effects among healthy subjects of the duration of regularly practicing a guided imagery program. *BMC Complementary and Alternative Medicine, 5*, 21.

Watkins, J., & Watkins, H. (1990). Dissociation and displacement: Where goes the "ouch"? *American Journal of Clinical Hypnosis, 33*, 1–10.

Wayne, P., Krebs, D., Wolf, S., Gill-Body, K., Scarborough, D., McGibbon, C., et al. (2004). Can Tai Chi improve vestibulopathic postural control? *Archives of Physical Medicine and Rehabilitation, 85*, 142–152.

Weber, S. (2004). The effects of relaxation exercises on anxiety levels in psychiatric inpatients. *Journal of Holistic Nursing, 14*, 196–205.

Weidenhammer, W., Linde, K., Streng, A., Hoppe, A., & Melchart, D. (2007). Acupuncture for chronic low back pain in routine care: A multicenter observational study. *Clinical Journal of Pain, 23*, 128–135.

Weinstein, E., & Au, P. (1991). Use of hypnosis before and during angioplasty. *American Journal of Clinical Hypnosis, 34*, 29–37.

Weiss, M., Nordlie, J., & Siegel, E. (2005). Mindfulness-based stress reduction as an adjunct to outpatient psychotherapy. *Psychotherapy and Psychosomatics, 74*, 108–112.

Weissbecker, I., Salmon, P., Studts, J., Floyd, A., Dedert, E., & Sephton, S. (2002). Mindfulness-based stress reduction and sense of coherence among women with fibromyalgia. *Journal of Clinical Psychology in Medical Settings, 9*, 297–307.

Werntoft, E., & Dykes, A.K. (2001). Effect of acupressure on nausea and vomiting during pregnancy: A randomized, placebo-controlled, pilot study. *Journal of Reproductive Medicine, 46*, 835–839.

Wharton, R., & Lewis, G. (1986). Complementary medicine and the general practitioner. *British Medical Journal, 292*, 1498–1500.

White, A., & Moody, R. (2006). The effects of auricular acupuncture on smoking cessation may not depend on the point chosen—An exploratory meta-analysis. *Acupuncture in Medicine, 24*, 149–156.

White, A., Foster, N., Cummings, M., & Barlas, P. (2007). Acupuncture treatment for chronic knee pain: A systematic review. *Rheumatology, 46*, 384–390.

White, P., Lewith, G., Prescott, P., & Conway, J. (2004). Acupuncture versus placebo for the treatment of chronic mechanical neck pain. *Annals of Internal Medicine, 141*, 911–919.

Whitehead, W. (2006). Hypnosis for irritable bowel syndrome: The empirical evidence of therapeutic effects. *International Journal of Clinical and Experimental Hypnosis, 54*, 7–20.

Wilk, C., & Turkoski, B. (2001). Progressive muscle relaxation in cardiac rehabilitation: A pilot study. *Rehabilitation Nursing, 26*, 238–243.

Wilkinson, S., Aldridge, J., Salmon, I., Cain, E., & Wilson, B. (1999). An evaluation of aromatherapy massage in palliative care. *Palliative Medicine, 3*, 409–417.

Wilkinson, S., Love, S., Westcombe, A., Gambles, M., Burgess, C., Cargill, A., et al. (2007). Effectiveness of aromatherapy massage in the management of anxiety and depression in patients with cancer: A multicenter randomized controlled trial. *Journal of Clinical Oncology, 25*, 532–539.

Williams, K., Kolar, M., Reger, B., & Pearson, J. (2001). Evaluation of a wellness-based mindfulness stress reduction intervention: A controlled trial. *American Journal of Health Promotion, 15*, 422–432.

Williams, K. A., Petronis, J., Smith, D., Goodrich, D., Wu, J., Ravi, N., et al. (2005). Effect of Iyengar yoga therapy for chronic low back pain. *Pain, 115*, 107–117.

Williams, N. H., Edwards, R. T., Linck, O., Muntz, R., Hibbs, R., Wilkinson, C., et al. (2004). Cost-utility analysis of osteopathy in primary care: Results from a pragmatic randomized controlled trial. *Family Practice, 21*, 643–650.

Wilson, K., Dowson, C., & Mangin, D. (2007). Prevalence of complementary and alternative medicine use in Christchurch, New Zealand: Children attending general practice versus paediatric outpatients. *New Zealand Medical Journal, 120*, 1–9.

Witt, C., Jena, S., Brinkhaus, B., Liecker, B., Wegscheider, K., & Willich, S. (2006). Acupuncture for patients with chronic pain. *Pain, 125,* 98–106.

Wolf, S. L., O'Grady, M., Easley, K. A., Guo, Y., Kressig, R. W., & Kutner, M. (2006). The influence of intense Tai Chi training on physical performance and hemodynamic outcomes in transitionally frail older adults. *Journals of Gerontology Series A: Biological Sciences and Medical Sciences, 61,* 184–189.

Wolpe, J. (1990). *The practice of behavior therapy.* New York: Pergamon Press.

Wu, G., & Keyes, L. (2006). Group tele-exercise for improving balance in elders. *Telemedicine Journal and e-Health, 12,* 561–570.

Wu, H. S., Wu, S. C., Lin, J. G., & Lin, L.C. (2004). Effectiveness of acupressure in improving dyspnoea in chronic obstructive pulmonary disease. *Journal of Advanced Nursing, 45,* 252–259.

Wynd, C. A. (2005). Guided health imagery for smoking cessation and long-term abstinence. *Journal of Nursing Scholarship, 37,* 245–250.

Xu, H., Lawson, D., Kras, A., & Ryan, D. (2005). The use of preventive strategies for bone loss. *American Journal of Chinese Medicine, 33,* 299–306.

Yagci, S., Kibar, Y., Akay, O., Kilic, S., Erdemir, F., Gok, F., & Dayanc, M. (2005). The effect of biofeedback treatment on voiding and urodynamic parameters in children with voiding dysfunction. *Journal of Urology, 174,* 1994–1997.

Yeh, G., Wood, M., Lorell, B., Stevenson, L., Eisenberg, D., Wayne, P., et al. (2004). Effects of Tai Chi mind–body movement therapy on functional status and exercise capacity in patients with chronic heart failure: A randomized controlled trial. *American Journal of Medicine, 117,* 541–548.

Yeh, M., Lee, T., Chen, H., & Chao, T. (2006). The influences of Chan-Chuang Qi Gong therapy on complete blood cell counts in breast cancer patients treated with chemotherapy. *Cancer Nursing, 29,* 149–155.

Yeh, S., Chuang, H., Lin, L., Hsiao, C., & Eng, H. (2006). Regular Tai Chi exercise enhances functional mobility and CD4CD25 regulatory T cells. *British Journal of Sports Medicine, 40,* 239–243.

Yogendra, J., Yogendra, H. J., Ambardekar, S., Lele, R. D., Shetty, S., Dave, M., & Husein, N. (2004). Beneficial effects of yoga lifestyle on reversibility of ischaemic heart disease: Caring heart project of International Board of Yoga. *Journal of the Association of Physicians of India, 52,* 283–289.

Yoo, H. J., Ahn, S. H., Kim, S. B., Kim, W. K., & Han, O. S. (2005). Efficacy of progressive muscle relaxation training and guided imagery in reducing chemotherapy side effects in patients with breast cancer and in improving their quality of life. *Supportive Care in Cancer, 13,* 826–833.

Yucha, C. B., Tsai, P. S., Calderon, K. S., & Tian, L. (2005). Biofeedback-assisted relaxation training for essential hypertension: Who is most likely to benefit? *Journal of Cardiovascular Nursing, 20,* 198–205.

Yussman, S. M., Ryan, S. A., Auinger, P., & Weitzman, M. (2004). Visits to complementary and alternative medicine providers by children and adolescents in the United States. *Ambulatory Pediatrics, 4,* 429–435.

Zaborowska, E., Brynhildsen, J., Damberg, S., Fredriksson, M., Lindh-Astrand, L., Nedstrand, E., et al. (2007). Effects of acupuncture, applied relaxation, estrogens and placebo on hot flushes in postmenopausal women: An analysis of two prospective, parallel, randomized studies. *Climacteric, 10,* 38–45.

Zachariae, R., & Bjerring, P. (1994). Laser-induced pain-related brain potentials and sensory pain ratings in high and low hypnotizable subjects during hypnotic suggestions of relaxation, dissociated imagery, focused analgesia, and placebo. *International Journal of Clinical and Experimental Hypnosis, 42,* 56–80.

Zainuddin, Z., Newton, M., Sacco, P., & Nosaka, K. (2005). Effects of massage on delayed-onset muscle soreness, swelling, and recovery of muscle function. *Journal of Athletic Training, 40,* 174–180.

Zhang, J., Dean, D., Nosco, D., Strathopulos, D., & Floros, M. (2006). Effect of chiropractic care on heart rate variability and pain in a multisite clinical study. *Journal of Manipulative and Physiological Therapeutics, 29,* 267–274.

Zhang, W., Leonard, T., Bath-Hextall, F., Chambers, C. A., Lee, C., Humphreys, R., & Williams, H. C. (2005). Chinese herbal medicine for atopic eczema. *Cochrane Database of Systematic Reviews, 4,* CD002291.

Zhao, H. L., Tong, P. C., & Chan, J. C. (2006). Traditional Chinese medicine in the treatment of diabetes. In J. P. Bantle & G. Slama (Eds.), *Nutritional management of diabetes mellitus and dysmetabolic syndrome: Nestlé nutrition workshop series: Clinical and performance programme* (Vol. 11, pp. 25–29). Basel, Switzerland: Karger.

Zinn, M., & Zinn, M. (2003). Psychophysiology for performing artists. In M. S. Schwartz & F. Andrasik (Eds.), *Biofeedback: A practitioner's guide* (3rd ed., pp. 545–559). New York: Guilford Press.

AUTHOR INDEX

Kabat-Zinn, J., 8, 127, 128
Kaiser, D. R., 142
Kaiser, J., 147
Kamei, T., 64, 131
Kankane, A., 65
Kantrowitz, F. G., 76
Kaplan, J. Z., 116
Kaptanoglu, B., 143
Karavidas, M. K., 122
Karst, M., 46
Kato, Y., 96
Katula, J., 57
Katz, J., 27
Katz, J. L., 47
Kaufman, C., 142
Kaur, J., 113
Kaur, P., 64
Kaur, S., 64
Kaushik, R. M., 123
Keck, J. F., 34
Keefer, L., 132
Keenan, N. L., 18
Kelley, G. A., 143
Kelley, K. S., 143
Kellner, H., 85
Kelly, A. S., 142
Kelmanson, I. A., 140
Kemp, J., 37
Kemps, E., 107
Kenchington, P., 66
Kern, P., 145
Kersig, S., 131
Keyes, L., 58
Khalsa, S. B., 65
Kharti, P., 75
Khumar, S. S., 64
Kiejna, A., 81
Kiive, E., 75
Kim, H. J., 94
Kim, J., 87, 94
Kim, J. H., 36
Kim, K., 92
Kim, M. J., 94
Kim, M. S., 36
Kim, S. B., 101
Kim, T. I., 40
Kim, W. K., 101

Kimata, H., 87
Kimura, H., 64
Kimura, K., 64
Kimura, T., 144
Kirkpatrick, N., 101
Kirkwood, G., 18
Kjaer, T., 130
Klerman, G. L., 9
Ko, G., 57, 59
Koger, S., 86
Kohen, D. P., 146
Kolar, M., 131
Kolasinski, S. L., 65
Kolich, M., 31
Kominski, G. F., 20
Koo, J., 15
Korpelainen, R., 77
Kosten, T. R., 47
Krakow, B., 106
Kralik, S., 141
Kranitz, L., 124
Kras, A., 56
Krasnegor, J., 31
Kristal, A., 68
Kuboki, T., 124
Kubota, N., 88
Kubsch, S. M., 34
Kuhn, C., 9, 29
Kumano, H., 64
Kumar, R. C., 28
Kuo, B. I., 40
Kuo, C., 57
Kuo, C. H., 40
Kuttner, L., 141
Kwon, I. S., 87
Kwon, Y., 48

Laaksonen, D. E., 77
LaBrot, T., 20
Lai, H. L., 83, 84, 144
Lai, J., 58
Lai, M. D., 15
Lajoie, Y., 126
Lam, P., 56
Lan, C., 58
Landers, D. M., 73
Lang, E., 116

Langevin, H. M., 16
Larun, L., 144
Lau, J., 59
Lau, M., 7, 8
Lau, M. A., 9
Lawlor, D. A., 75
Lawson, D., 56
Lazar, S., 130
Lazaroff, I., 82, 87
Leathem, J., 55
Lebaschi, A., 50
LeDoux, J., 90
Lee, D., 85
Lee, E., 56
Lee, E. S., 92
Lee, H., 50
Lee, H. K., 93, 140
Lee, M., 92, 94
Lee, S., 131
Lee, T., 60
Leger, A., 70
Lehr, S., 93
Lehrer, P. M., 124, 125
Lehrner, J., 93
Leivadi, S., 36
Leonard, A., 108
Leonard, C., 136
Leppäluoto, J., 77
Leppämäki, S. J., 74
Lerner-Geva, L., 41
Leung, P. C., 16
Leung, T. F., 15
Levine, P., 108
Levy, M., 65
Lewinsohn, P. M., 8
Lewis, D., 36
Lewis, G., 44
Lewith, G., 45
Lewith, G. T., 93
Li, F., 55, 56, 58
Li, K., 44
Li, P., 88
Liepert, J., 50
Lin, J. G., 40, 41
Lin, L., 57
Lin, L. C., 40, 41
Lin, M., 58

Lin, P. F., 41
Linde, K., 48
Liossi, C., 146
Lira, P. I., 145
Lis-Balchin, M., 92
Littman, A., 68
Liu, Y., 58
Loewy, J., 145
Lönnqvist, J. K., 74
Looney, S. W., 82
Lotman, D. G., 136
Louie, S. W., 110
Lowe, G., 101
Lu, L., 88
Lu, W., 57
Lucas-Polomeni, M. M., 146
Lucini, D., 98
Lutzenberger, W., 147

Ma, K. C., 15
Ma, S., 9, 131
Maaroos, J., 75
Maciaszek, J., 58
Mackay, E., 76
Mackinnon, L. T., 109
MacPherson, H., 49
Madanmohan, 67
Madeleine, P., 124
Madhu, S., 67, 74
Mahajan, S. K., 123
Mainous, R. O., 82
Maiorana, A., 77
Majumdar, M., 131
Malhotra, V., 67, 74
Manchanda, S. C., 66
Mangin, D., 136
Manjunath, N. K., 65, 141
Manocha, R., 66, 127
Margolin, A., 47
Marks, G. B., 66
Martin, A., 123
Martin, D., 48
Martinez, A., 11, 35, 83
Martinez, C., 145
Martyn-St James, M., 78
Marwinski, G., 93
Mason, O., 131

Mathews, A., 106
Matolic, M., 141
Mattos, S. S., 145
Mayumi, S., 95
Mazzone, M., 142
McCaffery, M., 97
McCallie, M., 99
McCubbin, J., 98
McGinnis, R. A., 125
McGlynn, F. D., 101
McGrady, A. V., 123, 125
McHugh, T., 106
McKinney, C., 84
McMain, S., 7, 8
Medlicott, M. S., 123
Mehl-Madrona, L. E., 17
Meier, M., 95
Meister, I. G., 104
Melchart, D., 49
Melzack, R., 45
Menniti-Ippolito, F., 21
Menzies, V., 108
Merboldt, K. D., 105
Metz, R. D., 20
Miansi, S., 83
Michalsen, A., 63
Middaugh, S. J., 123
Miglioretti, D. L., 65
Miguez, M. J., 140
Miller, A., 44
Miller, E. H., 85
Miller, K., 100
Mimura, K., 58
Minamino, M., 96
Ming, J. L., 40
Mior, S. A., 20
Misao, H., 92
Missaghian, M., 141
Mochel, M., 16
Modi, N., 28
Moffet, H., 45
Mohamed, A. I., 31
Mohapatra, R., 128
Mohn, A., 143
Mollasiotis, A., 101
Monahan, P. O., 87
Monastra, D. M., 147

Monastra, V. J., 146, 147
Money, M., 17
Monheim, C. J., 145
Montgomery, G., 116
Moody, R., 47
Moore, L. E., 116
Moore, N. C., 119, 122
Moos, R., 74
Moraska, A., 33
Morgenstern, H., 20
Mori, H., 38
Mori, M., 96
Moritani, T., 144
Moss, M., 91
Mosscrop, D., 50
Motivala, S., 57
Motomura, N., 91
Munro, B. J., 126
Mur, E. J., 123
Murray, J., 45
Mustian, K., 57

Nagai, N., 144
Nagarathna, R., 67
Nagendra, H. R., 67, 68
Nakao, M., 124
Nakata, Y., 78
Nam, E. S., 94
Narendran, S., 67
Narendran, V., 67
National Center for Complementary
    and Alternative Medicine, 3
National Institutes of Health, 46
Nauman, E., 17
Naveen, K., 68, 128
Nayak, S., 86
Nedstrand, E., 52
Nelson, C. F., 20
Nelson, J., 106
Nelson, V. S., 136
Neri, I., 50
Nestoriuc, Y., 123
Neveau, T., 34
Newton, M., 38
Newton, P., 110
Nickel, C., 100
Nilsson, U., 85

Robertson, M., 9
Rodriguez, M., 67
Rohan, K., 131
Rong, J. R., 41
Rooks, D. S., 76
Rosen, H., 114
Rosen, L., 137
Rosengren, K., 58
Rounsaville, B. J., 9
Roy, M., 87
Ruan, W. J., 15
Rubin, D. M., 137
Rull, M., 117
Ryan, D., 56
Ryan, S. A., 135
Rydeard, R., 70
Rykov, M. H., 145
Rymaszewska, J., 81

Saadat, H., 116
Sacco, P., 38
Saeki, Y., 95
Sahai, A., 68
Sajid, I., 126
Sakurai, A., 91
Sala, J., 117
Salmon, I., 95
Salome, C. M., 66
Salzberg, C., 44
Samdup, D. Z., 136
Sanders, C., 24, 92
Sando, W., 116
Sands, L., 100, 108
Sato, E., 47
Sayette, M. A., 94
Schanberg, S., 9, 29, 30
Schlicht, W., 75
Schluter, P., 82
Schmid, W., 83
Schneider, A., 51
Schroder, S., 50
Schulz-Stubner, S., 115
Schumacher, H. R., Jr., 65
Scott, D. L., 76
Seeley, J. R., 8
Segal, N., 70

Segal, Z., 131
Segal, Z. V., 8
Seki, K., 16
Sendelbach, S., 85
Sexton, H., 107
Sforzo, G. A., 38
Shapira, D. E., 145
Sharma, C., 65
Sharma, N., 65
Sharma, R., 21
Sharma, S., 113
Shatapathy, C. C., 68
Shaw, K., 37
Sheiman, U., 85
Shenefelt, P. D., 126
Sherman, K. J., 65
Shiflett, S., 86
Shimshoni, R., 82, 87
Shin, L. M., 106
Shin, M. S., 40
Shin, Y. H., 40
Shinagawa, N., 88
Shirakawa, T., 105
Shlik, J., 75
Shor-Posner, G., 140
Shulman, K. R., 27
Sibinga, E. M. S., 135
Siboni, L., 46
Sidorenko, V., 85, 86
Siegel, E., 131
Siev-Ner, I., 41
Silverman, C. B., 76
Silverstein, J. H., 116
Sims, J., 45
Singer, L., 85
Singh, K., 56, 67, 74
Singh, M. A., 142
Singh, S., 67, 74
Sinha, D., 137
Sjøgaard, G., 124
Sledge, R. B., 87
Sletten, C., 48
Sloan, P., 50
Sloman, R., 105, 109
Slothower, M. P., 146
Smith, C., 136

Smith, D., 70
Smith, J., 99
Smith, M. C., 37
Smith, M. J., 137
Smith, P., 50
Smith, R. G., 136
Smitherman, T. A., 101
Smolen, D., 85
Søgaard, K., 124
Sollers, J., 57
Solterbeck, L. A., 91
Song, R., 56
Sostero, E., 83
Speca, M., 130–132
Spies, G., 114
Spinelli, M. G., 9
Stadler, C., 147
Stano, M., 21
Steele, J. R., 126
Steinberg, K., 130
Steinberger, J., 142
Stemplewski, R., 58
Stephenson, N. L., 41
Strapp, C. M., 91
Strathopulos, D., 20
Streitberger, K., 51
Streng, A., 49
Strüder, H. K., 74
Stuart, S., 9
Sunic-Omejc, M., 147
Sunshine, W., 32, 33
Suzuki, M., 86
Sveistrup, H., 126
Sweeney, B., 44
Swensen, T., 38
Swerdlow, B., 33
Sykes, K., 57
Szeklicki, R., 58

Taboun, S. M., 31
Taggart, H., 56
Tagliaferri, M., 15
Takahashi, T., 51, 129
Talwar, N., 84
Tamir, R., 109
Tan, G., 117

Tanaka, K., 78
Tandon, O., 67, 74
Tang, B., 115
Tang, J. L., 141
Tang, W., 57
Tansey, M. J., 143
Tavakoli, A. S., 41
Tavola, T., 49
Taylor, A. G., 108
Taylor, L., 55
Taylor, M. J., 142
Taylor, S., 33
Taylor-Piliae, R., 55, 58
Teague, A., 84
Teasdale, J. D., 8, 9, 131
Tekintürk, S., 143
Telles, S., 65, 68, 128, 141
Thayer, J., 57
Theakston, H., 31, 35
Thimas, E., 56
Thomas, K., 49
Thomas, R., 131
Thompson, B. L., 18
Thomson, J., 81
Thornton, E., 57
Tian, L., 124
Tietjen, G. E., 123
Tiggemann, M., 107
Toljan, S., 141
Tong, P. C., 15
Topp, R., 85
Toriumi, Y., 64
Tornek, A., 84
Tõru, I., 75
Travis, F., 129
Trestman, R., 130
Trinh, K., 49
Tripathy, D., 15
Troosters, T., 76
Tryon, W. W., 101
Tsai, J., 57
Tsai, P. S., 124
Tsang, P., 57
Tsang, W., 59
Tsay, S. L., 41
Tse, M. M., 86

SUBJECT INDEX

AHR (Airway Hyperresponsiveness to Methacholine), 66
Air, 14
Airway Hyperresponsiveness to Methacholine (AHR), 66
Alertness, 58, 149, 150
Alexander technique, 26–27, 160
Almond oil, 94
Alpha-1 activity, 129
Alpha band, 120
Alpha power, 27, 28
Alzheimer's disease, 149
American Academy of Medical Acupuncture, 160
American Association of Acupuncture and Oriental Medicine, 165
American Board of Medical Acupuncture, 154
American Fitness Professionals and Associates (AFPA), 155
American Institute of Vedic Studies, 165
American Massage Therapy Association, 42, 153–154, 163
American Medical Association, 18, 114
American Music Therapy Association, 156
American Oriental Body Work Association, 160, 164
American Polarity Association, 164
American Psychiatric Association, 164
American Psychological Association, 164
American Society of Clinical Hypnosis, 117, 162
American Yoga Association, 165
Amygdala, 90
Anesthesia, 114
Anesthesiologists, 154
Angina, 149
Angina pectoris, 124
Angioplasty, 114
Animal magnetism demonstrations, 113
Ankhmahor tomb, 24
Anorexia nervosa, 30, 149
Anterior cingulate gyrus, 115
Antimicrobial effects, of essential oils, 90
Anxiety and anxiety disorders
    acupuncture for, 46–47

biofeedback for, 122
effective therapies for, 149
homeopathy for, 18
imagery for, 105
massage therapy for, 27–28
meditation for, 130–131
music therapy for, 10, 11, 82
in pediatric populations, 146
progressive muscle relaxation for, 99
Tai Chi for, 55
yoga for, 63–64
APRT. *See* Abbreviated progressive relaxation training
AQLQ (Asthma Quality of Life Questionnaire), 66
Aquatherapy, 136
Arab empire, 89
Aristotle, 103
Aroma massage, 92
Aromatherapy, 10, 11, 89–96
    for addictions, 94
    for cardiovascular conditions, 94–95
    for cognitive performance/mood, 91–93
    conditions/procedures treated by, 149–151
    defined, 89
    for dysmenorrhea, 94
    empirical support for effects of, 91–96
    for immune conditions, 95–96
    origins of, 89, 90
    for osteoarthritis, 94
    for pain syndromes, 94
    for pediatric populations, 137
    popular uses of, 90
    for postoperative pain, 94
    potential mechanisms of action for, 90–91
    referring clients for, 96
    resources for, 160
    for skin aging, 95–96
    for stress, 91
    training for, 156–157
Aromatherapy Institute and Research, 161
Aroma Vera, 161
Arteriosclerosis, 149
Arthritis, 149

Asanas, 62
Aspirin, 17
Associated Bodywork and Massage Professionals (ABMP), 163
Association for Applied Psychophysiology and Biofeedback, 126
Asthma
  biofeedback for, 125
  effective therapies for, 149
  imagery for, 109–110
  in pediatric populations, 137–139, 143, 146
  and progressive muscle relaxation, 101
  yoga for, 66
Asthma Quality of Life Questionnaire (AQLQ), 66
Atopic dermatitis
  biofeedback for, 126
  Chinese herbal medicine for, 15
  and music therapy, 87
Attention-deficit/hyperactivity disorder (ADHD)
  effective therapies for, 149
  in pediatric populations, 137, 146–147
  Tai Chi for, 56
Attentiveness, 149, 150
Auricular acupuncture, 46, 47
Australia, 136
Autism, 137, 145
Autoimmune conditions
  biofeedback for, 125–126
  imagery for, 109–110
  music therapy for, 87
  physical exercise for, 76–77
  yoga for, 66–67
Ayurvedic Institute, 161
Ayurvedic medicine
  in naturopathy, 18
  origins of, 13–14
  resources for, 161

Back pain
  acupuncture for, 49
  chiropractic for, 20
  effective therapies for, 149
  music therapy for, 84–85
Baird, James, 113

Balance
  and biofeedback, 126
  effective therapies for, 149
  of energy, 44
  of life forces, 14
  and Tai Chi, 55, 58, 59
Baseline measurements, for biofeedback, 120
Basil, 90
Benign imagery, 106
Bergamot, 94
Beta band, 120
Bikram yoga, 62, 71
Biofeedback, 119–126
  for anxiety disorders, 122
  for asthma, 125
  for autoimmune conditions, 125–126
  for blood pressure, 124
  for cardiovascular disorders, 124–125
  for chronic obstructive pulmonary disease, 125
  for chronic pain, 123
  conditions/procedures treated by, 149–151
  defined, 119
  for depression, 122
  for diabetes, 125
  EEG monitoring in, 120
  EMG monitoring in, 121
  empirical support for effects of, 122–126
  for fibromyalgia, 122–123
  heart rate/heart rate variability monitoring in, 120–121
  with hypnosis, 114
  for migraine headaches, 123
  for pain syndromes, 122–124
  for pediatric populations, 146–147
  for performance enhancement, 126
  potential underlying mechanisms for effects of, 121–122
  process of, 120–121
  referring clients for, 126
  for skin conditions, 126
  skin-conductance monitoring in, 121
  for temporomandibular joint disorder, 123

Central nervous system, 44, 104
Cerebral blood flow, 81–82
Cerebral palsy, 136–137, 141, 147, 149
Certification
    in acupuncture, 154
    in biofeedback, 158
    in hypnosis, 157–158
    in massage therapy, 153
    in music therapy, 156
    in Pilates instruction, 155–156
    in yoga instruction, 155
Certification Board for Music Therapists
    exam, 156
Cervical lordosis, 69
Cesarean deliveries, 82, 85
CES–D (Center for Epidemiological
    Studies–Depression), 64
Chair massage, 27
Chamomile, 92
Change-oriented mindfulness mediation,
    8
Chemotherapy
    acupressure with, 40
    with Chinese herbal medicine, 15
    effective therapies for, 149
    nausea/vomiting with, 149
    and progressive muscle relaxation,
        101
Chest infections, 90
Chi (Qi), 15, 44
Chi Gong, 11, 53, 59–60
Children, CAM therapies for. *See*
    Pediatric populations, CAM
    therapies for
Chinese martial arts, 53
Chinese medicine
    history of, 14–16
    massage therapy in, 24
    in naturopathy, 18
    resources for, 165
Chinese music, 87–88
Chiropractic, 19–21, 136, 137
Cholesterol
    effective therapies for, 149
    and physical exercise, 78, 143
    and Tai Chi, 57
Cholinergic function, 15

Chronic fatigue syndrome, 33, 149
Chronic lung disease, 76
Chronic obstructive pulmonary disease
    (COPD)
    acupressure for, 41
    biofeedback for, 125
    effective therapies for, 150
    imagery for, 110
    physical exercise for, 75–76
Chronic pain, 123
Circuit training, 77
Citronella, 90, 95
Clary sage, 93, 94
Classical music, 10, 11, 81, 86
Clay burners, 89
Cocaine users, 47
Cognitive–behavioral therapy, 7–9
Cognitive function, 141
Cognitive performance, 91–93, 150
Cold (with massage), 24
Colitis, 51, 150
Colonoscopy, 85, 150
Commission on Massage Training
    Accreditation, 154
Complementary and alternative medi-
    cine (CAM) therapies, 3
    Ayurvedic medicine, 13–14
    Chinese medicine, 14–16
    chiropractic, 19–21
    conditions/procedures effectively
        treated with, 149–151
    homeopathy, 17–18
    Native American medicine, 17
    naturopathy, 18–19
    osteopathy, 19
    resources for, 159–165
    shamanism, 16–17
    training for, 11
    Web site for, 159
Compression, 25
Concentration, 11
Concentrative meditation, 127
Constipation, 147
Contemplative Outreach, Ltd., 163
COPD. *See* Chronic obstructive pul-
    monary disease
Coronary artery bypass surgery, 100, 150

Massage therapy (*continued*)
    for burn pain, 31–32
    for carpal tunnel syndrome, 32
    and chiropractic, 19
    for chronic fatigue syndrome, 33
    conditions/procedures treated by,
        149–151
    defined, 23
    for depressed pregnant women, 9–10
    for depression, 28–29
    for eating disorders, 30
    empirical support for effects of, 27–38
    for exercise/sports performance, 38
    Feldendrais method of, 26
    for fibromyalgia, 32–33
    for headaches, 33, 34
    history of, 24
    for HIV, 37
    for hypertension/cardiac conditions,
        36
    for immune conditions, 36–37
    for insomnia, 30
    for labor pain, 33
    licensure for, 42
    for long-term joint pain, 34–35
    for low back pain, 31
    medical, 25
    moderate vs. light pressure in, 24,
        138, 140
    for musculoskeletal/neurological
        conditions, 35–36
    in naturopathy, 18
    for pain syndromes, 31–35
    for pediatric populations, 136,
        138–140
    for postoperative pain, 34
    for posttraumatic stress disorder, 30
    potential mechanisms of action for,
        23–24
    for premenstrual syndrome pain, 35
    for prenatal depression, 29–30
    referring clients for, 42
    resources for, 163
    Rosen method of, 26
    Rubenfeld method of, 26
    sports, 25
    Swedish, 25

    Thai, 26
    Trager method of, 26
    training for, 153–154
    for trauma pain, 34
    vagal activity increased with, 20
Mat Pilates certification, 155, 156
MBCT (mindfulness-based cognitive
    therapy), 8–9
MBSR. *See* Mindfulness-based stress
    reduction
Medical doctors, 154
Medical massage, 25
Medical resonance music therapy, 88
Meditation, 127–133
    for cardiac conditions, 132
    conditions/procedures treated by,
        149–151
    defined, 127
    for depression, 131
    empirical support for effects of,
        130–133
    for fibromyalgia, 132
    for immune conditions, 132–133
    for IBS, 131–132
    origins of, 127–128
    for pain syndromes, 131–132
    potential underlying mechanisms for
        effects of, 128–130
    referring clients for, 133
    research problems with, 130
    resources for, 163
    for stress/anxiety, 130–131
    training for, 157
Medline Plus Complementary and
    Alternative Medicine, 159
Megavitamins, 136
Menopausal symptoms
    acupuncture for, 51–52
    effective therapies for, 150
    naturopathic treatment of, 18–19
Menstrual cramps, 39, 94
Mental-rehearsal imagery, 104
Mentastics, 26
Meridians, 15, 39, 44
Mesmer, Franz Anton, 113
Mesmerism, 113
Metoprolol, 49

Mezger, Johan Georg, 25
Michigan State University, 82
Midazolam, 46
Migraine headaches
    acupuncture for, 49
    biofeedback for, 123
    effective therapies for, 150
    massage therapy for, 33, 34
    yoga for, 65
Miller, Neal, 119
Mindfulness-based cognitive therapy
        (MBCT), 8–9
Mindfulness-based stress reduction
        (MBSR), 128, 131, 132
Mindfulness meditation, 127, 128, 131,
        132
Moderate-pressure massage, 24, 138, 140
Mood
    aromatherapy for, 91–93
    and biofeedback, 121
    effective therapies for, 150
    imagery for, 105–106
    and meditation, 131
    Tai Chi for, 55
Mother–infant interactions, 29, 140
Mothers with depression, 28–29
Motor activity, 98, 105
Movement habits, 26
Moxibustion, 43
MRI (magnetic resonance imaging), 115
MT–BC (music therapist—board certi-
        fied), 156
Multiple-resistant tuberculosis, 95
Multiple sclerosis
    acupressure for, 41
    effective therapies for, 150
    massage therapy for, 35
    music therapy for, 83
    reflexology for, 41
    yoga for, 66
Muscle activity, 119
Muscle relaxation, 85
Muscle strength
    effective therapies for, 150
    physical exercise for, 75
    and Tai Chi, 55, 58
Muscle tone, 25

Musculoskeletal conditions and disorders
    acupuncture for, 50–51
    effective therapies for, 150
    imagery for, 108–109
    massage therapy for, 35–36
    music therapy for, 86–87
    yoga for, 66
Music
    entrainment, 82
    making vs. listening to, 87
    patient's preferred type of, 81–82
Musical performance, 104, 126
Music therapist—board certified
        (MT–BC), 156
Music therapy, 10–11, 81–88
    for anxiety, 82
    for autoimmune conditions, 87
    for back pain, 84–85
    for cancer, 87–88
    for cardiovascular conditions, 87
    conditions/procedures treated by,
        149–151
    defined, 81
    for dementia, 86
    for depression, 83–84
    empirical support for effects of,
        82–88
    for epilepsy, 86–87
    history of, 82
    for labor pain, 85
    for neurological/musculoskeletal
        conditions, 86–87
    for operative/postoperative pain,
        85–86
    for pain syndromes, 84–86
    for Parkinson's disease, 86
    for pediatric populations, 144–145
    for posttraumatic stress disorder, 84
    potential underlying mechanisms for
        effects of, 81–82
    referring clients for, 88
    for schizophrenia, 84
    for sleep problems, 84
    for stroke, 86
    training for, 156
Myelinated A neurons, 44–45
Myocardial infarction, 124

Nalaxone, 45

Natarajasana pose, 63

National Association for Music Therapy, 82

National Association of Holistic Aromatherapy, 161

National Association of Social Workers, 164

National Board of Certified Clinical Hypnotherapists (NBCCH), 157

National Cancer Institute, 159

National Center for Complementary and Alternative Medicine (NCCAM), 3, 161

National certification, in massage therapy, 153

National Certification Board for Therapeutic Massage and Bodywork, 153, 163

National Certification Commission for Acupuncture and Oriental Medicine, 160

National Coalition of Arts Therapies Associations, 160

National Council of Colleges of Acupuncture and Oriental Medicine, 154

National Guild of Hypnotists, 162

National Institute of Mental Health Treatment of Depression Collaborative Research Program, 9

National Institutes of Health, 3, 117

Nationally Certified in Therapeutic Massage and Bodywork (NCTMB) designation, 153

Native American medicine, 17

Natural killer (NK) cells
  effective therapies for, 150
  and imagery, 110
  and massage therapy, 36–37
  and music therapy, 88
  in pediatric population, 140

Naturopathy, 18–19

Nausea
  acupressure for, 40
  acupuncture for, 51
  effective therapies for, 149

and progressive muscle relaxation, 101
  self-acupressure for relief of, 39

NBCCH (National Board of Certified Clinical Hypnotherapists), 157

NCCAM. See National Center for Complementary and Alternative Medicine

NCCAM Newsletter, 159

NCCAM Research Grants, 159

NCTMB (Nationally Certified in Therapeutic Massage and Bodywork) designation, 153

Neanderthals, 90

Neck pain
  acupuncture for, 45–46, 49
  chiropractic for, 20
  effective therapies for, 150

Negative imagery, 106

Nerve conduction velocity, 150

Neurodermatitis, 87

Neurofeedback, 122

Neurological conditions and disorders
  acupuncture for, 50–51
  imagery for, 108–109
  massage therapy for, 35–36
  music therapy for, 86–87
  yoga for, 66

Neurologists, 154

Neurotransmitters, 74, 130

Neutrophils, 110

New Zealand, 136

Nitric oxide (NO), 47–48

NK cells. See Natural killer cells

NO. See Nitric oxide

Nonspinal conditions, chiropractic for, 20

Norepinephrine, 30, 114

North American Society of Teachers of the Alexander Technique, 160

Obesity
  and diabetes, 143
  effective therapies for, 151
  in pediatric population, 142

Obsessive–compulsive disorder, 122

Odor receptors, 89

Odors, 15
Olfactory bulb, 89
Olfactory nerve, 90
Operative pain, 85–86, 146
Opioid peptides, 45, 73
Opioid theory, 73–74
Oriental medicine, 154. *See also* Chinese medicine
Orphans, 140
Osteoarthritis
  acupuncture for, 48
  aromatherapy for, 94
  imagery for, 108
  progressive muscle relaxation for, 100
  Tai Chi for, 56
  yoga for, 65
Osteopathy, 19
Osteoporosis, 56–57, 151
Oxygen consumption, 151
Oxytocin, 50

Pain and pain syndromes
  acupuncture for, 47–50
  aromatherapy for, 94
  biofeedback for, 122–124
  chiropractic for, 20
  effective therapies for, 151
  hypnosis for, 116–117
  imagery for, 107–108
  massage therapy for, 31–35
  meditation for, 131–132
  music's effects on, 82
  music therapy for, 84–86
  physical exercise for, 76
  progressive muscle relaxation for, 100
  Tai Chi for, 56
  yoga for, 65
Palpation, 15
Panchakarma, 14
Parasympathetic activity, 120, 128
Parental CAM use, 135
Parents, CAM therapies provided by, 148
Parkinson's disease
  effective therapies for, 151

imagery for, 109
massage therapy for, 35
music therapy for, 86
Passive massage, 25
Passive stretching, 26
Patajali, 61
Pediatric populations, CAM therapies for, 135–148
  acupuncture, 140–141
  for asthma/HIV, 137–138
  for attention disorders/autism, 137
  biofeedback, 146–147
  with cerebral palsy, 136–137
  demographics associated with, 135–136
  empirical support for effects of, 136–138
  exercise, 142–144
  hypnosis, 145–146
  massage therapy, 138–140
  music therapy, 144–145
  Pilates, 141–142
  referring, 147–148
  relaxation therapy/imagery, 145
  spending on, 135
  yoga, 141
Penicillin-resistant staphylococcus aureus, 95
Peppermint, 90, 93
Peptides, 138
Performance enhancement, 126, 151
Peripheral neuropathy, 50–51
Petrissage, 25
Phobias, 101
Physical conditions, effective therapies for, 151
Physical exercise, 73–79
  for autoimmune conditions, 76–77
  for depression, 74–75
  for diabetes, 76–77
  empirical support for effects of, 74–78
  for fibromyalgia, 76
  for immune conditions, 77
  for pain syndromes, 76
  for pediatric populations, 142–144
  physiological effects of, 77–78

Physical exercise (*continued*)
  potential underlying mechanisms for
    effects of, 73–74
  for pulmonary health/disease, 75–76
  for quality of life, 75
  referring clients for supervised, 79
  training for, 11
Physical therapy, 18
"Physician's tomb," 24
Pilates, 69–71
  combining exercise/yoga with, 156
  conditions/procedures treated by,
    149–151
  empirical support for, 70
  origins of, 69
  for pediatric populations, 141–142
  physiological effects of, 70–71
  referring clients for, 71
  training for, 11, 155–156
Pilates, Joseph H., 69, 156
Pilates Instructor Certification, 155–156
Pitta, 14
Piyo, 156
Plants, 17
PMR. *See* Progressive muscle relaxation
Polarity, 164
POMS (Profile of Mood States), 66
Posterior parietal cortex, 104
Postmenopausal symptoms, 51–52, 151
Postoperative conditions
  aromatherapy for, 94
  effective therapies for, 151
  massage therapy for, 34
  music therapy for, 85–86
  in pediatric populations, 140–141,
    145
  progressive muscle relaxation for, 100
Postpartum mothers, 92
Posttraumatic stress disorder (PTSD)
  biofeedback for, 122
  effective therapies for, 151
  imagery for, 106
  massage therapy for, 30
  music therapy for, 84
Posture(s)
  in Alexander technique, 26–27
  and osteopathy, 19

  in Pilates, 69, 70
  in Rubenfeld method, 26
Prefrontal cortex, 130
Pregnancy-related conditions
  acupressure for, 39, 40
  effective therapies for, 151
  yoga for, 67
Pregnant women
  depression in, 9–10
  massage therapy for, 9–10, 29–30
  and progressive muscle relaxation,
    100–101
Premature contractions and delivery,
    29–30, 39, 151
Premature infants, 138, 140, 144–145
Premenstrual syndrome, 35, 151
Prenatal depression, 29–30
Preoperative conditions
  effective therapies for, 151
  hypnosis for, 116
  in pediatric populations, 146
Pressure, in massage therapy, 24, 25
Pressure points, 39
Pressure receptors, 74, 98
Preventive Chinese medicine, 14
Primary motor cortex, 104, 105
Profile of Mood States (POMS), 66
Progressive muscle relaxation (PMR),
    97–101
  for anxiety, 99
  for cardiovascular conditions, 100–101
  conditions/procedures treated by,
    149–151
  defined, 97
  empirical support for effects of, 99–101
  and hypnotic susceptibility, 115
  with imagery, 104
  for immune conditions, 101
  origins of, 97
  for osteoarthritis, 100
  for pain syndromes, 100
  for postsurgical pain, 100
  potential underlying mechanisms for
    effects of, 98
  referring clients for, 101
  research problems with, 98
  for stress, 99

for systematic desensitization, 101
    training for, 157
Prostate cancer, 132
Psoriasis, 87, 151
Psychological symptoms and disorders
    acupuncture for, 46–47
    biofeedback for, 122
    hypnosis for, 116
    imagery for, 105–107
    massage therapy for, 27–31
    music therapy for, 82–84
    in pediatric populations, 145
    physical exercise for, 74–75
    progressive muscle relaxation for, 99
    Tai Chi for, 55–56
    yoga for, 63–64
Psychotherapy
    combining CAM with, 7–12
    integrating CAM therapies into tra-
        ditional, 10–12
    resources for, 164
PTSD. *See* Posttraumatic stress disorder
Pulmonary health and disease, 68,
        75–76
Pulse taking, 14, 15

Qi. *See* Chi
Quail eggs, 138
Quality of life, 75

Radiation therapy, 82
Range of motion, 25, 26
Reaction time, 126
Referrals, need for, 12
Reflexology, 23, 39–41
    defined, 23
    empirical support for effects of, 40–41
    referring clients for, 42
    resources for, 164
Registered massage therapists, 153
Relaxation
    aromatherapy for, 11, 95
    effective therapies for, 151
    and music therapy, 85
    and Tai Chi, 11, 58
Relaxation therapy, 145. *See also* Pro-
        gressive muscle relaxation

Relaxation training, 114
Relaxing odors, 95
Renal disease, 41
Resistance training, 78
Respiratory sinus arrhythmia, 120
Reston, James, 43
Revascularization procedures, 66
Reynaud's syndrome, 124
Right anterior insula, 130
Ritalin, 147
Rock music, 11, 84
Rome, ancient, 24, 89
Rose, 90, 94
Rosemary, 11, 90, 92, 93, 95, 96
Rosen Institute, 164
Rosen method, 26, 164
Rostrum, 115
Royal jelly, 138
The Rubenfeld Center, 164
Rubenfeld method, 26, 164
Running performance, 68, 151

SAD (seasonal affective disorder), 74
Sandalwood, 90
Schizophrenia, 84, 151
Seasickness, 39
Seasonal affective disorder (SAD), 74
Self-acupressure, 39
Self-hypnosis, 115, 146
Self-massage, 30–31
Serotonin, 33, 45
Sexual abuse, 151
Sham acupuncture, 45–46
Shaman, 16
Shamanism, 16–17
Shiatsu, 38–39, 165
Shingles, 57
Shoulder pain, 35
SIgA immune cells, 101
Sigmoidoscopies, 85
Sitting meditation, 128
Skin, pressure receptors under the, 74
Skin aging, 95–96
Skin conditions, 15, 126
Skin-conductance monitoring, 121
Sleep apnea, 51
Sleep deprivation, 32–33

Tea tree oil, 95
Temporomandibular joint (TMJ)
    acupuncture for, 50
    biofeedback for, 123
    effective therapies for, 151
TENS. *See* Transcutaneous electrical
    nerve stimulation
Tension headaches, 33
Thai massage, 26
Theta activity, 129, 130
Theta:alpha ratio, 115
Theta band, 120
Thinking style, 8
Thoracic breathing, 69
Thoracic spine, 69
Thyme, 90
Thymol, 90
TMJ. *See* Temporomandibular joint
Tongue, 14–15
Touch, 14
Touch Research Institute, 27, 163
Trager approach, 26, 165
Trager Institute, 165
Training, 153–158
    for acupuncture, 154
    for aromatherapy, 156–157
    for biofeedback, 158
    for CAM therapies, 11
    for hypnosis, 157–158
    for massage therapy, 153–154
    for meditation, 157
    for music therapy, 156
    for Pilates, 155–156
    for progressive muscle relaxation,
        157
    for Tai Chi, 154–155
    for yoga, 155
Transcendental meditation, 128
Transcutaneous electrical nerve stimu-
    lation (TENS), 32, 50
Trauma pain, 34
Triglycerides, 143
Tuberculosis, 95
Turkey, 138, 147
Type 1 diabetes, 76–77, 143
Type 2 diabetes, 77, 125, 143

Unmyelinated C neurons, 44–45
Urinary infections, 90

Vagal activity. *See also* Heart rate
    variability
    and biofeedback, 120
    and chiropractic, 20
    effective therapies for, 151
    effects of increased, 4–5
    and massage therapy, 23–24
    and meditation, 128–129
    in pediatric populations, 144
Vagal tone, 140
Vagus, 23
Vata, 14
Ventral striatum, 130
Verbal expression, in Rosen method,
    26
Vietnam veterans, 106
Vision, 14
Vitamin therapy, 136, 137
Voiding dysfunction, 147
Vomiting
    acupressure for, 40
    acupuncture for, 51
    effective therapies for, 149
    and progressive muscle relaxation,
        101

Walking, 79
Web sites, 159
Weight-bearing exercise, 77–78, 143
Weight gain, 140
Weight reduction, 142, 151
Weight training, 76
Well-being, feelings of, 121
White blood cells, 110
White House Commission on Comple-
    mentary and Alternative Medi-
    cine Policy, 159
Willow, 17
Wolpe, Joseph, 97
Workplace
    massage therapy at, 27
    and meditation, 132–133
Work-related injuries, 124

Wrinkling, of skin, 151
Wushu Resources, U.S.A., 162

X-rays, 19

Yang, 14
Yang channels, 44
Yang treatment, 16
The Yellow Emperor's Classic of Internal Medicine, 24
Yin, 14
Yin channels, 44
Yin treatment, 16
Ylang-ylang, 90, 94
Yoga, 61–68
    for anxiety, 63–64
    for asthma, 66
    for autoimmune conditions, 66–67
    conditions/procedures treated by, 149–151
    for depression, 64
    for diabetes, 67
    empirical support for effects of, 62–68

    and exercise/sports performance, 68
    for headaches, 65
    for hypertension/cardiac conditions, 66
    for immune conditions, 67
    for low back pain, 65
    for multiple sclerosis, 66
    origins of, 61
    for osteoarthritis, 65
    for pain syndromes, 65
    for pediatric populations, 141
    physical effects of, 68
    physiological effects of, 67–68
    potential mechanisms of action for, 62
    for pregnancy-related conditions, 67
    referring clients for, 71
    resources for, 165
    sessions of, 62, 63
    for sleep problems, 65
    training for, 11, 155
Yoga poses, 62, 63
Yoga Sutras (Patajali), 61

ABOUT THE AUTHOR

Tiffany Field, PhD, is director and founder of the Touch Research Institute and professor of pediatrics, psychiatry, and psychology at the University of Miami School of Medicine, Miami, Florida, and is on the faculty of Fielding Graduate University, Santa Barbara, California. She is a recipient of the American Psychological Association Boyd McCandless Young Scientist Award and has received a number of research scientist awards from the National Institutes of Health. Dr. Field is the author of *Infancy, The Amazing Infant, Touch, Advances in Touch, Touch Therapy*, and *Massage Research;* the editor of a series of volumes on high-risk infants and a series on stress and coping; and the author of more than 450 journal articles.